THE DIVERSITY DELUSION

ALSO BY HEATHER MAC DONALD

The War on Cops:
How the New Attack on Law and Order
Makes Everyone Less Safe

Are Cops Racist?
How the War Against the Police Harms Black Americans

The Burden of Bad Ideas:
How Modern Intellectuals Misshape Our Society

The Immigration Solution:
A Better Plan Than Today's
(with Victor Davis Hanson and Steven Malanga)

THE DIVERSITY
DELUSION

How Race *and* Gender Pandering
Corrupt *the* University
and Undermine Our Culture

HEATHER MAC DONALD

ST. MARTIN'S PRESS ⧓ NEW YORK

Versions of these chapters originally appeared in the following publications and websites: *City Journal*, chap. 1–2, 4–6, 9–11, 13–16; *The Wall Street Journal*, chap. 1, 12; *The Weekly Standard*, chap. 3, 7; *The National Review Online*, chap. 3, 9, 12; FoxNews.com, chap. 6.

www.stmartins.com

The Library of Congress Cataloging-in-Publication Data is available upon request.

ISBN 9781250200914 (hardcover)
ISBN 9781250200921 (ebook)

Our books may be purchased in bulk for promotional, educational, or business use. Please contact your local bookseller or the Macmillan Corporate and Premium Sales Department at 1-800-221-7945, extension 5442, or by email at MacmillanSpecialMarkets@macmillan.com.

10 9 8 7 6 5 4

CONTENTS

Introduction   1

Part I: Race

1. The Hysterical Campus   9
2. Elites to Affirmative Action Voters: Drop Dead   35
3. Affirmative Disaster   53
4. The Microaggression Farce   63
5. Are We All Unconscious Racists?   87

Part II: Gender

6. The Campus Rape Myth   117
7. Neo-Victorianism on Campus   139
8. The Fainting Couch at Columbia   149
9. Policing Sexual Desire: The #MeToo
   Movement's Impossible Premise   155

Part III: The Bureaucracy

10. Multiculti U.   171
11. How Identity Politics Is Harming
    the Sciences   189
12. Scandal Erupts Over the Promotion
    of Bourgeois Behavior   201

Part IV: The Purpose of the University

13. The Humanities and Us   211
14. Great Courses, Great Profits   223
15. The True Purpose of the University   237
16. From Culture to Cupcakes   243

Notes   249
Index   265

ACKNOWLEDGMENTS

Thank you to the Thomas W. Smith Foundation for its generous support of my fellowship at the Manhattan Institute, as well as for its support of this volume. I am also indebted to the Andrea Waitt Carlton Family Foundation, Peter Farrell, Randy Kendrick, the Dian Graves Owen Foundation, and the Arthur N. Rupe Foundation for helping to make *The Diversity Delusion* possible.

THE DIVERSITY DELUSION

INTRODUCTION

In 1903, during America's darkest period of hate, W. E. B. Du Bois heartbreakingly affirmed his intellectual affinity with Western civilization. "I sit with Shakespeare and he winces not. Across the color line I move arm in arm with Balzac and Dumas," Du Bois wrote in *The Souls of Black Folk*. "I summon Aristotle and Aurelius and what soul I will, and they come all graciously with no scorn nor condescension."[1]

Half a century earlier, Frederick Douglass had paid tribute to the eighteenth-century British orators whom, at age twelve, he had discovered in a collection of political speeches. "Every opportunity afforded me, for a time, was spent in diligently perusing [*The Columbian Orator*]," Douglass recalled in his autobiography. "This volume was, indeed, a rich treasure," he wrote, for the speeches—by Richard Sheridan, Charles James Fox, and William Pitt—"gave tongue to many interesting thoughts, which had frequently flashed through my soul, and died away for want of utterance."[2]

How much things have changed.

In 2016, a student petition at Yale University called for dismantling the college's decades-long requirement that English majors take a course covering Chaucer, Spenser, Milton, and Wordsworth. Reading these authors "creates a culture that is especially hostile to students of color,"[3] complained the students. Sadly, there was by then nothing remarkable in this demand. Attacks on the canon as an instrument of exclusivity and oppression have flourished since the 1980s, when Jesse Jackson famously joined Stanford students in chanting, "Hey, hey, ho, ho, Western Civ has got to go." But in the past few years the world-view behind such antagonism has become even more militant, transforming not just universities but the world at large. The demand for "safe spaces," reflexive accusations of racism and sexism, and contempt for Enlightenment values of reason and due process are no longer an arcane species of academic self-involvement—they increasingly infuse business, government, and civil society. *The Diversity Delusion* is an attempt to investigate how this transformation happened and why.

The roots lie in a charged set of ideas that now dominate higher education: that human beings are defined by their skin color, sex, and sexual preference; that discrimination based on those characteristics has been the driving force in Western civilization; and that America remains a profoundly bigoted place, where heterosexual white males continue to deny opportunity to everyone else.

These ideas, which may be subsumed under the categories of "diversity" and identity politics, have remade the university. Entire fields have sprung up around race, ethnicity, sex, and gender identity. Coursework in traditional departments also views the past and present through that same self-engrossed lens. A vast administrative apparatus—the diversity bureaucracy—promotes the notion that to be a college student from an ever-growing number of victim groups is to experience daily bigotry from your professors and peers. In fall 2015, black Princeton students chanted: "We're sick and tired of being sick and tired"—a phrase first used by Fannie Lou Hamer, a civil rights activist from the deep South who was beaten in the 1950s for trying to vote. Hamer had grounds aplenty to be sick and tired, but *any* Princeton student who thinks of himself as downtrodden is in the grip of a terrible delusion. That delusion, however, is actively encouraged by Princeton's administrators, including the vice provost for institutional equity and diversity, who in early 2018 erected posters throughout campus inviting students to report "problematic experiences based on identity." In 2016, Brown students occupied their provost's office to demand exemption from traditional academic requirements such as class attendance because they were so focused, they said, on staying alive at Brown. *Fact-check*: No Brown student is at risk of his life from going to classes and trying to learn.

This victimology fuels the sometimes violent efforts to shut down speech that challenges campus orthodoxies. Taught to believe that they are at existential threat from circumambient bias, students equate nonconforming ideas with "hate speech," and "hate speech" with life-threatening conduct that should be punished, censored, and repelled with force if necessary. In March 2017, a mob of Middlebury College students assaulted a professor, giving her a concussion and whiplash, following their successful effort to prevent social scientist Charles Murray from speaking to a live audience by shouting, pounding on walls, and activating fire alarms. Murray just missed being knocked down and beaten himself.[4] After this attack, 177 professors from across the country signed an open letter protesting that the assailants had been disciplined, however minimally. The professors blamed the Middlebury administration for the violence, since its decision to allow Murray to lecture constituted a "threat" to students. A few days later, another group of faculty members described the tribulations that students and faculty "of color" on that bucolic campus allegedly encounter: marginalization, neglect, objectification, and exclusion from full participation in campus life. The protest was a matter of "active resistance against racism, sexism, classism, homophobia, transphobia, ableism, ethnocentrism, xenophobia, and all other forms of unjust discrimination," they wrote.[5]

In May 2017 students from Evergreen State College in Washington state stormed into a class taught by biology professor Bret Weinstein and began cursing and hurling racial epithets. "Fuck you, you piece of shit," screamed one student. "Get the fuck out of here," screamed another. Weinstein, a lifelong progressive, had refused to obey an edict from Evergreen's Director of First Peoples Multicultural Advising Services that all white faculty cancel their courses for a day and stay off campus. White students were also ordered to absent themselves from the school, to show solidarity with the supposed struggles of Evergreen's minority students. Weinstein told the mob that he did not believe that science professors at Evergreen were "targeting" students of color, contrary to the premises of a newly announced equity initiative. "Fuck what you have to say," a student responded. "This is not a discussion." Evergreen's president, after being subjected to a similar expletive-filled mob tirade, expressed his "gratitude for the [students'] passion and courage." In September 2017, Weinstein and his wife, also an Evergreen biology professor, accepted a $500,000 settlement to resign from the college.

Universities should be the place where students encounter the greatest works of mankind and learn to understand what makes them touchstones of human experience. History should convey the hard work it took over centuries to carve stability and prosperity out of violence, tyranny, and corruption. Instead, victim ideology encourages ignorant young adults to hate the monuments of Western civilization without bothering even to study them. (Bruce Bawer and Roger Kimball previously called out these trends in *The Victims' Revolution* and *Tenured Radicals,* respectively.) Faculty respond to students' know-nothing tantrums with silence—when they are not actively colluding in the destruction of humanistic learning.

None of this campus self-pity is justified. American college students are among the most privileged human beings in history. But the claim of ubiquitous "racism, sexism, classism, homophobia, transphobia, ableism, ethnocentrism, and xenophobia" is now lodged in the non-academic world as well, where it is being used to silence speakers and ideas with which favored victim groups disagree. Civility is shrinking and civil peace may be in jeopardy. Masked anarchists use force to block conservatives from speaking in public forums. The free speech crisis on and off campus will not be solved until the premises of victimology are challenged directly and exposed as fraudulent, as this book aims to do.

The academic obsession with identity is ironic, since its roots lie in a philosophy that denied the very existence of the self. In the 1970s, the literary theory of deconstruction took over humanities departments with a curious set of propositions about language. Because linguistic signs were arbitrary, successful communication was said to be impossible. Most surprisingly, the human subject was declared to be a fiction, a mere play of rhetorical tropes. In the 1980s, however, the self came roaring back with a vengeance as feminists and race theorists took the mannered jargon of deconstruction and turned it into a political weapon. The key deconstructive concept of linguistic "*différance*" became identity difference between the oppressed and their oppressors; the prime object of study became one's own self and its victimization. The most significant change concerned attitudes toward the Western intellectual tradition. Deconstructive theorists such as Paul de Man and Jacques Derrida performed their interpretive sleights of hand on Proust, Rousseau, Plato, Shelley, and Wordsworth, among other leading philosophers and writers. They did not disparage these complex texts as the contemptible products of dead, white males. Multiculturalism, which took over literary studies in the 1980s, destroyed that respect for the canon while continuing the deconstructive stance of exposing alleged subtexts and suppressed meanings. What had been an epistemological project became a political one.

And now multiculturalism's cover for unblemished ignorance of the past—the reflexive "dead, white male" taunt—is being used to further rationalize formal and informal censorship. A twenty-three-year-old theater student at the University of California, San Diego, circulated a petition in February 2018 to cancel a course on Woody Allen's movies, due to Allen's alleged sexual improprieties. Asked if the demand to efface the course raised free speech problems, the student dismissed the First Amendment as an "outdated" law "written by a bunch of white men." (It is a certainty that she has read neither the amendment nor the history of the Bill of Rights.) The university rejected the petition, but the multicultural excuse for trashing Enlightenment principles continues to wreak havoc elsewhere.

Even the one remaining bright spot in the universities is vulnerable. Academic science is in the crosshairs of the victimologists. For now, university researchers are still accomplishing astounding feats of intellectual discovery. But the incessant demand from administrators and government officials that science departments hire by gender and race, rather than established accomplishments, may take a toll on their intellectual capital. That demand continues into the marketplace, where activist groups and the media exert identical pressure on for-profit science and technology firms in Silicon Valley and elsewhere.

"Diversity" in the academy purported to be about bridge-building and broadening people's experiences. It has had the opposite effect: dividing society, reducing learning, and creating an oppositional mind-set that prevents individuals from seizing the opportunities available to them. It is humanistic learning, by contrast, that involves an actual encounter with diversity and difference, as students enter worlds radically different from their own. Humanistic study involves imaginative empathy and curiosity, which are being squelched in today's university in favor of self-engrossed complaint. Teaching the classics is the duty we owe these great works for giving us an experience of the sublime. Once we stop lovingly transmitting them to the next generation, they die.

For decades, universities have drifted further and further away from their true purpose. Now they are taking the rest of the world with them.

PART I
RACE

1

THE HYSTERICAL CAMPUS

Where are the faculty? American college students are increasingly resorting to brute force, and sometimes criminal violence, to shut down ideas that they don't like. Yet when such travesties occur, the faculty are, with few exceptions, missing in action, though they have themselves been given the extraordinary privilege of tenure to protect their own liberties of thought and speech. It is time for them to take their heads out of the sand.

I was the target of such silencing tactics two days in a row in 2017, the more serious incident at Claremont McKenna College in Claremont, California, and a less virulent one at UCLA.

The Rose Institute for State and Local Government at Claremont McKenna had invited me to meet with students and to give a talk in April about my book *The War on Cops*. Several calls went out on Facebook to "shut down" this "notorious white supremacist fascist Heather Mac Donald." A Facebook post from "we, students of color at the Claremont Colleges" announced grandiosely that "as a community, we CANNOT and WILL NOT allow fascism to have a platform. We stand against all forms of oppression and we refuse to have Mac Donald speak." A Facebook event titled "Shut Down Anti-Black Fascist Heather Mac Donald" and hosted by "Shut Down Anti-Black Fascists" encouraged students to protest the event because I allegedly "condemn [the] Black Lives Matter movement," "support racist police officers," and "support increasing fascist 'law and order.'"[1] (My supposed fascism consists in trying to give voice to the millions of law-abiding minority residents of high-crime areas who support the police and are desperate for more law-enforcement protection.)

The event organizers notified me a day before the speech that a protest was planned and that they were considering changing the venue from CMC's Athenaeum to one with fewer glass windows and easier egress. When I arrived on campus, I was shuttled to what was, in effect, a safe house: a guest suite for campus visitors, with blinds drawn. I could hear the growing crowds chanting and drumming, but I could not see the auditorium that the protesters were surrounding. One female voice rose above the chants with particularly shrill hysteria. From the balcony, I saw a petite blond female walk by, her face covered by a Palestinian keffiyeh headscarf and carrying an amplifier on her back for her bullhorn. A lookout was stationed about forty yards away, and students were seated on the stairway under my balcony, plotting strategy.

Since I never saw the events outside the Athenaeum, which remained the chosen venue, an excellent report from the student newspaper, *The Student Life*, provides details of the scene:

> The protesters, most of whom wore all black, congregated outside Honnold/Mudd Library at 4 p.m. to stage the action. "We are here to shut down the fucking fascist," announced an organizer to a crowd of around 100 students. The protesters subsequently marched to the Ath around 4:30 while chanting. An organizer shouted "How do you spell racist?" into a megaphone; the marchers responded "C-M-C."
>
> When they arrived, the protesters were greeted by around two dozen Campus Safety officers and Claremont police officers, stationed at various locations around the building. Protestors ignored the officers (who did not obstruct them) and the makeshift white fences sectioning off areas of Flamson Plaza, enveloping each of the Ath's entrances with multiple rows of students linking arms. White students were encouraged to stand in front to form a barrier between students of color and the police.
>
> The protesters continued their chants, including "hey hey, ho ho, Heather Mac has got to go," "shut it down," and—most frequent and sustained—"black lives matter." Some of the officers appeared visibly

uncomfortable during the chant of "from Oakland to Greece, fuck the police."

Keck Science professor Anthony Fucaloro pushed against and grappled with the crowd of protesters in an unsuccessful attempt to reach the door. Garrett Ryan, CM '17, brought a large speaker to the Hub's patio, blasting Sousa's patriotic march "The Stars and Stripes Forever" to provoke the protesters. A woman who ran up to him managed to steal his audio cable after a brief scuffle, cutting off the music and garnering cheers from the protesters when she returned to the crowd.

"It was not well-received," Ryan told *TSL*.

Steven Glick, PC '17, coeditor-in-chief of the conservative *Claremont Independent* publication, attempted to livestream the protest but was swarmed by protesters who blocked his phone.

Several administrators attended the protest and stood to the side. They told *TSL* that they saw their role as ensuring student safety, but they also sympathized with the protesters' views. "Black Lives Matter is really at my heart," said Pomona associate dean Jan Collins-Eaglin.

Of all the chants, "How do you spell racist?" "C-M-C," was the most absurd (and didn't even rhyme). "Racist" CMC is so eager for "diverse" students that it has historically admitted black and Hispanic students with an average 200-point-lower SAT score than white and Asian students.

Shortly before 6 PM, I was fetched by an administrator and a few police officers to take an out-of-the-way elevator into the Athenaeum. The massive hall, where I was supposed to meet with students for dinner before my talk, was empty—the mob, by then numbering close to two hundred, had succeeded in preventing anyone from entering. The large plate-glass windows were covered with translucent blinds, so that from the inside one could see only a mass of indistinct bodies pounding on the windows. The administration had decided that I would live stream my speech in the vacant room in order to preserve some semblance of the original plan. The podium was moved away from a window so that, as night fell and the lights inside came on, I would not be visible to the agitators outside.

I prefaced my speech by observing that I had heard chants for the last two hours that "black lives matter." I hoped, therefore, that the protesters had been equally fervent in expressing their outrage when five-year-old Aaron Shannon Jr. was killed on Halloween 2010 in South Central Los Angeles, while proudly showing off his Spider-Man costume. A twenty-six-year-old member of Watts's Kitchen Crips sent a single bullet through Aaron's head, and also shot Aaron's uncle and grandfather. I said that I hoped the protesters also objected when nine-year-old Tyshawn Lee was lured into an alley in Chicago with the promise of candy in November 2015 and assassinated by gang enemies of Tyshawn's father. The murderers' original plan had been to cut off Tyshawn's fingers and send them to his mother. While Black Lives Matter protesters have, in fact, ignored all such mayhem, the people who *have* concerned themselves are the police, I said. And though it was doubtful that any of the protesters outside had ever lost a loved one to a drive-by shooting, if such a tragedy ever did happen, the first thing that he or she would do would be to call the police.

I completed my speech to the accompaniment of chants and banging on the windows. I was able to take two questions from students via live streaming. But by then, the administrators and police officers in the room, who had spent my talk nervously staring at the windows, decided that things were growing too unruly outside to continue. I was given the cue that the presentation was over. Walkie-talkies were used to coordinate my exit from the Athenaeum's kitchen to the exact moment that a black, unmarked Claremont Police Department van rolled up. We passed startled students sitting on the stoop outside the kitchen. Before I entered the van, one student came up and thanked me for coming to Claremont. We sped off to the police station.

The previous night, I actually succeeded in delivering a talk on policing to the audience who had come to hear it; such heretofore ordinary circumstances are now noteworthy. My hosts, the UCLA College Republicans, had titled my presentation "Blue Lives Matter," which campus activists viewed as an unspeakable provocation. After I finished speaking and welcomed questions, pandemonium broke out. Protesters stormed the front of the classroom, demanding control of the mic and chanting loudly: "America was never great" and "Black

Lives Matter, they matter here," among other insights. After nearly ten minutes of shouting, one of the organizers managed to persuade some students to line up for questions. *The College Fix* paper captured the subsequent interaction:

> A black female asked whether "black victims killed by cops" mattered.
>
> "Yes," Mac Donald replied. "And do black children that are killed by other blacks matter to you?"
>
> At that the room erupted in gasps and angry moans and furious snaps, and the young lady who asked the original question began to yell at Mac Donald, pointing her finger and repeating the original question. . . .
>
> "Of course I care [that black victims are killed by cops], and do you know what," Mac Donald said. "There is no government agency more dedicated to the proposition that black lives matter than the police."
>
> Again, gasps and moans filled the auditorium. "Bullshit! Bullshit!" a young woman off camera could be heard screaming.
>
> Mac Donald continued: "The crime drop of the last 20 years that came to a screeching halt in August 2014 has saved tens of thousands of minority lives. Because cops went to those neighborhoods and they got the dealers off the street and they got the gang-bangers off the street."
>
> Mac Donald took more questions and at times was able to articulate her points during the Q&A, but was also often interrupted by angry audience members shouting out things such as:
>
> "I don't trust your numbers."
>
> "Why do white lives always need to be put above everybody else? Can we talk about black lives for one second?"
>
> "The same system that sent police to murder black lives . . ."
>
> "You have no right to speak!"
>
> "What about white terrorism?!"

To the inevitable claim that poverty causes gun violence, I responded that if students really believed in that causation, they should be concerned that mass low-skilled immigration was driving down wages for the American poor. That provoked a new chant: "Say it loud! Say it clear! Immigrants are welcome here."

At 8 PM, the organizers decided to end the event, and I was hustled out of the room with a police escort.

The UCLA administration never acknowledged the disruption of my presentation and interaction with students. The Claremont Mc-Kenna administration did, however, respond both before and after the incident. Two days ahead of my speech, the director of the Rose Institute, Andrew Busch, sent out an email decrying the use of the epithet "racist" "as a bludgeon with which to shut up critics or keep friends in line." Busch optimistically put matters in the conditional: "If we ever accept that approach we will have taken a giant step toward surrendering freedom of thought and expression"—as if intimidation via the R-word is not already routine on and off campuses. Busch graciously tried to provide a neutral summary of my views and noted that I, too, aim to protect black lives.

A few minutes after I was escorted out of the Athenaeum, a campus-wide missive from Vice President for Academic Affairs and Dean of the Faculty Peter Uvin expressed disappointment that people could not attend the lecture, but lauded the fact that the lecture was live streamed. Uvin, a government professor specializing in development and human rights, went on to establish his bona fides with the social-justice crowd: "I fully understand that people have strong opinions and different—often painful—experiences with the issues Heather Mac Donald discusses. I also understand that words can hurt. And in a world of unequal power, it is more often than not those who have a history of exclusion who are being hurt by words. I support everyone's right to make this world a better one." This may not have been the best moment to reaffirm the idea that undergirds such silencing protests: that speech can damage allegedly excluded or marginalized minorities.

The next day, CMC president Hiram Chodosh, a former international law professor, weighed in. He explained the failure to intervene against the protesters: "Based on the judgment of the Claremont Police Department, we jointly concluded that any forced interventions or arrests would have created unsafe conditions for students, faculty, staff, and guests. I take full responsibility for the decision to err on the side of these overriding safety considerations."[2] Chodosh said that students who violated school policies by blocking access to buildings would be held accountable.

A poorly written editorial in the student newspaper attributed to me positions I have never taken and quoted me wildly out of context. Such misunderstanding goes with the territory. But the editorialists' explanation for why my talk had to be shut down revealed the "racism is everywhere" brainwashing that students at even a once relatively conservative campus like Claremont now receive: "If we allow her to speak at the Ath or attend her talk, we are amplifying her voice and enhancing her credibility. Last month, we proposed that writing and publishing an article, even if it's 'free of opinion,' is not passive. This is a through line for many of our editorials this year: many actions that seem neutral in theory are actually entrenched in unconscious bias."[3]

When speakers need police escort on and off college campuses, an alarm bell should be going off that something has gone seriously awry. Of course, an ever-growing part of the faculty is the reason that police protection is needed in the first place. Professors in all but the hardest of hard sciences increasingly indoctrinate students in the belief that to be a non-Asian minority or a female in America today is to be the target of nonstop oppression, even, uproariously, if you are among the privileged few to attend a fantastically well-endowed, resource-rich American college. Those professors also maintain that to challenge that claim of ubiquitous bigotry is to engage in "hate speech" and that such speech is tantamount to a physical assault on minorities and females. As such, it can rightly be suppressed and punished. To those faculty, I am indeed a fascist, and a white supremacist, with the attendant loss of communication rights.

Hyperbole is part and parcel of political speech. But I would hope that there are some remaining faculty with enough of a lingering connection to reality who would realize that I and other conservatives are not a literal threat to minority students. To try to prevent me or other dissenting intellectuals from connecting with students is simply an effort to maintain the Left's monopoly of thought. The fact that this suppression goes under the title of "antifascism" is particularly rich. I am reluctant to wield the epithet "fascist" as promiscuously as my declared opponents do. But it must be observed that if campus conservatives tried to use physical force to block Senator Elizabeth Warren from giving a speech, *The New York Times* would likely put the obstruction on the front page and the term "fascist" would be flying around like a swarm of hornets, followed immediately by the epithet "misogynist." And when students and their fellow anarchists start breaking glass, destroying businesses, and assaulting perceived opponents, as they did during the Berkeley riots against Milo Yiannopoulos's scheduled talk in February 2017, and to prevent sociologist Charles Murray from speaking at Middlebury College the following month, it is hard not to hear echoes of 1930s fascism.

It is not enough for professors to sign statements in support of free speech (and surprisingly few have actually done so).* When word goes out of a plan to "shut down" nonconforming political views, that plan must be taken deadly seriously. Claremont McKenna took obvious pains to protect my talk, but they were not enough. I won't second-guess President Chodosh's decision not to arrest the mob blocking access to the Athenaeum. Administrators and campus police are loath to do anything that might necessitate the use of force against student darlings. But if arrests are all but foreclosed, enough police manpower must be summoned to maintain open access through sheer command presence.

Before a planned blockade, the faculty must reaffirm in their classes the institution's belief in free expression. And the faculty must show up to the threatened event itself to give meaning to the ideal of free speech; they must shame the students trying to prevent their fellow students from hearing ideas that challenge campus orthodoxies. Unfortunately, since the Claremont McKenna shutdown, professors across the country have either continued their silence in the face of student censorship or actively joined it. In January 2018, dozens of faculty at the University of Chicago urged the cancellation of a planned debate

---

* Heterodox Academy, an organization devoted to viewpoint diversity in universities, has approximately 1,800 faculty and graduate student members. It is an essential counterweight to academia's ideological monoculture, but its 1,800 members represent 1 percent of the country's 1.6 million full- and part-time faculty.

on nationalism featuring Steve Bannon, President Trump's former political adviser. Ironically, the administration of the University of Chicago has distinguished itself by explicitly disavowing the cloying rhetoric of safe spaces and trigger warnings. Apparently the administration's admirable commitment to open debate does not run particularly deep among Chicago's own professoriate.

Punishment for violating school rules is essential. In July 2017, Claremont McKenna handed down three one-year suspensions, two single-semester suspensions, and two conduct probations against seven CMC students for their involvement in the blockade. While the number of students disciplined is not overwhelming, those suspensions nevertheless represent the most serious discipline meted out anywhere to date against students who forcibly deny free speech. Middlebury College claims to have put dozens of students on probation in connection with the Murray incident, but none have been suspended, despite their use of criminal violence. The neighboring Claremont colleges, whose students also blocked my talk, have abstained from sanctions.

Naturally, the CMC discipline did not sit well with the students and their supporters. In May 2017, a coalition of CMC students, faculty, and alumni denounced the school's investigation as the "further criminalization of already marginalized students." After the suspensions were announced, the students' attorney, who hails from Justice Warriors 4 Black Lives, called the administration's actions "completely outrageous" and an attempt to "intimidate and bully" the blockaders. The only people bullying and intimidating others were the students themselves, but that fact does not penetrate the upside-down world of campus victimology.

We are cultivating students who lack all understanding of the principles of the American Founding. The mark of any civilization is its commitment to reason and discourse. The great accomplishment of the European Enlightenment was to require all forms of authority to justify themselves through rational argument, rather than through coercion or an unadorned appeal to tradition. The resort to brute force in the face of disagreement is particularly disturbing in a university, which should provide a model of civil discourse.

But the students currently stewing in delusional resentments and self-pity will eventually graduate, and some will seize levers of power more far-reaching than those they currently wield over toadying campus bureaucrats and spineless faculty. Unless the campus zest for censorship is combated now, what we have always regarded as a precious inheritance could be eroded beyond recognition, and a soft totalitarianism could become the new American norm.

■ ■ ■

A few weeks after my Claremont appearance, black students at Pomona College and neighboring schools in Claremont, California, published an open letter declaring their hostility to free speech—other people's free speech, that is. The letter shows that the faculty of the Claremont colleges are failing in their most basic educational duties. The manifesto, written by "We, few of the Black students here at Pomona College and the Claremont Colleges," was provoked by a bland statement on academic freedom by outgoing Pomona College president David Oxtoby.

Oxtoby's statement, in turn, responded to the student blockade that tried to shut down my talk. Leave aside for a moment the letter signatories' unblemished ignorance regarding free speech and the role of unfettered discourse in creating their own liberties. Viewed purely formally, the letter is a major embarrassment to the faculty of Pomona and the Claremont colleges.

It is filled with excruciating solecisms ("Though this institution as well as many others including this entire country, have been founded upon the oppression and degradation of marginalized bodies, it has a liability to protect the students that it serves") and garbled regurgitations of high theory ("The notion of discourse, when it comes to discussions about experiences and identities, deters the 'Columbusing' of established realities and truths [coded as 'intellectual inquiry'] that the institution promotes").[4]

Does this student writing demonstrate the value of a Pomona education? Are the signatories' professors satisfied with their command of the English language? What grade would this incoherent tract receive if turned in as a term paper—an A?

Faculty undoubtedly fear correcting the writing of "marginalized students," lest they suffer the same scourging we will hear about in chapter 4 that was inflicted on UCLA education professor Val Rust.

The content of the letter, such as it is, should alarm the faculty as well (at least those faculty who have not inspired "We, few"'s labored efforts at Foucauldian postmodernism). The students appear to argue that the ideal of free speech is based on a mystifying and oppressive concept of unitary truth and that such a concept solidifies white supremacy: "The idea that there is a single truth—'the Truth'—is a construct of the Euro-West that is deeply rooted in the Enlightenment. . . . This construction is a myth and white supremacy, imperialism, colonization, capitalism, and the United States of America are all of its progeny. The idea that the truth is an entity for which we must search, in matters that endanger our abilities to exist in open spaces, is an attempt to silence oppressed peoples."

"We, few of the Black students here at Pomona, etc." have it exactly backward. Free speech is the best tool for challenging hegemonic power. Absolute rulers seek to crush nonconforming opinion; the censor is the essential bulwark of tyrants. Without the Enlightenment and its challenge to unquestioned authority, "We, few of the Black students" would not even be at the Claremont colleges, because those secular, independent colleges might not even exist. (It would be interesting to know how many Enlightenment philosophers "We, few" can even name; it is virtually certain that they have closely studied none.) Rhetorical persuasion was essential in the fight against slavery and Jim Crow. Frederick Douglass declared in 1860 that "slavery cannot tolerate free speech. Five years of its exercise would banish the auction block and break every chain in the South." A mob in Boston had just stormed a meeting to prevent him and others from commemorating the radical abolitionist John Brown. Like today's student censors, newspapers in the North had been calling for a ban on abolitionist speech. After the Boston mob attack, Douglass warned that "liberty is meaningless where the right to utter one's thoughts and opinions has ceased to exist. That, of all rights, is the dread of tyrants. It is the right which they first of all strike down." "We, few of the Black students" would presumably deem Douglass a dupe.

"We, few" only pretended to be postmodern relativists. They were fully confident that they possessed the truth about me and about their oppressed plight at the Claremont schools.

Typical of all such censors and despots, "We, few of the Black students" also wanted to crush dissent. They asked the Claremont University Consortium to take action, both disciplinary and legal, against the editors of the conservative student paper, *The Claremont Independent*, for the open-ended sins of "continual perpetuation of hate speech, anti-Blackness, and intimidation toward students of marginalized backgrounds." These are the demands not of relativists but of absolutists determined to solidify their power.

As for "We, few"'s gross misreading of my work, it showed that reading skills are in as short supply at the Claremont colleges as writing skills. My entire argument about the necessity of lawful, proactive policing is based on the value of black lives. I have decried the loss of black life to drive-by shootings and other forms of street violence. I have argued that the fact that blacks die of homicide at six times the rate of whites and Hispanics combined is a civil rights abomination. Black children should be able to walk to school with as little risk of a gang attack as white children face.

The ungrammatical list of attributes that "We, few of the Black students" say disqualify me from speaking—"Heather Mac Donald is a fascist, a white supremacist, a warhawk, a transphobe, a queerphobe, a classist, and ignorant of interlocking systems of domination that produce the lethal conditions under which oppressed peoples are forced to live"—unsurprisingly displayed the ignorance already familiar from the rest of their letter, since I was an early and documented opponent of the Iraq War and all such efforts at regime change. The other epithets are not worth responding to.

■ ■ ■

My campus experience has become an all-too-familiar one over the last several years.

The anti–Milo Yiannopoulos episode at Berkeley was a particularly resounding echo of a darker political era. A flamboyantly provocative Donald Trump supporter who revels in violating politically correct taboos, Yiannopoulos had been scheduled to give a talk on campus in February 2017. Both Berkeley campus and city police were woefully understaffed in preparation for his speech—undoubtedly due to the prevailing law-enforcement philosophy of not looking "confrontational." Bay Area activists had complained during the 2014 "F—k the Police" protests, as such anticop riots are locally known, that seeing police in riot gear made them feel anxious, and the police since then had been reluctant to use traditional crowd control tactics. But serious conflict at the Milo event was a certainty, and the appearance of dozens of so-called black bloc anarchists should not have been a surprise; these lawless assailants have been a regular feature of Bay Area protests since the early 2000s.

When flaming rockets started flying at the student union where Yiannopoulos was scheduled to speak, the University of California campus police retreated to the inside of the building and didn't re-emerge until well after the event. The event was canceled after black-masked anarchists beat and pepper-sprayed supposed attendees and hurled explosive devices at police officers. When the rioters fanned out to city streets, police commanders had neither the tactical tools nor the manpower to crack down on the chaos. The vandals ransacked and torched banks and retail businesses, breaking windows, lighting fires, and annihilating ATMs. The police made only one arrest the entire night: an arrest for failing to disperse. The rioters most certainly took notice of their unimpeded reign. The violence continued the next day, with physical assaults against Berkeley College Republicans, both on and off campus.

The next week, the Berkeley student newspaper invited several current and former columnists to justify the anti-Milo violence. It was an easy assignment. The writers needed merely to recycle the melodramatic rhetoric that university administrators and faculty had fed them for years.

One of the proviolence columnists wrote that he would "fight tooth and nail for the right to exist." (And fight he did, by his own proud confession.) Allowing Yiannopoulos to speak "could have endangered campus students . . . over their identities," he said.[5] Another columnist opined that the black bloc's attacks were "not acts of violence. They were acts of self-defense."[6] Such thinking accords with the hundred-plus faculty who sought to close down the speech on the ground that Yiannopoulos "actually harm[s] students through defamatory and harassing actions."[7]

Several Berkeley professors circulated emails downplaying the significance of the violence. Déborah Blocker, associate professor of French, reported to her fellow profs about the anarchy on campus: "Mostly this was typical Black Bloc action, in a few waves—very well-organized and very efficient. They attacked property but they attacked it *very sparingly,* destroying just enough University property to obtain the cancellation order for the MY event and making sure no one in the crowd got hurt" [emphasis in original]. (In fact, a woman was pepper-sprayed while giving an interview and her husband was beaten so badly that several ribs were broken, among other assaults on campus.) Katrin Wehrheim, associate professor of mathematics, reported on the rioters' progress downtown: "yes, some Bloc members did attack large corporation buildings." But hey! Thanks to everyone "for coming out—in person or spirit!" to what was "a mostly cheerful and peaceful crowd."

College graduates have been told for years that the United States is systemically racist and unjust. The rioters' nauseating sense of entitlement to destroy other people's property and to sucker punch ideological foes is a natural extension of this profound delegitimation of the American polity.

■ ■ ■

In autumn 2015, the pathological narcissism of American college students found a potentially devastating new source of power in the sports-industrial complex. University of Missouri president Timothy Wolfe resigned in the face of a threatened boycott by black football players of an upcoming game. Wolfe's alleged sin was an insufficient appreciation for the "systematic oppression" experienced by students of color at the university. A graduate student announced a hunger strike, claiming that he had been assaulted by white students and that the N-word had been painted on his door. The administration had allowed these attacks, he said.

The university's board of overseers convened in emergency session to discuss the football boycott; Wolfe resigned before meeting with them, issuing the standard mea culpa: "I take full responsibility for this frustration, and I take full responsibility for the inaction that has occurred." According to *The New York Times*, the university could have lost more than $1 million had it forfeited its football game with Brigham Young University. A group called "Concerned Faculty" had walked off the job in solidarity with the student activists and was calling on other faculty to join them.

There is no evidence that the University of Missouri denies equal opportunity to its black students. Those black students—like every other student on campus—are surrounded by lavish educational resources, which are available to them for the asking on a color-blind basis. Nor is there any evidence of the attacks alleged by the graduate student; he reported none of them to the university or to city law enforcement. The university's faculty and administrators are surely among the most prejudice-free, well-meaning group of adults on the planet. Thousands of Chinese students would undoubtedly do anything for the chance to be "systemically oppressed" by the University of Missouri's stupendous laboratories and research funding.

But Missouri's political class has embraced the patent delusion that the university is rife with racism. Governor Jay Nixon called on college officials to "ensure the University of Missouri is a place where all students can pursue their dreams in an environment of respect, tolerance and inclusion." In truth, the only barrier to such pursuit is a student's own lack of academic preparedness, as will be discussed in chapters 2 and 3. Mayor Bob McDavid of Columbia, Missouri—where the university's main campus is located—told CNN after Wolfe's resignation that he congratulated the "students on achieving their goal." McDavid insisted that we need to "deal with the pain of minorities" and that we will be "done" only "when every student has the freedom to fulfill his dream unimpeded by racial epithets."

The precedent set here was monumental. Any student protester who can persuade his college's football or basketball team to threaten a strike will be able to bring administrators to their knees even more quickly than usual. Administrative cupidity and alumni fanaticism have turned the collegiate sports-industrial complex into the most powerful force on campus. If that behemoth can be reliably persuaded to support the latest racial agitation—and there will often be a critical mass of black athletes to appeal to—then an already supine leadership class will discard the reality principle once and for all.

Even without the sports-boycott tool, however, the takeover of the college campus by racial hysteria appears all but complete. A notorious video of a black female student at Yale screaming and cursing at her college master in November 2015 is a chilling portrait of self-engrossed, bathos-filled entitlement that has never been corrected by truth, much less restrained by manners: "Be quiet!" she shrieks at the frozen administrator. "Why the fuck did you accept the [master] position, who the fuck hired you?!" she continues at full, self-righteous cry. "You should not sleep at night! You are disgusting!"[8]

The master's wife, child psychologist Erika Christakis, had recently suggested in an email that the Yale multiculturalism bureaucracy did not need to oversee Halloween costumes. Her email prompted an open letter signed by nearly a thousand faculty, deans, and students accusing her of racism and white supremacy and calling for her and her husband's immediate removal from their jobs and campus home. A hundred or so mostly minority students then mobbed her husband, Nicholas Christakis, a renowned physician and sociologist, for an hours-long abuse session in the college quad that included the "Be quiet!" shriek, among equally horrifying displays of rudeness. "You are disgusting!" screamed another student. "I want your job to be taken from you. Look at me in my face first of all and understand that you are such a disappointment to this university, to your students, to yourself; you are the disgusting male you were twenty seconds ago, a day ago, and a month ago." *Time* magazine had named Nicholas Christakis one of the hundred most influential people in the world in 2009, but the students knew better. When Christakis meekly tells the students that he was trying to understand their predicament, a tall male strides up to him and, inches from his face, issues the usual demand that Christakis look at him (which Christakis was already doing). Christakis later hugs the student, Abdul-Razak Mohammed Zachariah, in a conciliatory gesture, but Zachariah orders Christakis to understand that the "situation right now doesn't require you to smile." Another female student, Alexandra Zina Barlowe, cries that Christakis's invocation of free speech creates "a space to allow for violence to happen on this campus." Christakis responds: "That I disagree with." Barlowe shouts at him: "It doesn't matter whether you agree or not. . . . It's not a debate."[9]

No administrator ever reprimanded these students for their insubordination.

Instead, Yale's president, Peter Salovey, issued the usual fawning declarations of sorrow for the tribulations experienced by Yale's minority students. "Their concerns and cries for help made clear that some students find life on our campus profoundly difficult," he wrote in November 2015, following up ten days later with further empathy: "In my thirty-five years on this campus, I have never been as simultaneously moved, challenged, and encouraged by our community—and all the promise it embodies—as in the past two weeks. You have offered me the opportunity to listen to and learn from you."[10]

And in case anyone misunderstood where the administration's sympathies lay, Yale conferred on Alexandra Zina Barlowe and Abdul-Razak Mohammed Zachariah its graduation prize for accomplishment in the "service of race and ethnic relations." Yale lauded Barlowe for her "womanist, feminist, anti-racist work" and for teaching her peers, faculty, and administration about "inclusive leadership." That inclusive leadership does not require a respect for debate, apparently.

Erika and Nicholas Christakis's careers have been devoted to social-justice concerns. Nevertheless, Erika Christakis resigned from teaching at Yale and Nicholas Christakis canceled his spring 2016 courses, after students marched on their home and chalked hostile messages outside their bedroom window. They resigned from their roles as college master in May 2016 after some students refused to accept their diplomas from Nicholas Christakis. The Chinese Cultural Revolution was hardly more efficient.

. . .

A similar capitulation—minus the expletives—took place at Emory University, when several dozen Emory students barged into the school's administration building to demand protection from "Trump 2016" slogans that had been written in chalk on campus walkways. Acting out a by-now standardized psychodrama of oppression and vulnerability, the students claimed that seeing Trump's name on the sidewalk confirmed that, as minorities, they were "unsafe" at Emory. College sophomore Jonathan Peraza led the allegedly traumatized students in a chant: "You are not listening! Come speak to us, we are in pain!"

As the Emory protesters entered the administration building, they drew on *The Communist Manifesto* (probably the only political theory they have even heard of) to express their plight: "It is our duty to fight for our freedom. It is our duty to win. We must love each other and support each other. We have nothing to lose but our chains."[11]

The order of the day was feelings. "What are we feeling?" protest leader Peraza asked his fellow sufferers, consistent with the neo-Victorian sentimentalism currently dominant on campuses. "Frustration" and "fear" were the answers. "I'm supposed to feel comfortable and safe [here]," a student told an *Emory Wheel* reporter. "I don't deserve to feel afraid at my school."

Emory protesters leveraged their Trump-induced "pain" and "unsafety" into the all-too-familiar demand for more diversity hires. The Emory students also picked up on an exculpatory meme to explain why affirmative action admits are not competitive scholastically: because they are so burdened by the need to create safe spaces for themselves. An Emory student told President James Wagner that "people of color are struggling academically because they are so focused on trying to have a safe community."

Put aside for a moment the students' demand for protection from political speech. ("Trump 2016" chalked on a sidewalk cannot be classed as a provocation.) Their self-image as immiserated proletarians, huddled together for safety and support, is pure fantasy. In fact, they are supremely fortunate, enjoying unfettered access to intellectual, scientific, and social resources that would have been the envy of every monarch in the age of absolutism. And any administrator who wants to prepare students for an objective relationship to reality would seek to convey that truth. By contrast, rewarding students' delusional self-pity only increases the likelihood that they will fail to take advantage of the enormous intellectual riches at their fingertips and go through life with self-defeating chips on their shoulders. But President Wagner followed obsequiously in the footsteps of virtually every other college president confronted by student claims of "unsafety"— he rolled over completely.

After initially declining, to his credit, to send a campus email decrying support for the "fascist, racist" Trump, Wagner nevertheless penned a missive that validated every aspect of the students' self-pity. He told the "Emory Community" that the students "voiced their genuine concern and pain in the face of this perceived intimidation" from the Trump chalkings, and that he "cannot dismiss their expression of feelings and concern as motivated only by political preference or oversensitivity."

Therefore, he was announcing a four-point plan to "recognize, listen to, and honor the concerns of these students." That plan included "a formal process to institutionalize identification, review, and addressing [sic] of social justice opportunities and issues." An annual Racial Justice Retreat and better procedures for reporting and responding to bias was promised. The university would be reviewing security videotape to identify the chalkers and submit them to the "conduct violation process," according to the *Wheel*, for possible violations of regulations requiring preapproval for chalkings. Would the same policies and procedures have been enforced if the chalking had read "Clinton 2016"?

Wagner paid lip service to free speech—only to qualify it with "safe spaces" jargon: "As an academic community, we must value and encourage the expression of ideas, vigorous debate, speech, dissent and protest. At the same time, our commitment to respect, civility, and inclusion calls us to provide a safe environment that inspires and supports courageous inquiry."[12] Why does "courageous inquiry" require a "safe environment"? If inquiry is "courageous," presumably it can withstand the pampered, hothouse climate of a college campus.

Any college president who adopts the rhetoric of "safe spaces" is already lost. Such rhetoric implies that there is somewhere on his campus that is not "safe"—a complete fiction. Wagner is an engineer by training, suggesting that a science background, with its grounding in the empirical method, does not inoculate a college president against cowardice when facing student neurasthenia.

Wagner wrapped up his campus-wide message with an echo from Yale: a paean to the protesters for teaching him so much. "I learn from every conversation like the one that took place yesterday and know that further conversations are necessary," Wagner wrote, recalling Salovey's even more revolting love letter to disruptive students.

Obviously, the Emory students need some basic civics lessons in political debate. They are likely to encounter more names of candidates they deplore over the course of their lives. They will not have a campus bureaucracy to run to for protection, in what has become the reflex reaction of students today to any behavior they don't like. The mature response to political speech that you disagree with is argument.

But the Emory students need something even more fundamental than an understanding of free speech and democratic persuasion. They need to stop feeling sorry for themselves and gain some perspective on their own privilege as members of a great university.

■ ■ ■

What's behind this soft totalitarianism? It is routinely misdiagnosed as primarily a psychological disorder. Young "snowflakes," the thinking goes, have been overprotected by helicopter parents, and now are unprepared for the trivial conflicts of ordinary life.

"The Coddling of the American Mind," a 2015 article in *The Atlantic* (now expanded into a book), has been the most influential treatment of the psychological explanation. The movement to penalize certain ideas is "largely about emotional well-being," argues Greg Lukianoff of the Foundation for Individual Rights in Education and Jonathan Haidt of New York University. The authors take activists' claims of psychological injury at face value and propose that freshmen orientations teach students cognitive behavioral therapy so as to preserve their mental health in the face of differing opinions.

But if risk-averse child-rearing is the source of the problem, why aren't heterosexual white male students demanding "safe spaces"? They had the same kind of parents as the outraged young women who claim to be under lethal assault from the patriarchy. And they are the targets of a pervasive discourse that portrays them as the root of all evil. Unlike any other group on a college campus, they are stigmatized with impunity, blamed for everything from "rape culture" to racial oppression.

Campus intolerance is at root not a psychological phenomenon but an ideological one. At its center is a worldview that sees Western culture as endemically racist and sexist. The overriding goal of the educational establishment is to teach young people within the ever-growing list of official victim classifications to view themselves as existentially oppressed. One outcome of that teaching is the forceful silencing of contrarian speech.

Such maudlin pleas for self-preservation are typical. An editorial in the Wellesley College student newspaper defended "shutting down rhetoric that undermines the existence and rights of others."

Offending "rhetoric" frequently includes the greatest works of Western civilization. In November 2015, a Columbia University sophomore announced on Facebook that his "health and life" were threatened by a core curriculum course taught by a white professor. The comment thread exploded with sympathetic rage: "The majority of why?te [*sic*] students taking [Contemporary Civilization] and on this campus never have to be consistently aware of their identities as white ppl while sitting in CC reading racist, patriarchal texts taught by white professors who most likely are unaware of the various forms of impact that CC texts have on people of color."

Another sophomore fulminated: "Many of these texts INSPIRED THE RACISM THAT I'M FORCED TO LIVE WITH DAILY, and to expect, or even suggest, that that doesn't matter, is fucking belittling, insulting, and WAY OUT OF FUCKING LINE."[13] Those "racist" texts include works by Plato, Aristotle, Kant, Rousseau, and Mill.

Many observers dismiss such ignorant tantrums as a phase that will end once the "snowflakes" encounter the real world. But the graduates of the academic victimology complex are remaking the world in their image (as we will see at length in chapter 11). Consider the firing of Google engineer James Damore in August 2017 for questioning the company's diversity ideology. After attending a diversity training session, Damore wrote a ten-page memo titled "Google's Ideological Echo Chamber." He observed that "differences in distributions of traits between men and women may in part explain why we don't have 50% representation of women in tech and leadership." Among those traits are assertiveness, a drive for status, an orientation toward things rather than people, and a tolerance for stress. He acknowledged that many of the differences in distribution are small and overlap significantly between the sexes, so that one cannot assume on the basis of sex where any given individual falls on the psychological spectrum. Considerable research supports Damore's claims regarding male and female career preferences and personality traits.

Damore affirmed his commitment to diversity and suggested ways to make software engineering more people-oriented. But he pointed out that several of Google's practices for engineering diversity discriminated in favor of women and minorities. And he called for greater openness to ideas that challenge progressive dogma, especially the "science of human nature," which shows that not all differences are "socially constructed or due to discrimination."

Google CEO Sundar Pichai employed the academy's bathetic language of injury in his response to Damore. "The memo has clearly impacted our co-workers, some of whom are hurting and feel judged based on their gender," he asserted in a memo of his own.[14] Yonatan Zunger, a recently departed Google senior engineer, claimed in an online essay that the speculations of Damore, a junior employee, have "caused significant harm to people across this company, and to the company's entire ability to function." He added that "not all conversations about ideas even have basic *legitimacy*"[15] [emphasis in original].

Ironically, Google is making even stronger claims than Damore is about the company's lack of bias against women. US Labor Department auditors allege that the company's salary differentials reflect sex discrimination; Google strenuously denies it. "We remain committed to treating, and paying, people fairly and without bias with regard to factors like gender or race," Eileen Naughton, vice president of "people operations," said in July 2017. "We are proud of our practices and leadership in this area." But typical of the cognitive dissonance affecting every diversity-obsessed company, Google puts its workers through "implicit bias" training on the theory that such biases inevitably cloud their ability to judge female and minority employees and job applicants fairly.

The corporate world is even mimicking academia in its inhospitality to nonconforming speakers. Earlier in 2017, a Google employee had asked me if I would be interested in speaking there about the police. The employee ultimately decided he could not go through with the invitation, however, citing "personal/professional matters" that he had to take into account for himself. An affiliation, however remote, with someone who challenges the Black Lives Matter narrative is apparently a job hazard at Google. A discrimination lawsuit filed by Damore in January 2018 alleges that Google keeps a black list of right-wing commentators who set off silent security alarms if they try to enter the Google campus.

Don't assume that the discipline of the marketplace will prevent this imported academic victimology from harming business competitiveness. Google sets managerial goals for increased diversity. Damore wrote that he has observed such goals resulting in discrimination. That is fully believable. A comment on an internal anonymous discussion app warned that more Google employees need to stand up "against the insanity. Otherwise 'Diversity and Inclusion' which is essentially a pipeline from Women's and African Studies, will ruin the company."[16]

The more resources that US companies spend on engineering diversity while global competing firms base themselves on meritocracy, the more we blunt our scientific edge. Employees are thinking about leaving Google because of its heavy-handed ideology, Damore said in an interview after his firing. While the prestige of elite companies may outweigh the burden of censorship for now, there may come a point when the calculus changes.

Eric Schmidt, outgoing chairman of Google parent Alphabet Inc., told a June 2017 shareholder meeting that Google was founded on the principle of "science-based thinking." It says a lot about the corporate world that it makes universities look like an open marketplace of ideas. Research into biological differences may be unwelcome in much of academia, but it proceeds on the margins nevertheless. In the country's most powerful companies, however, it is enough to disparage a scientific finding as a "stereotype" to absolve the speaker from considering the question: But is it true?

And now that zeal for censoring politically incorrect facts is working its way into the apparatus of government itself. In February 2018, an associate general counsel of the National Labor Relations Board released an official "Advice Memorandum" holding that Google was justified in firing Damore. Damore had filed a complaint with the NLRB in August 2017, but withdrew it in January 2018 after filing a lawsuit in state court. The associate general counsel went ahead and published her opinion anyway, though the issue was moot.

Damore's statements about "purported biological differences between men and women" were "discriminatory and constituted sexual harassment," declared NLRB counsel Jayme Sophir. Sophir sneers that Damore tried to cloak his comments with "'scientific' references and analysis." She makes no effort to determine whether that science met traditional research standards, which it does. If it contradicts feminist ideology, it must be both wrong and suppressed. Sophir notes that some of Google's employees had complained that Damore's memo made them feel "unsafe at work." Thus does bathos-filled academic victimology get bootstrapped into further assaults on rational inquiry outside the academy.

Sophir's advice memo does not have the force of law, but it is a barometer of which way the wind is blowing in government bureaucracies. As we will see, her views are hardly unique. The logic of her ruling means that any academic researcher investigating biological differences between the sexes is at risk of his job. Evolutionary biologists, psychologists, linguists, neurologists, or economists—anyone who has documented different risk preferences, ways of communicating, emotional bonding, or levels of aggression between males and females—could be fired for engaging in what Sophir labels "harmful, discriminatory, and disruptive" practices. This ruling, were it to become the standard governmental response to research on the sexes, would end that field of science entirely and create a chilling effect in many other areas.

■ ■ ■

Faculty and campus administrators must start defending the Enlightenment legacy of reason and civil debate. But even if dissenting thought were welcome on college campuses, the ideology of victimhood would still wreak havoc on American society and civil harmony. The silencing of speech is a massive problem, but it is a symptom of an even more profound distortion of reality. This distortion has its roots partly in well-intentioned public policies designed to advance minorities in the American education system, particularly in higher education; the objective failure of these policies has led to ever-more contorted theoretical efforts to explain their failures as the result of systemic racism, leading to an ideology of victimization that largely defines the campus environment today.

2

ELITES TO AFFIRMATIVE ACTION VOTERS: DROP DEAD

In 1996, Californians voted to ban race and gender preferences in government and education. Ten years later, the chancellor of the state-funded University of California at Berkeley, Robert Birgeneau, announced a new vice chancellor for equity and inclusion, charged with making Berkeley more "inclusive" and "less hostile" to "under-represented minority . . . groups." This move became just another expression of the University of California's unrelenting resistance to the 1996 voter initiative, in every way possible short of patent violation. Stasi apparatchiks disappeared more meekly after the Soviet Empire's collapse than California's race commissars have retreated after voters tried to oust their preference regime.

California shows the power, and the limitations, of the crusade for a color-blind America led by Ward Connerly, architect of the 1996 antipreference initiative. Without a doubt, Proposition 209, as that measure is called, has cut the use of race quotas in the Golden State's government. But it has also exposed the contempt of the elites—above all, in education—for the popular will. "Diversity"—meaning socially engineered racial proportionality—is now the official ideology of the education behemoth, and California shows what happens when that ideology comes into conflict with the law.

When Prop. 209 passed, a few politicians, such as San Francisco mayor Willie Brown, loudly vowed to disobey it. Most public officials, though, were more circumspect. Doubtless they counted on a highly publicized lawsuit, filed the day after the election, to eviscerate the new constitutional amendment before it affected their operations. A coalition of ethnic advocacy groups and big labor, represented gratis by some of the state's top law firms, had sued to block the amendment from taking effect. The plaintiffs argued, remarkably, that requiring government to treat everyone equally violated the Equal Protection Clause of the Fourteenth Amendment.

The plaintiffs could not have found a more sympathetic audience than Judge Thelton Henderson, one of the federal bench's most liberal activists. He quickly issued an injunction against Prop. 209, on the grounds that American society is so racist and sexist that only special preferences for minorities and women could ensure their constitutional right to equal protection. Henderson's 1996 ruling was the high point of the preference racket's reception in the courts. The Ninth Circuit Court of Appeals reversed Henderson's ruling the next year, declaring that Prop. 209's ban on discrimination and preferential treatment was fully compatible with the Equal Protection Clause—a point evidently not obvious to the crème of the state's lawyers.

From then on, state and federal judges would show an admirable respect both for voter intent and for the plain meaning of the state's new constitutional amendment. Not so for California's bureaucrats and pols. Many chose passive resistance or tried to hide noncompliance under Orwellian name changes: San Jose's affirmative action bureaucracy rechristened itself the "Office of Equality Assurance," for instance.

Without the efforts of a small public interest law firm, some of the state's largest government employers would still be using racial preferences for hiring and would be requiring contractors to do the same. The Pacific Legal Foundation had to drag into court the city and county of San Francisco, the Sacramento municipal utility district, the state lottery commission, the state bond commission, and the California community college system, among others, to vindicate the people's will. The Los Angeles and Berkeley school districts continued to assign students and teachers by race, even though the foundation had won suits challenging the practice in other school districts.

California's then–attorney general, Bill Lockyer, filed an amicus brief supporting San Jose's continuing preferential-outreach requirements for contractors. As for enforcing the state constitution against violators of 209, Lockyer could not be bothered. Members of the state legislature also busily tried to thwart the voters' fiat, often under pressure from Latino advocates. In a particularly strained move, the state assembly in 2003 adopted a definition of discrimination put forward by the 1969 UN International Convention on the Elimination of All Forms of Racial Discrimination, whose terms would have restored racial preferences in contracting. California courts saw through this ruse and overruled it in 2004.

Ward Connerly estimated in 2006 that 65 to 75 percent of California's agencies no longer use race in hiring or contracting—hardly resounding compliance but a huge improvement over the pre-209 era. A propreference organization claimed in 2004 that transportation-construction contracts awarded to minority-owned businesses had dropped 50 percent since 1996 and that the percentage of women in the construction trades had declined by one third. These figures suggest the extent to which race and gender discrimination had been keeping many noncompetitive enterprises afloat.

California's university system is a different matter entirely. That diehard center of race and gender obsession has managed to stay out of court (except for one sweetheart suit brought by propreference advocates) through fiendishly clever compliance with the letter of the law, while riding roughshod over its spirit. In doing so, university officials have revealed a fatalism about the low academic achievement of blacks and Hispanics that they would decry as rankest bigotry in a 1950s Southerner.

After Prop. 209's passage, UC Berkeley, like the rest of the UC system, "went through a depression figuring out what to do," says Robert Laird, Berkeley's propreferences admissions director from 1993 to 1999. The system's despair was understandable. It had relied on wildly unequal double standards to achieve its smattering of "underrepresented minorities," especially at Berkeley and UCLA, the most competitive campuses. The median SAT score of blacks and Hispanics in Berkeley's liberal arts programs was 250 points lower (on a 1600-point scale) than that of whites and Asians. This test-score gap was hard to miss in the classroom. Renowned Berkeley philosophy professor John Searle, who judges affirmative action "a disaster," recounted that "they admitted people who could barely read."

The downward trajectory of those students was inevitable, Searle said. "You'd be delighted to find that your introductory philosophy class looked like the United Nations, but that salt-and-pepper effect was lost after six to eight weeks," he recalled. "There was a huge drop-out rate of affirmative-action admits in my classes by mid-terms. No one had taught them the need to go to class. So we started introducing BS majors, in an effort to make the university ready for them, rather than making them ready for the university." Searle recalled a black studies class before his that was "as segregated as Mississippi in the 1950s." One day, Searle recounted, the professor had written on the blackboard that a particular tribe in Africa "wore colorful clothing."[1]

Even though preference beneficiaries often chose the easiest majors—there were few blacks and Hispanics in the most competitive engineering and computer science majors, for example—graduation rates also reflected the qualifications gap. The average six-year graduation rate for blacks and "Chicanos" (California-speak for Mexican Americans) admitted from 1991 to 1997, the last year of preferences, was about 20 percent below that of whites and Asians. The university always put on a happy face when publicly discussing the fate of its "diversity" admits. Internally, however, even the true believers couldn't ignore the problems. A psychology professor at UC San Diego recalled that "every meeting of the faculty senate's student affirmative-action committee was a lugubrious affair. They'd look at graduation rates, grades, and other indicators and say, 'What we're doing is failing.'"[2]

Yet for the preference lobby, a failing diversity student is better than no diversity student at all—because the game is not about the students but about the self-image of the institution that so beneficently extends its largesse to them. Thus, when "underrepresented minorities" accepted at Berkeley dropped by half in 1998, the first year that Prop. 209 went into effect, and by nearly that much at UCLA, the university sprang into action. Never mind that the drops at other campuses were much smaller. Berkeley's then-chancellor, Robert Berdahl, came to the Berkeley Law School and demanded that the faculty increase its shrunken minority admissions. When a professor asked how the school was supposed to do that consistent with 209, Berdahl responded testily that he didn't care how they did it, but do it they must. UCLA law professor Richard Sander was on a committee to discuss what could be done after 209. "The tone among many of the faculty and administrators present was not 'How do we comply with the law in good faith?' but 'What is the likelihood of getting caught if we do not comply?'" he said. "Some faculty observed that admissions decisions in many graduate departments rested on so many subjective criteria that it would be easy to make the continued consideration of race invisible to outsiders."[3]

Like Proteus caught in a net, the University of California struggled furiously over the next decade to rework its admissions formulas, trying to re-create its former "diversity" profile without explicitly using race. If, in 1967, an Arkansas fire department had devised pretextual, ostensibly nonracial, job qualifications to foil a desegregation order, it would have been judged in violation of the Constitution. But legal elites will never object to such pretextual surrogates for race in order to engineer a certain level of representation for "underrepresented minorities."

The university's attitude was as damaging as its actions. How to explain the significant drop-off in black and Hispanic applications to UC's most elite campuses after Prop. 209 passed? The then-dean of Berkeley Law School, Herma Hill Kay, gave PBS's *NewsHour* the pro-preference answer: "I think that there was a feeling that California in general had turned its back on minority applicants. People felt that they didn't have to come here if they weren't welcome here." Another explanation, of course, might be that minority students, well aware of how much they had previously benefited from preferences, realized that without those preferences they stood little chance of getting in to the most selective campuses.

UC could have responded to the charge of being "unwelcoming" with something like the following rebuttal: "We welcome students of all races and ethnicities. Every student will be judged according to his accomplishments, and anyone who meets our standard—equally high for all—will win admission. UC has never discriminated and never will." Instead, UC continued throwing its weight behind the argument that the only way to "welcome" minority students is to make sure that they get in whether or not they match the academic qualifications of white and Asian students.

University spokesmen constantly convey the idea that 209 is forcing them to do something unjust. "It's a hard message to send—persuading kids that they have a place at the university, when we deny so many qualified students," observed administrator Nina Robinson.[4] (Robinson masterfully blended the "unwelcoming" topos with the university's current line that students who would be admitted only under affirmative action are all "highly qualified.") But the University of California rejects almost all white and Asian applicants with combined SAT scores of 1000 and 2.85 GPAs, say, and no one accuses UC of being unwelcoming to rejected white and Asian students. If proportionally far fewer black and Hispanic students qualify for admission than whites and Asians, the problem lies with the systemic academic weakness of those students, not with the admissions standards. But this is a truth that, post-209, the university has persistently denied.

Only in 1998 did the university's admissions processes operate without either explicit racial preferences or stealthy surrogates for race. The results were telling: At Berkeley, the median SAT gap shrunk nearly in half, to 120 points; black and Hispanic admits logged an impressive 1280 on their combined SATs. The six-year graduation rates of this class would increase 6.5 percent for blacks and 4.9 percent for Hispanics, compared with the class admitted two years earlier.

The more pedagogically sound environment that resulted didn't matter to the race mongers, however. They flung themselves into their long experimentation with different admissions schemes, with one purpose: "To maintain a racially and ethnically diverse student body," as former UC associate president Patrick Hayashi wrote in 2005. The first scheme that the university tried was to give an admissions preference to low-income students. This device backfired, however, when it yielded a wealth of Eastern European and Vietnamese admits—not the kind of "diversity" that the university had in mind. So the campuses cut their new socioeconomic preferences in half and went back to the drawing board.

Various components in the system began diluting their academic requirements. Berkeley Law School reduced the role of the Law School Admission Test (LSAT) and college grade-point average (GPA) in ranking students, and it lowered the LSAT cutoff score that would disqualify a student for consideration. Previously these lowered expectations had applied only to minorities but they would now technically apply to all students. The school also removed the quality adjuster for high school GPAs, so that a 3.8 from a school where half the students drop out before graduating counted as much as a 3.8 from a school where the student body is frantically competing to rack up academic honors.

Other schools created pretextual institutions in the hope that they would be minority magnets. UCLA's law school established a specialization in critical race studies, a branch of legal theory contending that racism pervades nearly every category of the law and that writing about one's personal experiences grappling with that racism is real legal scholarship. College seniors who say that they want to specialize in critical race studies on their UCLA law school applications get a boost in the admissions process. As the school discreetly put it, a student's interest in the program "may be a factor relevant to the overall admissions calculus." In 2002, UCLA rejected all white applicants to the program, even though their average LSAT score was higher than the average score of the blacks who were admitted.

The university as a whole started admitting all students in the top 4 percent of their high school class, regardless of their standardized test scores, hoping that this would net more applicants from all-minority schools. The public justification for this practice, which Texas and Florida also implemented in response to affirmative action bans, is that getting to the top of one's class signals the same academic talents regardless of whether your school awards As just for showing up. But a 2005 college board study found that 30 percent of the African American and Hispanic students with an A average have mediocre SAT verbal scores of 500 or lower.[5] Indeed, while only half of the blacks and Hispanics who rank in the top tenth of their class also score over 600 on either section of the SAT, all the whites in the top 10 percent do. And contrary to the claims of affirmative action proponents, the evidence is strong that students with combined SAT scores of 1000, say, are less likely to do well in competitive colleges than students with test scores several standard deviations above that. In addition, UC also started giving preferences to students who had attended university-sponsored tutoring programs, which, while technically open to students of all races, target underrepresented minorities.

None of these new admissions measures produced the numbers of "underrepresented minorities" at Berkeley and UCLA that the diversity ideologues and the ethnic lobbies in the state legislature demanded, however. The legislature's Latino caucus told the university that more of "their people" at Berkeley and UCLA was the price of budgetary support. Clearly, the university remained too wedded to its old, meritocratic ways to achieve the "critical mass" of minorities that diversity advocates claim is necessary for a sound education. So the university began to "question all criteria, including criteria that have long been regarded as reflecting high academic achievement," in the words of former associate president Hayashi. Incredibly, it began to ignore entirely its applicants' objective academic rankings.

For several decades, the university had divided its applicants into two categories: It admitted one half only by objective tests of academic merit, such as standardized test scores and honors classes; it evaluated the other half subjectively, weighing such factors as race, economic status, or leadership. From this tier, where racial preferences had free rein, the vast majority of blacks and Hispanics were drawn.

After 209, the university could no longer use race within this second tier, and the surrogates for race it had developed netted a lower percentage of minorities from this tier than pure racial targeting. The solution? Junk the academic tier and evaluate the entire applicant pool on subjective and "contextual" factors. The hope, obviously, was that by eliminating the academic admits, the process would open up more spaces for students admitted on "holistic" factors—who just happened to be black and Hispanic.

UC president Richard Atkinson proposed in 2001 that all campuses adopt this new "comprehensive review" process. Under comprehensive review, already in use at diversity-mad Berkeley, perfect 1600 scores on the SATs would have to be understood "contextually." They might end up being given the same weight as 1100s, say, if the 1600-scoring student had come from a stable two-parent family and had attended a top high school. And 900s on the SATs might count more than 1600s, if the student with the 900s came from a school with many low-achieving students or if he came from a single-parent home or spoke a foreign language at home. Admissions officers perked up when they read that a student lived in a gang area or had been shot. Tutors in UC outreach programs taught students to emphasize their social and economic disadvantages in their application essay.

Precious few faculty members in the UC system had the guts to oppose Atkinson's comprehensive-review proposal publicly (though a plurality of professors polled by Roper opposed preferences—in private, of course). Berkeley political scientist Jack Citrin was one of the few who spoke out. Citrin observed that a UC Davis study showed that comprehensive review inevitably decreases the quality of the freshman class. Indeed, average SAT scores for entering freshmen at Berkeley dropped from 1330 in 1998 to 1290 in 2001, according to *USA Today*; and the test-score gap between whites and Asians, on the one hand, and blacks and Hispanics, on the other, widened.

Citrin exposed the vacuity of UC's claim that it was necessary to "refine and redefine" the "concept of merit to make it more inclusive." "How do we 'refine' the meaning of merit for a political science or electrical engineering major that goes beyond knowledge of subject matter and the capacity for critical thinking?" Citrin wrote in an op-ed. "Clearly, the concept of 'evaluation-in-context' is an invitation to introduce a new set of group preferences. I personally believe that poverty should not be a handicap to attending UC and strongly support generous student aid from all sources. But I do not believe that such a background factor should be a positive advantage, outweighing factors more directly linked to academic success and discriminating against middle-class students."

The university found even this criticism too much to tolerate. President Atkinson and his minions went ballistic when they learned that the UC regents chairwoman had invited Citrin to speak to that body before it voted on Atkinson's comprehensive-review proposal. An Atkinson aide threatened to engineer a faculty vote of censure against the chairwoman if she did not cancel Citrin's appearance. She held her ground, but not without further tongue-lashing from Atkinson.

Atkinson needn't have bothered. The regents duly rubber-stamped his plan, and UC swept away the concept of objective academic merit. If anyone had any doubt as to comprehensive review's purpose, a 2003 legal settlement dispelled it. The NAACP and a bevy of other "civil rights" groups had sued Berkeley in 1999 for "discriminating" against "people of color" in its admissions process—i.e., for failing to extend them overt racial preferences. If ever there was a sweetheart suit, this was it, since Berkeley wholly embraced the plaintiffs' cause. The parties settled amicably, agreeing that comprehensive review fully satisfied the plaintiffs' demands by "taking into account the full range of indicators of 'merit,'" according to the NAACP's press release.

A 2002 *Wall Street Journal* article provided eye-opening details about how comprehensive review worked in practice. UCLA had accepted a Hispanic girl with SATs of 940, while rejecting a Korean student with 1500s. The Korean student hardly lived in the lap of luxury: He tutored children to pay the rent for his divorced mother, who had developed breast cancer. But he went to a highly competitive school with a high Asian population in Irvine, while the Hispanic girl came from a school filled with failing students in overwhelmingly Hispanic South Gate. Students from South Gate got into UCLA and Berkeley at twice the overall acceptance rate. Indeed, an analysis of UCLA admissions rates in the four years following Prop. 209—even before comprehensive review—found that going to a school with a high-achieving student body decreased one's admissions chances sevenfold. An engineer's son with near-perfect SATs from University High in Irvine, for instance, was rejected from both Berkeley and UCLA.

It's remarkable in the post-209 world how explicitly university administrators speak about their racial intentions—and get away with it. Thus, a 2003 report by the UC president's office lauded comprehensive review, the 4 percent automatic admissions mechanism, and the preferences for tutoring-program attendees for boosting the admissions chances of minorities, even as other groups faced decreased admissions. As long as the mechanisms that administrators use for engineering a certain racial outcome are ostensibly color-blind, they appear safe.

Comprehensive review gives university administrators a face-saving explanation for admissions disparities that appear racially motivated. In 2003, for example, John Moores Sr., who was the one remaining regent committed to color-blind meritocracy, disclosed that Berkeley had admitted 374 applicants in 2002 with SATs under 1000—almost all of them "students of color"—while rejecting 3,218 applicants with scores above 1400. UCLA had similar admissions disparities. In a *Forbes* column, Moores, who had fought tooth and nail to get the data, accused Berkeley of continuing to discriminate against Asians and of admitting students who were unprepared for Berkeley's rigors.

Predictably, the administration exploded, engineering a censure resolution against Moores by his fellow regents. Backed up by a huge coalition of left-wing professors, civil rights groups, ethnic advocates, and opponents of standardized testing, administrators argued that the students admitted with extremely low scores had unique leadership skills or character and that their test scores said nothing about their ability to succeed at an elite institution. Race, they huffed, was irrelevant to their admission.

But the few independent studies that were published on admissions processes continued to show racial disparities that such "contextual factors" cannot explain away. A study of UCLA admissions from 1998 to 2001—before the official onset of comprehensive review—showed that, even controlling for economic status and school ranking, blacks were 3.6 times as likely to be admitted as whites, and Hispanics 1.8 times as likely. An unpublished study of Berkeley Law School admissions by Richard Sander revealed disparities between minorities and whites of such magnitude that to posit any explanation other than race seems fanciful. The school assigns each applicant a numerical index based on college grades and LSAT scores. In 2002, it admitted 92 percent of white applicants with an index of 250 or higher but only 5 percent with an index between 235 and 239. By contrast, it admitted 75 percent of black applicants in the 235 to 239 range in 2002 and 65 percent in 2003. No black applicants had an index of 250 or higher. Even a 2004 university study acknowledged that there were admissions disparities by race that nonacademic, nonracial factors could not account for.

Even if race were not motivating admissions decisions in violation of 209, it is ludicrous to imagine that it is a favor to let someone into an elite institution where most students scored much higher on the SATs. But preference advocates deny that standardized tests measure anything relevant about academic aptitude or preparedness. The standard line at UC is that "everyone whom we admit is highly qualified"—which just boils down to a tautology: If we admit you, you are by definition highly qualified.

Yet the argument that objective tests reveal no meaningful distinctions among students contains implications that preference advocates don't want to accept. If everyone above a certain minimum floor is equally qualified for elite institutions, Berkeley prof Jack Citrin asked during the debate over comprehensive review, why not admit people by lottery? A lottery would reflect the diversity of the applicant pool exactly and would admit more minorities. But it would also lower academic quality. "If you think they don't care about that, of course they care," said Citrin. "God forbid Berkeley should resemble [less elite] UC Riverside!"

Citrin's lottery proposal went nowhere, of course. Race-conscious schools are perfectly content to use objective tests of aptitude to judge Asians and whites, and even to rank black and Hispanic students within their own group. But if you suggest using objective standards to evaluate students on a common universal scale, those standards suddenly lose all their validity.

Why? "It's not the case that test takers are uniformly capable of displaying what they know during standardized tests," argued Mark Rashid,[6] a civil engineering prof at UC Davis and chair of UC's admissions committee. He invoked a theory propounded by Stanford education professor Claude Steele, who claims that blacks and Hispanics get so worried that they'll confirm the stereotype that minorities score lower on standardized tests that they freeze up and *do* score lower. Unanswered, of course, is the question of how the stereotype arose in the first place. At any rate, if the so-called stereotype threat really were inhibiting minorities from showing what they know and can do, standardized tests should predict that black and Hispanic students will do worse in college than they actually do. The opposite is the case. Blacks and Hispanics do worse than their SATs predict.

Affirmative action defenders have yet another explanation for the poor SAT performance of minorities. Low-income applicants from schools with underperforming student bodies, they contend, have never gotten the chance to develop their academic talents and so should not be held to the same standards. A 900 for them is the equivalent of a 1400 for a more privileged applicant. Colleges can compensate for deficiencies in K–12 education, said Rashid, "if you devise a process that identifies applicants with the willingness to succeed. Initially they need services, but by their third year, they're really screaming along." Yet while undoubtedly some ill-taught high school students end up trouncing their peers in college, such cases are not the norm. And college admissions have to be about averages.

The most radical preference advocates simply dismiss the validity of tests—for everyone. One UC report, for example, stressed that high school GPAs and standardized test scores combined predict only about 25 percent of freshman-year grades at the university—which, the authors imply, is a pathetically low predictive validity. Such objective measures, therefore, should give way to "holistic" factors for determining eligibility. But the 25-percent validity that they scorn in this case is higher than the correlation between SATs and socioeconomic status, which they invoke as a reason to discontinue the use of SATs in college admissions (SATs unfairly disadvantage the poor, goes the argument). If, as ex–Berkeley admissions director Laird put it, there is an "absolute correlation between income and SAT scores," then the correlation between SATs and academic performance is beyond absolute. By contrast, the factors that the 209 foes want to use instead of SATs for admission, such as "spark" and leadership, have predictive powers of about 2.5 percent—in other words, almost no relationship to academic success.

In 2004, a groundbreaking study of affirmative action in law schools blew away every rationale for racial double standards ever put forth. Richard Sander found that law schools that admit black students with lower GPAs and LSAT scores than their nonblack peers—almost all law schools, in other words—actually lowered those students' chances of passing the bar.[7] Because of the "mismatch" between their academic preparedness and the academic sophistication of the school that has bootstrapped them in, the preference beneficiaries learn less of what they need to pass the bar than they would in a school that matched their capabilities. Far from increasing the supply of black lawyers, affirmative action actually decreases the diversity of the bar.

The data that Sander offered about black performance in law school were stunning. After the first year, 51 percent of black students were in the bottom tenth of their class, compared with 5 percent of white students. Two-thirds of black students were in the bottom fifth of their class. Blacks were twice as likely to drop out as whites, and only 45 percent of black law school graduates pass the bar on their first try, compared with 80 percent of white grads. Blacks were six times as likely to fail the bar after multiple efforts.

Law school is the perfect place to evaluate whether aptitude tests such as the LSAT and SAT do or do not predict academic success. College gives no objective exit exam that measures what undergraduates actually learned. Grades are imperfect measures, since courses vastly differ in difficulty, and grade inflation is rampant. Law school grades, by contrast, provide a more reliable gauge, since they are often calculated blind and on a curve. The bar is an objective exit exam.

The correlation between black law students' rock-bottom LSATs and their performance in law school and on the bar exam was overwhelming. Sander's study demolished the two mainstays of the preferences regime: the argument that objective aptitude tests do not anticipate minorities' academic performance, and the argument that admitting affirmative action beneficiaries to schools where their academic skills are below the norm is in their interest.

Clearly, Sander's work was a mortal threat and had to be treated as such. The article was "a piece of crap that never should have been published and has no merit of any sort," Stanford law professor Michele Landis Dauber huffed.[8] Berkeley law professor Goodwin Liu (now an associate justice of the California Supreme Court) misrepresented the article's message, charging Sander with telling blacks that they "should lower their sights"[9] in choosing a law school—as if blacks can aspire to the top tier only with the crutch of affirmative action.

Other law professors offered increasingly tortured explanations of Sander's data. All involved the phlogiston of modern liberalism: racism—which can neither be perceived nor measured but can be invoked as an explanation in the face of ignorance or (as here) bad faith. Harvard law professor David Wilkins, for instance, ascribed the racial achievement gap to some law professors' low expectations of black students—a fanciful explanation, given that the classroom interaction between law professors and all students at Harvard is only slightly more intimate than that between a marquis and a peasant, and is not much more engaged elsewhere.

In the wake of Sander's paper, preference advocates were wildly casting about, like sailors on a sinking ship, to find aspects of legal education that they could toss overboard to try to improve black performance. Liu suggested that law schools might jettison time-limited exams, for instance. "But don't lawyers need to think quickly under pressure, especially in a courtroom?" I asked. "What percentage of lawyers make courtroom arguments?" he responded. Timothy Clydesdale, a College of New Jersey sociologist, argued in response to Sander's article that law professors' method of publicly grilling students on their understanding of the law intimidates black students.[10] Never mind that litigators can expect far rougher treatment from judges. (Clydesdale did not answer a request to explain why he thinks that black law students are uniquely sensitive to aggressive questioning.)

Sander's research empirically exploded the argument that affirmative action benefits its recipients. But the practice of pushing unprepared black and Hispanic students into elite schools raises a logical question as well: If it would be so injurious to their life chances to attend a school that they can handle academically, however less elite, why should any student suffer the fate of going to California State University, Northridge, instead of UCLA, say, or Santa Clara Law School instead of Berkeley's? Why not close down those allegedly career-destroying second- and third-tier schools, so that everyone can get an elite degree?

Affirmative action's condescension toward lesser-ranked schools received its perfect expression in Berkeley's then-chancellor Robert Birgeneau. In a 2006 interview, Birgeneau opined: "One of my most important practical concerns is that the communities most in need of educated, strong leadership are also the communities most profoundly underrepresented at the state's flagship university. . . . [T]here are just too few people here from those communities at present to provide that leadership going forward."[11] In other words, don't expect UC Riverside or Cal State Long Beach to turn out "community" leaders.

I asked leading UC affirmative action proponents why we inflict on *any* student the handicap of attending a nonelite college. I never got an answer. UC admissions committee head Mark Rashid simply parried one question with another. I tried again: "Why is it okay for a white kid to go to Cal State Hayward and not a Hispanic?"

"That should be the point of the admissions process," he responded, "to figure out what are various degrees of deserving. What if we knew that more African Americans are capable of succeeding at Berkeley?" Is that only true of blacks, not of whites? "It's probably more true of blacks than whites or Asians," he said. "The bottom line is: Race is important, it has a lot to do with how we see ourselves. The critical mass argument for affirmative action should not be casually dismissed."

Another question I never got answered was whether minorities were doing everything that *they* could to qualify themselves for the university. Even supposing that California were inequitably distributing its educational resources, are minorities grasping such opportunities as are available to them? Or does a culture of underachievement—truancy, failure to do homework, indifference to learning, and so on—also impede the proportional representation of blacks and Hispanics? I learned that nothing riles an affirmative action proponent more than the suggestion that academic achievement is an individual, as well as a social, responsibility.

"Why not encourage the same commitment to learning in underrepresented minorities as in Asians, a group that once suffered discrimination?" I asked Patrick Hayashi, the former UC associate president. Though only 12 percent of California's population, Asians made up nearly half of Berkeley's freshman class a decade after Prop. 209. "A lot of Asians are deeply committed to education," Hayashi advised me, "but a lot are deeply involved in gangs, drugs. Be careful how you generalize."

"Doesn't the stigma against 'acting white'—i.e., achieving academically—hold back minority achievement?" I asked Robert Laird, Berkeley's ex–admissions chief. "There's some truth to the allegation," he said, "but you can't blame the victim. It's really shallow [to say] that this is just a matter of cultural indifference. There are a lot of reasons why that cultural indifference is in place. You can't simply say, 'Okay, here are the opportunities, why don't you just do it?' You need to overcome the cultural damage that has led to that indifference."

I emailed former UC admissions chair Michael Brown, a UC Santa Barbara education professor. (Brown was appointed provost of the UC system in 2017.) Rather than worry about UC eligibility standards, I suggested, more might be accomplished by trying to foster among underrepresented minorities the same fanaticism about academic overachievement that a significant portion of Asians demonstrates. "It saddens me," Brown emailed back, "that you are comparing groups based on stereotypes. Asians are not monolithic and neither are URMs [underrepresented minorities]. 'Whites' aren't either. Individual merit— properly identified, supported, and rewarded—should be what we *all* care about, at least it seems to me."

If only.

3
AFFIRMATIVE DISASTER

A growing body of empirical evidence is undermining the claim that racial preferences in college benefit their recipients. Students who are admitted to schools for which they are inadequately prepared learn less, in fact, than they would in a student body that matches their own academic level. A controversy at Duke University demonstrated, however, that such pesky details may have no effect on the preference regime.

Duke admits black students with SAT scores on average over one standard deviation below those of whites and Asians (blacks' combined math and verbal SATs are 1275; whites' are 1416; and Asians', 1457). Not surprisingly, blacks' grades in their first semester are significantly lower than those of other ethnic groups, but by senior year, the difference between black and white students' grades has shrunk almost 50 percent.[1] This convergence in GPA might seem to validate preferential admissions by suggesting that Duke identifies minority students with untapped academic potential who will narrow the gap with their white and Asian peers over their college careers.

Three Duke researchers demonstrated in 2012 that such catching-up is illusory. Blacks improve their GPAs because they switch disproportionately out of more demanding science and economics majors into the humanities and soft social sciences, which grade much more liberally and require less work. If black students stayed in the sciences at the same rate as whites, there would be no convergence in GPAs. And even after their exodus from the sciences, blacks don't improve their class standing in their four years of college.)

This study, by economics professor Peter Arcidiacono, sociology professor Ken Spenner, and then-economics graduate student Esteban Aucejo (now a professor at Arizona State University), has major implications for the nationwide effort to increase the number of minority scientists.[2] The federal government alone has spent billions of dollars of taxpayers' money trying to boost minority participation in science; racial preferences play a key role in almost all college science initiatives. The Arcidiacono paper suggests that admitting aspiring minority scientists to schools where they are less prepared than their peers is counterproductive.

The most surprising finding of the study is that, of incoming students who reported a major, more than 76 percent of black male freshmen at Duke intended to major in the hard sciences or economics, higher even than the percentage of white male freshmen who anticipated such majors. But more than half of those would-be black science majors switched track in the course of their studies, while less than 8 percent of white males did, so that by senior year, only 35 percent of black males graduated with a science or economics degree, while more than 63 percent of white males did. Had those minority students who gave up their science aspirations taken introductory chemistry among students with similar levels of academic preparation, they would more likely have continued with their original course of study, as the record of historically black colleges in graduating science majors suggests. Instead, finding themselves in classrooms pitched at a more advanced level of math or science than they have yet mastered, preference recipients may conclude that they are not cut out for quantitative fields—or, equally likely, that the classroom "climate" is racist—whereas the problem may just be that they have not yet laid the foundations for more advanced work.

Attrition from a hard science major was wholly accounted for in the paper's statistical models by a freshman's level of academic qualifications; race was irrelevant. While science majors had SATs that were fifty points higher than students in the humanities in general, students who had started out in science and then switched had SATs that were seventy points lower than those of science majors. Any student in a class that assumes knowledge of advanced calculus is likely to drop out if he has not yet mastered basic calculus.

Predictably, a number of black students, alumni, and professors portrayed the research, whose methodology was watertight, as a personal assault. Members of Duke's Black Student Alliance (BSA) held a silent vigil outside the school's Martin Luther King Day celebration in protest of the paper and handed out flyers titled "Duke: A Hostile Environment for Its Black Students?" In an email to the state NAACP, the BSA called the paper "hurtful and alienating" and accused its authors of lacking "a genuine concern for proactively furthering the well-being of the black community."[3]

Naturally, the BSA leveraged its protest into demands on the Duke administration for more black faculty and administrators and for more funding of black-themed programs. A Duke professor of English, women's studies, and law, Karla Holloway, tweeted that the study "lacks academic rigor"—this women's studies professor neglected to specify which of its algorithms she found flawed—and that it "re-opens old racial wounds."[4] A senior research scholar, Tim Tyson, wrote in an op-ed that the paper was a "political tract disguised as scholarly inquiry," representing a "crusade to reduce the numbers of black students at elite institutions."[5] (Both Tyson and Holloway were active in the witch hunt against the three Duke lacrosse players who were falsely accused in 2006 of raping a black stripper.) A group of recent black Duke graduates called on the study's authors to "stop their attack on students of color."

To the extent that these critics tried to address the paper's arguments, they missed its gist entirely. The Duke alumni alleged that black students "shy away" from "so-called 'difficult' majors" because they've been told all their lives that they are "inferior"—overlooking the fact that Duke's black students "shied away" from the sciences only *after* starting out in those fields. Tyson claimed that black students choose the humanities over the sciences because they "come from cultural and intellectual traditions different than—not less than—most white students at Duke"—again, ignoring the fact that black students overwhelmingly intend to major in the sciences when they arrive at Duke. An essay by a professor of critical culture, gender, and race studies at Washington State University faulted the researchers for not exploring the "countless" ways in which "racism" denies black high school students equal access to SAT prep and advanced placement courses. But the focus of the major-switching paper was on what happened to minority students *after* they arrived at Duke, not before. Moreover, the paper did note that the racial difference in academic preparation is "not surprising, given disparities in resources between black and white families."

The study's critics also asserted that the intellectual demands of humanities and science majors are indistinguishable. Applying Ferdinand de Saussure (a nineteenth-century Swiss linguist invoked today only in literature classes) to *The Matrix*, it was claimed, is as challenging as mastering the Heisenberg Uncertainty Principle. Here, too, the protesters ignored the paper's empirical evidence: Duke seniors in the hard sciences have lower grades than *freshmen* in humanities and social sciences, even though the SATs of science majors are, on average, higher than those of humanities majors. For blacks, the disparity in grading is even greater. Black freshmen at Duke get higher grades in the humanities and social sciences than freshmen of all races get in the hard sciences, though black students' test scores and overall grades are significantly lower than other students'. As for the coursework demands in the various fields, it is students themselves who report spending 50 percent more time studying for the hard sciences, and who rate those courses as more difficult than those in the humanities and the social sciences.

In a different world, the Duke administration might have tried to dispel the critics' distortions of the Arcidiacono paper, given the authors' patent lack of invidious intent and the rigor of their work. Instead, Duke's top bureaucrats let the authors twist in the wind. In an open letter to the campus, provost Peter Lange and a passel of deanlings declared: "We understand how the conclusions of the research paper can be interpreted in ways that reinforce negative stereotypes."[6] It is hard to imagine a more hypocritical utterance. To the extent that the paper reinforced "negative stereotypes," it did so by describing the effects of Duke's policy of admitting black students with lower academic qualifications than whites and Asians. It is Duke's predilection for treating black students as a group whose race trumps their individual academic records that constitutes "stereotyping," not the authors' analysis of the consequences of that groupthinking. (Campus spokesman Michael Schoenfeld ignored a request to specify the "negative stereotypes" that the paper might reinforce.)

But perhaps a concession to black anger had to be made to clear some space for a defense of the Arcidiacono paper? Not a chance. The deanlets and provosts followed their invocation of "negative stereotypes" with an anodyne generalization about academic freedom: "At the same time, our goal of academic success for all should not inhibit research and discussion to clarify important issues of academic choice and achievement." In other words, don't blame us for what these wacky professors might say.

The bureaucrats went on to explain the origins of the student database that the professors had used for their study, as if the very gathering of information had been called into question by the paper. (The Duke data repository was a response to William Bowen and Derek Bok's 1999 study of college affirmative action, *The Shape of the River*, which had exposed the low grades of preference beneficiaries nationwide; the Duke data project was intended to identify and help resolve similar problems of underachievement locally. In other words, the Arcidiacono paper was squarely within the mandate of the Duke student database.) Duke has worked to create an "empowering, safe, and stigma-free environment" for students to get help in science, the administrators added, implicitly acknowledging that the administration has known for years about (minority students' struggles with science.)

Finally, as is de rigueur in all such flaps over "diversity," the administration pledged to try even harder to be sensitive to Duke's black students. "We welcome the call to action. Many people have been working for a long time to create a positive climate for African-American students. We look forward to ongoing conversations with BSA and others about ways that we can improve," Schoenfeld penitently announced. Of course, as Schoenfeld meekly hinted, Duke has been engaged in color-coded programming and funding for decades, pouring money into, to name just a few endeavors, a black student center, a black student recruiting weekend, and such bureaucratic sinecures as a vice provost for faculty diversity and faculty development and an associate vice provost for academic diversity, who, along with the faculty diversity task force and faculty diversity standing committee, ride herd over departmental hiring and monitor the progress of the ongoing Faculty Diversity Initiative, which followed upon the previous Black Faculty Strategic Initiative. But no college administration in recent history has ever said to whining students of *any* race or gender: "Are you joking? We've kowtowed to your demands long enough, now go study!" And why should the burgeoning student services bureaucracy indulge in such honesty? It depends on just such melodramatic displays of grievance for its very existence.

The BSA may have misunderstood the paper's argument, but it was right about one thing: The Duke administration had completely ducked the substance of the study. Referring to the bureaucrats' open letter, the BSA's executive vice president told the campus newspaper: "They didn't mention the words 'race,' 'black' or the phrase 'affirmative action' in their response, and we feel that this was a deliberate attempt to avoid directly addressing the issues at hand." No kidding. The Duke hierarchy uttered not a word on whether the school's black students were dropping out of the sciences because of their relative lack of preparation. It was as if Arcidiacono, Spenner, and Aucejo had committed a social transgression so embarrassing that the only polite thing to do was to ignore it.

A handful of scholars have been documenting the negative consequences of so-called academic mismatch, but the scourging of Arcidiacono and his fellow authors cannot encourage many others to enter the fray. Nevertheless, the evidence is already strong that preferences are contributing to the undereducation of minorities. In 2004, as we have seen, UCLA law professor Richard Sander demonstrated that (blacks admitted to law schools because of their race end up overwhelmingly in the lowest quarter of their class and have much greater difficulties passing the bar than students admitted on their merits) A working paper by Sander and UCLA statistician Roger Bolus extended the Arcidiacono analysis of students at Duke to a comparative setting: Science students with credentials more than one standard deviation below their peers' are half as likely to graduate with science degrees as students with similar qualifications attending schools where their academic preparation matches that of their peers.

As such findings mount, the conclusion will become inescapable: College leaders who continue to embrace affirmative action do so simply to flatter their own egos, so that they can gaze upon their "diverse" realm and bask in their noblesse oblige. Faced with the Arcidiacono analysis and other research like it, the responsible thing for Duke administrators to do would be to admit all students on the same basis, so that all would stand an equal chance of success in the most challenging majors. Getting rid of racial preferences would reduce Duke's black population, now 10 percent of the student body, by half, but the half that remained would be fully competitive with their peers. Admittedly, such a drop in the black student census would trigger charges that Duke was hostile to minorities. And unless other schools reformed their own admissions policies, the students whom Duke would have admitted through racial preference would simply go to other elite institutions, where they would be just as handicapped by deficiencies in their academic preparation. All the more imperative, then, to air mismatch research as widely as possible. But until it becomes possible to discuss the effects of preferences without being accused of racial animus, it may be impossible to dislodge academic affirmative action, no matter how discredited its purported justifications.

A DEVASTATING AFFIRMATIVE ACTION STORY

In 2013, the *Los Angeles Times* published a case study in the malign effects of academic racial preferences. The University of California at Berkeley followed the diversocrat playbook to the letter in admitting

Kashawn Campbell, a South Central Los Angeles high school senior, in 2012: It disregarded his level of academic preparation, parked him in the black dorm—the "African American Theme Program"—and provided him with a black studies course. The results were thoroughly predictable. After his first semester, reports the *Times,* Kashawn had barely passed an introductory science course.

In College Writing 1A, his essays—pockmarked with misplaced words and odd phrases—were so weak that he would have to take the class again. His writing often didn't make sense. He struggled to comprehend the readings. "It took a while for him to understand there was a problem," his instructor said. "He could not believe that he needed more skills. He would revise his papers and each time he would turn his work back in having complicated it. The paper would be full of words he thought were academic, writing the way he thought a college student should write, using big words he didn't have command of." His grade-point average was 1.7, putting him at risk of expulsion if he didn't raise it by the end of the year. The one bright spot in his academic record? Why, African American Studies 5A, of course! Kashawn had received an A on an essay and a B on a midterm, the best grades of his freshman year: Kashawn reveled in the class, a survey of black culture and race relations, in a way he hadn't since high school.

He would often be the first one to speak up in discussions, even though his points weren't always the most sophisticated, said Gabrielle Williams, a doctoral student who helped teach the African American Studies class. He still had gaps in his knowledge of history. But, Williams said, "you could see how engaged he was, how much he loved being there."

Did Kashawn's good grades in African American Studies 5A mean that he had suddenly learned how to think and to write? Not at all. He was advancing little in his second go-round at expository writing: "On yet another failing essay, the instructor wrote how surprised she was at his lack of progress, especially, she noted, given the hours they'd spent going over his 'extremely long, awkward and unclear sentences,'" reported the *Los Angeles Times*. His (to him) unforeseen academic struggles took a psychological toll: "He had never felt this kind of failure, nor felt this insecure," wrote the *Times*. "Each poor grade [was] another stinging punch bringing him closer to flunking out. None of the adults in his life knew the depth of his pain: not his professors, his counselors, or any of the teachers at his old high school."

He tried to rally his spirits with heart-wrenching pathos: "'I can do this! I can do this!' he had written [in a diary]. 'Let the studying begin! . . . It's time for Kashawn's Comeback!'" A counselor in the campus psychologist's office urged him to scale back his academic ambitions. "Maybe he didn't have to be the straight-A kid he'd been in high school anymore," the counselor advised him. This "be content with mediocrity" message sums up the attitude that many a struggling affirmative action "beneficiary" has adopted to get through college.

The black-themed dorm and student center also operated exactly as one would expect, confirming their members' belief in their own racial oppression: "Sometimes we feel like we're not wanted on campus," Kashawn said, surrounded at a dinner table by several of his dormmates, all of them nodding in agreement. "It's usually subtle things, glances or not being invited to study groups. Little, constant aggressions." Of course, the only reason that Kashawn and many of his fellow dormmates are at Berkeley is because the administration "wants" them so much, regardless of their chances of success.

It is unlikely, however, that African American Studies 5A discussed the academic-achievement gap in Berkeley's admissions between black, white, and Asian students. That gap, not racism, explains why Kashawn was not a sought-after addition to study groups. (Kashawn came to Berkeley through one of the University of California's many efforts to evade California's ban on governmental racial preferences: an admissions guarantee for students in the top decile of their high school classes, regardless of their test scores or the caliber of their school.) As his freshman year drew to a close, Kashawn was on tenterhooks waiting to learn if his second-semester grades would allow him to continue into sophomore year.

Which course gave him an A–, to pull his GPA over the top? *Hint*: it wasn't College Writing. The *Times* could not have produced a more resounding confirmation of mismatch theory if it had tried. But the *Times* story conveys a subtler point as well: Racial preferences are not just ill advised; they are positively sadistic.

It is primarily the preening self-regard of University of California administrators and faculty that is served by admitting such underprepared students.

4

THE MICROAGGRESSION FARCE

In November 2013, nearly two dozen graduate students at the University of California at Los Angeles marched into an education class and announced a protest against its "hostile and unsafe climate for Scholars of Color." The students had been victimized, they claimed, by racial "microaggression"—the hottest concept on campuses today, used to call out racism otherwise invisible to the naked eye. UCLA's response to the sit-in was a travesty of justice. The education school sacrificed the reputation of a beloved and respected professor in order to placate a group of students making a specious charge of racism.

The pattern would repeat itself twice more at UCLA that fall: Students would allege that they were victimized by racism, and the administration, rather than correcting the students' misapprehension, penitently acceded to it. Colleges across the country behave no differently. In the process, they are creating what tort law calls "eggshell plaintiffs"—preternaturally fragile individuals injured by the slightest collisions with life. The consequences will affect us for years to come.

UCLA education professor emeritus Val Rust was involved in multiculturalism long before the concept even existed. A pioneer in the field of comparative education, which studies different countries' educational systems, Rust spent over four decades mentoring students from around the world and assisting in international development efforts. He has received virtually every honor awarded by the Society of

Comparative and International Education. His former students are unanimous in their praise for his compassion and integrity. "He's been an amazing mentor to me," said Cathryn Dhanatya, a former assistant dean for research at the USC Rossier School of Education. "I've never experienced anything remotely malicious or negative in terms of how he views students and how he wants them to succeed."[1] Rosalind Raby, director of the California Colleges for International Education, said that Rust pushes you to "reexamine your own thought processes. There is no one more sensitive to the issue of cross-cultural understanding."[2] A spring 2013 newsletter from UCLA's ed school celebrated Rust's career and featured numerous testimonials about his warmth and support for students.[3]

It was therefore ironic that Rust's graduate-level class in dissertation preparation was the target of student protest just a few months later—ironic, but in the fevered context of the UCLA education school, not surprising. The school, which trumpets its "social-justice" mission at every opportunity, is a cauldron of simmering racial tensions. Students specializing in critical race theory play the race card incessantly against their fellow students and their professors, leading to an atmosphere of nervous self-censorship. Foreign students are particularly shell-shocked by the school's climate. "The Asians are just terrified," says a recent graduate. "They walk into this hyper-racialized environment and have no idea what's going on. Their attitude in class is: 'I don't want to talk. Please don't make me talk!'"[4]

Val Rust's dissertation-prep class had devolved into a highly charged arena of competing victim ideologies, impenetrable to anyone outside academia. For example: Were white feminists who use "standpoint theory"—a feminist critique of allegedly male-centered epistemology—illegitimately appropriating the "testimonial" genre used by Chicana feminists to narrate their stories of oppression? Rust took little part in these "methodological" disputes—if one can describe "Chicana testimonials" as a scholarly "method"—but let the more theoretically up-to-date students hash it out among themselves. Other debates centered on the political implications of punctuation. Rust had changed a student's capitalization of the word "indigenous" in her dissertation proposal to the lowercase, thus allegedly showing disrespect for the student's ideological point of view. Tensions arose over Rust's insistence that students use the more academic *Chicago Manual of Style* for citation format; some students felt that the less formal American Psychological Association style conventions better reflected their political commitments. During one of these heated discussions, Rust reached over and patted the arm of the class's most vociferous critical race-theory advocate to try to calm him down—a gesture typical of the physically demonstrative Rust, who is prone to hugs. The student, Kenjus Watson, dramatically jerked his arm away, as a burst of nervous energy coursed through the room.

After each of these debates, the self-professed "students of color" exchanged emails about their treatment by the class's "whites." (Asians are not considered "persons of color" on college campuses, for reasons that no one seems willing to explain.) Finally, on November 14, 2013, the class's three militant students of color, accompanied by at least eighteen students of color from elsewhere at UCLA, as well as by a reporter and photographer from the campus newspaper, made their surprise entrance into Rust's class as a "collective statement of Resistance by Graduate Students of Color." The protesters formed a circle around Rust and the remaining four students (one American, two Europeans, and one Asian national) and read aloud their "Day of Action Statement." That statement suggests that Rust's modest efforts to help students with their writing faced obstacles too great to overcome.

The Day of Action Statement contains hardly a sentence without some awkwardness of grammar or usage. "The silence on the repeated assailment of our work by white female colleagues, our professor's failure to acknowledge and assuage the escalating hostility directed at the *only* Male of Color in this cohort, as well as his own repeated questioning of this male's intellectual and professional decisions all support a complacency in this hostile and unsafe climate for Scholars of Color," the manifesto asserts. The Day of Action Statement denounces the class's "racial microaggressions," which it claims have been "directed at our epistemologies, our intellectual rigor and to a misconstruction of the methodological genealogies that we have shared with the class." (Though it has only caught on in recent years, the "micro-aggression" concept was first coined in the 1970s by a black psychiatrist.) Reaching its peroration, the statement unleashes a few more linguistic head-scratchers: "It is, at its most benign, disingenuous to the next generations of Scholars of Color to not seek material and systematic changes in this department. It is a toxic, unsafe and intellectually stifling environment at its current worse."

The PhD candidates who authored this statement are at the threshold of a career in academia—and not just any career in academia but one teaching teachers. The Day of Action Statement should have been a wake-up call to the school's authorities—not about UCLA's "hostile racial climate," but about their own pedagogical failure to prepare students for scholarly writing and advising. Rust is hardly the first professor to be called a bigot for correcting students' grammar and spelling. "Asking for better grammar is inflammatory in the school," said an occasional TA. "You have to give an A or you're a racist." Rather than examining their pedagogy, the authorities chose a different course.

As word of the sit-in spread in the press and on the internet, the administration began its sacrifice of Rust. Dean Marcelo Suárez-Orozco sent around a pandering email to faculty and students, announcing that he had become "aware of the last of a series of troubling racial climate incidents at UCLA, most recently associated with [Rust's class]"—thus conferring legitimacy on the preposterous claim that there *was* anything racially "troubling" about Rust's management of his class. Suárez-Orozco went on: "Rest assured I take this extremely seriously. I humbly dedicate myself to listening and to learning from this experience. As a community, we will work towards just, equitable, and lasting solutions. Together, we shall heal."

Of course, the very idea of taking "this" "extremely seriously" presupposes that there was something to be taken seriously and solved, as opposed to a mere outburst of narcissistic victimhood. The administration announced that Rust would not teach the remainder of the class by himself but would be joined by three other professors, one of whom, Daniel Solórzano, was the school's leading proponent of microaggression theory and critical race theory. This reorganization implicitly confirmed the charge that Rust was unfit to supervise "graduate students of color."

Unsatisfied with the administration's response, the protesters posted an online petition riddled with a new crop of grammatical puzzlers. "Students consistently report hostile classroom environments in which the effects of white supremacy, patriarchy, heteronormativity, and other forms of institutionalized oppression have manifested within the department and deride our intellectual capacity, methodological rigor, and ideological legitimacy," limped one typical sentence.

A few weeks later, a town hall convened to discuss the Day of Action's charge of a "hostile and toxic environment for students of Color." Professor Solórzano presented his typology of microaggressions to explain the school's racial tensions. Protest organizer Kenjus Watson read a long bill of particulars accusing Rust of lying about his microaggressions. Another black student argued that no reconciliation in the school was possible because Rust had not apologized for his transgressions. Several of Rust's faculty colleagues in the Division of Social Sciences and Comparative Education attended; none publicly defended him.

After the meeting, Rust approached the student who had berated him for not seeking forgiveness and tried to engage him in conversation. Ever naïve, Rust again reached out to touch his interlocutor. The student, a large and robust young man, erupted in anger and eventually filed a criminal charge of battery against the seventy-nine-year-old professor. Rust's employers presented him with a choice: If he agreed to stay off the education-school premises for the remainder of the academic year, they would not pursue disciplinary charges against him. The administration then sent around a letter to students, alerting them that the school would be less dangerous—for a while, at least—with Rust out of the picture.

The dean and his assistants were just warming up. They formed a committee charged with "examining all aspects of the [school's] operations and culture from the perspective of race and ethnic relations." Oblivious to conflicts of interest, they appointed Watson, leader of the anti-Rust protests, as "graduate student researcher" for the committee. None of the allegedly racially "hostile" students who had been penned inside the protest circle was invited to participate. Solórzano would chair the committee.

The committee's final report unctuously thanked the student protesters for their brave stand against racial oppression: "Recently, a group of our students have courageously challenged us to reflect on how we enact [the school's social-justice] mission in our own community. We owe these students a debt of thanks," opened the report. Watson, in other words, was thanking himself. To laud the students as courageous is absurd: They faced no prospect of negative repercussions from their protest.

The committee said nothing about the students' embarrassing writing skills, perhaps because it had almost as much difficulty as they did crafting clear prose: "We welcome the opportunity to step up to the leadership role that accompanies our social justice mission to work on remedying the unsafe and not brave learning spaces within our community and pledge to improving our pedagogical practices and classrooms so that all our students feel their work is valued," the committee announced.[5]

If UCLA were serious about preparing its graduate students for a life of scholarship, it would have rebutted the protesters' assumption that their work should be off-limits to questions. (According to the Day of Action Statement, "the barrage of questions by white colleagues and the grammar 'lessons' by the professor have contributed to a hostile class climate.") Intellectual debate is essential to the academic endeavor and in no way constitutes a "microaggression," the administration should have said. There is no likelihood that the class discussions were motivated by racism; virtually every American student in the education school embraces its "social-justice" mission. A graduate student who defended Rust in the UCLA student newspaper opened her op-ed on the dispute with the observation that racism "is deeply embedded within the institutions that make up UCLA" before denouncing Rust's "unjust . . . demoniz[ation] as a symbol of white male oppression."

But the most stunning failure of the committee's report and of the school's leadership more generally was the unwillingness to make any public effort to rebut the students' calumny against Rust. Surely Rust's colleagues knew that he lacks any trace of racial condescension or "hostility." As one of his students put it: "He is pure of heart." No more poisonous charge can be lodged against someone in today's university than racial bias or insensitivity. Yet the education-school administration sacrificed Rust's honor and feelings, not to mention the truth, to avoid further inflaming the protesters. This is not just a moral lapse; it is also an educational one. Rust's "students of color" profoundly misinterpreted the dynamics of the classroom, seeing racial animus where none existed. Not only did the education school not correct the students' misperceptions, it celebrated those students as heroes. The administration and complicit faculty have thus all but guaranteed that the protesters and their supporters will go through life lodging similar complaints against equally phantom racism and expecting a similarly laudatory response.

I asked Dean Suárez-Orozco whether his administration believed that Rust was an appropriate target of a racial protest; he refused to answer, citing through a spokesman "personnel privacy rights." In light of the open humiliation of Rust, as well as the administration and committee's existing public comments, it is cowardly to hide behind alleged "privacy rights" to avoid answering questions about a painfully public affair.

The closest that the administration came to acknowledging the possibility that the protesters had misconstrued the classroom dynamics was a brief passage in the Race and Ethnic Relations Committee report. According to the committee, there exists no right or wrong interpretation in alleged racial incidents—just different perspectives, each equally valid: "Any incident or experience shared by a community will always generate multiple narratives, each of which has the right to be respected and validated as an experience of events. No single version of any incident is a full explanation of a complex situation, particularly one that carries the heavy weight of issues emotionally charged by historical legacies of racism, power imbalance, and systematic abuses that often go unrecognized and without articulation in our culture." Though the committee gave no indication that it had considered, much less "validated," a narrative about Rust's class that *discounted* the claim of racism, implicit in its invocation of "issues emotionally charged by historical legacies of racism" is the hint that there may be another side to the protesters' portrayal of Rust's class. That's cold comfort, though, to Rust or anyone who cares about the truth. In fact, the committee's seemingly evenhanded gesture of epistemological inclusiveness was even more of a moral dodge than it first appeared. It let the committee sidestep its responsibility of deciding whether the racial accusation was justified; in practice, the racism charge will always trump a denial of racism. Once such a charge is launched, every campus administration will act as if it were true and will introduce a host of measures to counteract the alleged bias.

The committee concluded by congratulating itself and the school's leadership for identifying "the racial climate challenges that emerged in the Fall Quarter and mov[ing] quickly and decisively to address them." The authors lacked the integrity to name these "racial climate challenges" or to specify how the school addressed them, but presumably the administration did so by cordoning off the school from Rust's dangerous presence. The report went on to recommend the bureaucracy inflation that is every school's default response to racial protest: in this case, a new associate dean for equity and diversity, a permanent committee on equity and diversity, diversity training for the faculty, and a beefed-up grievance process for lodging complaints of racial discrimination, among other measures lifted directly from the protesters' petition.

Kenjus Watson, the *"only* Male of Color" in Rust's class and lead protest organizer, moved on to codirect the "Intergroup dialogue program" at Los Angeles's Occidental College the following summer. In fact, Watson became a font of "Intergroup dialogue" across the country, yet another content-free academic fraud. "Intergroup dialogue" courses, in the words of the Occidental catalog, seek to "enhance students' knowledge, understanding, and awareness about diversity and social justice while nurturing the development of constructive intergroup relations and leadership skills"—all for academic credit. Watson has taught "Intergroup dialogue" courses at Penn State, St. Louis University, and the University of Michigan, covering such topics as "Gender, Race, Sexuality, and Black Masculinity." The Day of Action Statement had denounced Rust's arm pat: "this singling out of this Male Student of Color reached an inexcusable culmination when the professor physically shook this student's arm in a questionable, patronizing and facetious effort to remind student of the importance of dialogue." Someone who felt so offended by Rust's innocuous gesture is not the ideal candidate for promoting "constructive intergroup relations," even if that were a legitimate academic field. But Watson has undoubtedly spread his version of "dialogue" and "social justice" to numerous receptive "Students of Color," who will have learned to see everything through a lens of racial offense.

For the next three years, Suárez-Orozco and his administration colleagues would hound Rust, driving him from one makeshift off-campus office space to another and filing baseless charges against him. Finally, in August 2017, Suárez-Orozco sent out a one-line memo to the ed school faculty affirming that Rust had full status as emeritus professor—the closest thing to an apology that Rust ever received.

Barely a week after the 2013 Day of Action at the education school, a different microaggression incident convulsed UCLA's law school. Once again, the administration failed to push back against clearly ungrounded student claims of racial injury.

Richard Sander, whom we met in previous chapters, taught an enthusiastic group of students in his first-year property class in the fall of 2013. Building on that class spirit, he proposed a softball match between his students and the other first-year property-law section. Sander's students wanted to make team T-shirts and came up with a design featuring the logo #teamsander and a picture of their professor holding a baseball bat, embellished with such property terms as "replevin" and "trover." A few days before the game, a number of Sander's students wore their T-shirts to class. An email storm immediately broke out among the first-year black students, charging Sander's class with microaggression.

Because of Sander's work on mismatch theory, UCLA's minority law students saw in the Team Sander T-shirts a racial slight against them. In the words of the school's Diversity Action Committee on Campus Climate, the students "felt triggered" by the shirt—an au courant phrase of campus victimology meaning that the shirt had engendered traumatic recollections of other racist abuse that the students had experienced. The shirts were a manifestation of "white privilege," according to a Facebook commenter, consistent with "racist/classist/sexist comments made inside and outside of the classroom."

This racial interpretation was wholly fanciful. Affirmative action had never come up during Sander's class; most of his students were not even aware of mismatch theory. Their choice of team name was solely an expression of gratitude for the class's camaraderie. Nevertheless, the first-year black students called a meeting for the next day to discuss their response to the alleged microaggression. Several of Sander's property-law students attended, in the hope of rebutting the idea that the T-shirt was a political statement; some of the minority students objected to their presence, and the meeting devolved into a shouting match.

Sander's students left the T-shirts at home for the softball game, but tensions remained high. Several students notified the legal gossip blog *Above the Law* about the T-shirt offense, and the blog gleefully ran a series of posts about "racism" at the UCLA law school. One post included an anonymous claim from a black student that the law school no longer assigns blacks to Sander's first-year property classes (there were none that year in his section) because taking a class taught by an opponent of racial preferences is too "awful." The anonymous source claimed that black students wouldn't feel comfortable seeking additional help from Sander for fear of "contributing to his research" on mismatch theory by admitting that they didn't understand a concept.[6] This is an understandable, if unfortunate, reaction to Sander's work, but it's hard to see any way around the dilemma. Sander pursues his research on racial preferences in good faith and goes where the facts lead him. He happens to be a committed liberal, passionately dedicated to racial equality, who has empirically come to the conclusion that affirmative action impedes black academic progress. No one has ever alleged that he treats all his students with anything other than respect. In any case, the creation of the Team Sander T-shirts had nothing to do with mismatch theory.

The day after the softball game, which the first-year black students and a few others in the opposing property-law section boycotted, law school dean Rachel Moran sent an email to the first-year class about the T-shirt incident and the "hurt feelings" that it had caused. Rather than rebutting the idea that the T-shirts were racially disrespectful, Moran took refuge in epistemological agnosticism, like the UCLA ed school bureaucrats. She urged students to be "respectful of one another's feelings and open to understanding different points of view." In theory, this is anodyne advice, but unless Moran believed that the T-shirts were justifiably viewed as a racial insult, she should have corrected the students' misperception and helped them gain some perspective on what constitutes a true racial offense. Moreover, if T-shirts with Sander's name and picture could legitimately be seen as an attack on black students, then Sander's very presence on campus must also constitute an attack on black students. Moran let that possibility hang out there.

The rest of Moran's email signaled where her heart lay. She promised that her administration would "facilitate constructive conversations in safe spaces for all of our students." This melodramatic "safety" rhetoric, deployed so promiscuously during the Rust incident (and constantly thrown around by campus feminists as well), lies at the heart of academic victimology. Any college bureaucrat who uses it has cast his lot with the fiction that his college is dangerous for minority and female students outside a few places of sanctuary.

Meanwhile, Sander asked a dean if the school had, in fact, stopped assigning black students to his class, as *Above the Law* had reported. The school has no such policy, the dean told him. Another T-shirt-inspired rumor held that Sander somehow penalizes blacks in grading, even though grading throughout the school is blind to students' identities. To the contrary, Sander learned, his first-year black students do better in his classes than in their other classes, earning a B on average, compared with a B– elsewhere. Sander asked the administration to put those facts out there to rebut the various falsehoods; it declined to do so, for fear of stirring up more protest.

Racial agitation continued into the new semester. The Black Law Students Association held a demonstration in February 2014, protesting the fact that there were only 33 blacks out of 1,100 students at the law school—apparently, the law school is to blame for the small pool of black college graduates nationwide and in California with remotely competitive LSAT scores and grades. The school twists itself into knots trying to admit as many black students as possible without violating California's ban on racial preferences so flagrantly that even the press takes notice. In fact, both UCLA and UC Berkeley law schools admit blacks at a 400 percent higher rate than can be explained on race-neutral grounds, according to a paper by a pro–affirmative action economist at Berkeley, Danny Yagan. No matter. The protesters wore T-shirts with "33/1,100" on them and made a YouTube video titled *33*, containing personal testimonials about the stress of being one of UCLA's black law students: "It's so far from being a safe space that it would be better for my mental health if I stayed at home," said one girl. Other students complained that they were looked to in class to represent the black perspective—precisely the role that the "diversity" rationale for racial preferences assigns to minority students.[7]

Meanwhile, a string of robberies near UCLA was prompting a discussion on the law school's student Facebook page about self-defense tips. The school's most vociferous critic of alleged white privilege and institutional racism, first-year student Alexis Morgan Gardner, argued that the robbery perpetrators were "clearly victims to life circumstances (and probably poverty) as well" and that the discussion should address the root causes of crime, not just "reactionary" measures. A few other students replied that a "root causes" discussion, however important, was secondary to the security issue. Gardner responded, mangling English idiom along the way: "I FEAR FOR MY SAFETY MORE HERE (at the law school) in this hostile space where the future 'leaders of America' are so intolerable to alternative perspectives" than in her own home, with "extremely higher" crime statistics. "It sounds like a lynch mob in the making," she added.

Several days later, a male student unknown to Gardner accosted her on a school elevator and asked her how she could feel at greater risk of physical harm at the law school than in a high-crime area. Gardner wrote about the encounter on Facebook as an example of why she felt unsafe at the school, adding a string of other purported abuses that suggested a paranoid streak: "people . . . publicly mock, disrespect, and dismiss me when it appeals to the majority. . . . everyone knows exactly who I am and stares at me when I walk through the halls because essentially, I am a fly in the milk. . . . there's some deep-seated abhorrence and intolerance of me among the masses, but they hide it in their microaggressions and behind their keyboards."

A day later, Gardner published on Facebook an anonymous hate-mail note that she said had been left in her mailbox: "stop being such a sensitive [n—r]." Gardner added: "And to all those of you who disrespectfully took part in that fb thread [presumably the one about crime and root causes], who liked comments and encouraged our classmates detestable behavior (on and off of fb), YOU actively contributed to this racially hostile campus environment. . . . I hope you are all proud of yourselves."

The school immediately went into crisis mode, outstripping its Sander T-shirt response. After the Black Law Students Association presented Dean Moran with a petition denouncing the school's "lack of institutional commitment to student of color presence and safety," she wrote to the student body that she was "personally sensitive to and aware of the kinds of challenges faced by students of color, in and out of the classroom." In a breathtakingly condescending gesture, Moran announced that the school would be holding seminars "to help students with cross-cultural competency and communication skills," an agenda later expanded to include "practical strategies for becoming a better ally."[8] This increasingly popular "ally" mission may come as a surprise to the average student, who thought that he had enrolled in college to get an education, not to be enlisted in the allegedly titanic struggle of black and Hispanic students against hostile academic forces. The school encouraged incoming first-year law students in the fall of 2014 to be tested for unconscious bias, for which they could receive counseling at the school's expense. (For more on the idea of implicit bias, see chapter 5.) The faculty needed an antiracism tune-up as well, in Dean Moran's eyes: The school would offer a faculty workshop on the neuroscience of unconscious bias and its impact on legal education, followed by workshops on "facilitating classroom discussions about race, diversity, and discrimination." Of course, the administration trotted out the usual parade of additional diversity initiatives, including a new Director of Student Learning Environment and Academic Affairs, tasked with "promoting and supporting diversity," and a new grievance procedure for student-bias complaints.

The chance that the hate-mail note was real is far lower than the chance that it was a hoax, to apply David Hume's test for miracles. UCLA's law students, like law students everywhere, are almost obsessively career-oriented. They have most likely spent their previous four years strategizing about law school admissions, with the hope of landing a lucrative job down the road with their newly minted JD. It would be an act of utter folly, contrary to the future orientation that helped land them at UCLA, to put their future career in jeopardy by sending so crude and juvenile a note, one that would simply serve as a pretext for more racial agitation.

Dean Moran announced on February 20, 2014, that a police investigation into the origin of the note was underway. That was the last mention of the investigation from the administration. Rumors circulated among the faculty that the note had proved a hoax. Eventually, the UCLA police department declared the incident "unfounded," meaning, according to a sergeant, that the message, even if real, did not rise to the level of a crime. The police department did not attempt to determine the note's provenance.

But in the unlikely event that the note *was* real, Moran's reaction was still excessive. Even if one law student sent a hate note, that aberrant behavior doesn't represent the daily reality at the school. It is ludicrous to suggest that UCLA's white and Asian students need "cross-cultural competency" training in how to talk to blacks and

Hispanics. The Facebook comments defending a self-help discussion in response to the local robberies were civil and reasoned, contrary to Gardner's characterization of them as "disrespectful" and "detestable." As for the faculty, no evidence exists that they are guilty of "unconscious bias" in their teaching, and it is an insult to imply otherwise. The entire law school environment is a paragon of racial tolerance, as any fair-minded administrator should recognize.

Moran should have condemned the hate note, if real, as the action of one immature, unmoored individual who grossly violated everything that the law school embodies, promised an investigation, and left it at that. Instead, she chose to feed the patent delusion that black students are under siege and "unsafe" at the school, thus encouraging in them a lifelong disposition toward similarly baseless perceptions. (Moran announced without explanation at the start of the 2014 fall semester that she would be leaving her position as soon as a replacement could be found.)

UCLA's third outbreak of racial complaint, in November 2013, prompted a response from the head of the university itself. A student-made video blamed UCLA for the allegedly low number of black male undergraduates at the school—3.3 percent—in a state with only a 6-percent black population. The film quickly received more than 2 million views on YouTube.

Black Bruins opens with a shot of the names of two Black Panthers killed by a rival radical at a UCLA student meeting in 1969. *Implication*: UCLA is responsible for their deaths. Apparently, that shooting was just the start of UCLA's long war against men of color. The camera pans to a group of hostile-looking black male students standing outside a campus building behind the filmmaker, third-year African American–studies major Sy Stokes. Accompanied by ominous music, Stokes recites a frequently unintelligible rap denouncing UCLA as a "fraudulent institutionalized racist corporation" that deliberately excludes blacks and that "refuses to come to [their] defense."

One passage concerns black paint, which Stokes claims black children were taught to avoid and which symbolized the melanin in their skin. Since black paints are only used to write words on a white background, Stokes proposes, and "if words are all we are good for, then don't you dare tell us to silence our voices when we dare to speak." We are left to wonder not just at the passage's logic, but also at who is telling blacks to silence their voices.

According to *Black Bruins,* UCLA is as much at fault for the 74-percent black-male graduation rate as it is for the 3.3-percent black-male enrollment rate.

Never mind that the school has poured millions into academic support services and the usual panoply of multicultural programming. Never mind that the school has come up with scheme after scheme, as noted earlier, to get around California's constitutional ban on governmental racial preferences, admitting black students at more than double the rate than can be explained by their credentials and socio-economic status, and at three times the rate of much poorer Asians. Never mind that *all* males—at less than 45 percent—are underrepresented in the undergraduate population and that whites—at 28 percent—are also underrepresented compared with their 39-percent share of California's population. UCLA's overall black enrollment—3.8 percent in 2013, when females are included—is actually higher than one would expect, given that the entire state population of 6 percent includes children and adults who would not be applying for admission to college. (And it is virtually identical to black enrollment in the entire University of California system.) But other factors also limit enrollment.

In 2013, when this controversy was raging, only 11 percent of black eighth-graders in California were proficient in math, compared with 42 percent of whites and 61 percent of Asians; 15 percent of black eighth-graders were proficient at reading, compared with 44 percent of whites and 51 percent of Asians.[9] Black elementary school students in California are chronically truant at nearly four times the state average. Only 5 percent of applications to UCLA even come from black students.[10] *Black Bruins* mentioned none of these facts, of course, but they show that UCLA has used every possible lever, legal or not, to boost its black student population.

UCLA's administrators couldn't line up fast enough to thank Stokes for his work and praise its artistic qualities. Janina Montero, UCLA's vice chancellor for student affairs, was first out of the gate. "In their video 'Black Bruin [The Spoken Word],' a number of UCLA students eloquently and powerfully expressed their frustration and disappointment with the low number of African-American male students on campus," she said in a published statement. "As a public institution that values a diverse student body, we share their dissatisfaction and frustration."[11] Was UCLA a "fraudulent institutionalized racist corporation" that tries to ruin the "hopes and dreams" of black students and that "refuses" to come to their "defense"? Apparently so, given Montero's fulsome "Amen" to the entirety of Stokes's message. Montero provided none of the academic or demographic data that would explain the 3.3-percent black-male enrollment figure. The only cause of that "low" number, according to Montero, is California's ban on "considering race in the admissions process." Montero eagerly reminded readers that the University of California was trying to overturn that ban in the Supreme Court. Why it should be necessary to consider race in the admissions process to achieve "diversity" went unexplained.

UCLA soon concluded that a mere vice chancellor was insufficient to respond to Stokes's masterpiece. Chancellor Gene Block stepped up to the plate, anticipating the servility of Yale's Peter Salovey and Emory's James Wagner. "We are proud when [our students] convey their thoughts, experiences and feelings—as they have done recently in several now viral videos," Block wrote in a campus-wide memo.[12] These students' "powerful first-hand accounts" testify to the "true impacts" of California's ban on racial preferences, the chancellor said. As Stokes had done, Block painted a dire picture of black student life at UCLA: "Too often, many of our students of color feel isolated, as strangers in their own house. Others feel targeted—mocked or marginalized, rather than recognized and valued." Were "students of color" *right* to "feel targeted—mocked and marginalized"? It would appear so. Block left unsaid who was doing the "mocking" and "marginalizing," but he seemed to believe that he presided over a student body and faculty of bigots. Block went on to chastise UCLA for its reluctance to have "conversations about race." "Make no mistake: [such conversations] can be very difficult. They are inevitably emotional. They can make people defensive. They sometimes lead to accusations. But we cannot be afraid to have these conversations, because they are so critically important not just to our university, but to society."

Pace Block, UCLA spends vast amounts of time having "conversations about race." But if he wants to engender even more, a good place to start would be with some facts. He could rebut the baseless allegation that UCLA deliberately destroys blacks' "dreams." He could lay out the vast academic-achievement gap, whose existence demolishes the claim that the absence of racial proportionality in the student body or faculty results from bias. Most important, he could provide a dose of reality. "This campus is one of the world's most enviable educational institutions," he could say, "whose academic splendors lie open to all its students. You will never again have as ready an opportunity to absorb knowledge. Exploit the privilege. You are surrounded by well-meaning, compassionate faculty who only want to help you. Study, write, and immerse yourself in timeless books. Apply yourself with everything you've got, and you will graduate prepared for a productive, intellectually rich life."

Rather than opting for the truth, Block kowtowed further. "I also appreciate that trust is earned and, among our critics, we must and will work harder to earn it," he wrote, in closing. He did not explain why UCLA should be mistrusted. Had it misled its black students? Discriminated against them? Block did not say. He did, however, remind them of UCLA's soon-to-be-hired new vice chancellor for equity, diversity, and inclusion and the two inaptly named "diversity prevention officers," the latter of whom would "investigate . . . racial and ethnic bias or discrimination among our faculty as well as providing education and training." And he bludgeoned the faculty yet again to pass a "diversity" course requirement for undergraduates, something of a sacred crusade for Block.

More layers of diversity bureaucracy won't have the slightest effect on black high schoolers' inadequate academic skills, which is the sole reason that blacks are not proportionally represented in the college student body. Stokes came closer to this fact than the administration did in an MSNBC interview following the breakout video: "I feel the focus is, you know, there's this general consensus within the black community, mostly, you know, the lower socioeconomic-status areas, that you either become a rapper, or a basketball player, or football player to become successful," he said. "The stress on academics isn't there anymore—or it actually never was." Stokes immediately obliterated this inadvertent acknowledgment of personal responsibility with more victimology, however: "It's used against us to keep us at that low point," he said.[13] The problem, in other words, is not blacks' lack of engagement in school; it's that society somehow "uses" that lack of engagement to keep blacks down.

Other colleges embrace the academic-racism fiction just as fervently. In March 2014, for example, Harvard's black students posted their own viral photo series, *I, Too, Am Harvard*, displaying the alleged microaggressions to which Harvard's own eggshell plaintiffs have been subject (the series' creator, the daughter of two critical race-theory law professors, explained: "We have to show that, like, these little daily microaggressions are just, like, part of the bubbling up of greater tensions that are, like, underlying this whole, like, post racial, this, like, post racial surface"). Students at Oberlin, Fordham, and numerous other schools have created webpages to catalog their racial slights at the hands of other students.

The indulgence of this fiction is far from innocuous. (Any student who believes that the university is an "unsafe," racially hostile environment is unlikely to take full advantage of its resources). Growing up means learning the difference between a real problem and a trivial one. Being asked: "So, like, what are you?" (a Fordham "microaggression") belongs in the trivial category, especially in a world that has been taught for the last three decades that the most important thing about an individual *is* his racial and ethnic identity. The time spent agitating about such innocent, if clumsy, inquiries would be far better dedicated to studying for an organic chemistry or a French literature exam. (As this book will show, the equally preposterous conceit that the university is "unsafe" for females has similarly distorting effects, creating more perpetual victims whose fragile egos are constantly threatened by the ordinary give-and-take of life and who see a "war on women" at every turn.)

The universities' encouragement of victimology has wider implications beyond the campus. The same imperative to repress any acknowledgment of black academic underachievement as the cause of black underrepresentation in higher education is more fatefully at work in repressing awareness of disproportionate black criminality as the cause of black overrepresentation in the criminal-justice system. When a police officer in Ferguson, Missouri, shot Michael Brown, an unarmed black teen, in August 2014, for example, the media suppressed any information about the incident that complicated its favored narrative about police brutality, all the while pumping out strained stories about racism in law enforcement and public life more generally. The result was days of violence, looting, and arson, from a populace that had been told at every opportunity that it is the target of ubiquitous discrimination.

Colleges today are determined to preserve in many of their students the thin skin and solipsism of adolescence. They build ever more monumental bureaucracies to indulge those traits. By now, of course, many of the adults running colleges are indistinguishable from their eggshell-plaintiff students. The rest of us bear the costs, in the maintenance of public policies founded on an equally spurious victimology.

MICROAGGRESSION, MACRO-CRAZY

Early in 2015, the University of California's new president, Janet Napolitano, asked all deans and department chairs in the university's ten campuses to undergo training in overcoming their "implicit biases" toward women and minorities. The department heads also needed training, according to the UC president, in how to avoid committing microaggressions. A more insulting and mindless exercise would be hard to imagine. But Napolitano's seminar possesses a larger significance: It demolishes any remaining hope that college administrators possess a firmer grip on reality than the narcissistic students over whom they preside.

The "Fostering Inclusive Excellence: Strategies and Tools for Department Chairs and Deans" seminar presumes that University of California faculty are so bigoted that they will refuse to hire the most qualified candidate for a professorship if that candidate happens to be female or an "underrepresented minority"—i.e., black or Hispanic. Attendees at the seminar were subjected to an "interactive theater scenario" called "Ready to Vote?" that showed white male computer-science professors on a fictional hiring committee failing to "value diversity." The author of the scenario, a professor of performance studies and ethnic studies at the University of California at San Diego, seems never to have attended a faculty-hiring committee meeting in her life. Nor, it would seem, has Napolitano. How otherwise could they not know that faculty searches in the sciences, far from shunning females and minorities, are often a determined exercise in tracking down female and non-Asian minority candidates who haven't already been snapped up by more well-endowed competitors? (See chapter 11 on STEM.) Females in the sciences are hired and promoted nationwide at rates above their representation in applicant pools. Too few black and Hispanic science PhDs exist to have inspired many reliable studies analyzing their hiring chances.

To voice these realities, however, is to commit a microaggression, according to University of California diversity enforcers. One handout inflicted on "Fostering Inclusive Excellence" attendees presents a long list of microaggressions, categorized by "Theme" and "Message." The "Myth of Meritocracy" "theme" includes such statements as: "Of course he'll get tenure, even though he hasn't published much—he's Black!" The "message" conveyed by this particular microaggression, according to UC's "Recognizing Microaggressions Tool," is that "people of color are given extra unfair benefits because of their race." Now where would anyone get that idea? Well, you might ask any high school senior, steeped in his class's SAT rankings, if it's true that "people of color" are given "extra benefits" in college admissions. He will laugh at your naïveté. A 2004 study of three top-tier universities, published in *Social Science Quarterly,* found that blacks were favored over whites by a factor of 5.5 and that being black got students an extra 230 SAT points on a 1600-point scale. Such massive preferences are found at every selective college and graduate school. Every student knows this, and yet diversity protocol requires pretending that preferences don't exist. The race (and gender) advantage continues into the academic workplace, as everyone who has sat on a hiring committee also knows.

Other alleged microaggressions include uttering such hurtful words as "I believe the most qualified person should get the job" or "America is the land of opportunity." Someone who has been through the "Fostering Inclusive Excellence" seminar may call you out for giving voice to such ideas. Why, exactly, saying that the most qualified person should get the job is a microaggression is a puzzle. Either such a statement is regarded simply as code for alleged antiblack sentiment, or the diversocrats are secretly aware that meritocracy is incompatible with "diversity."

Equally "hostile" and "derogatory," according to the "Tool," is the phrase "Everyone can succeed in this society, if they work hard enough." Such a statement is obviously an insult to all those career victims whose primary occupation is proclaiming their own helplessness and inability to accomplish anything without government assistance.

Many purported microaggressions arise from the contradictions in diversity ideology. Authorities in a diversity regime are supposed to categorize people by race and ethnicity—until that unpredictable moment when they are *not* supposed to. Assigning a black graduate student to escort a black visiting professor, for example, is a microaggression, per the "Tool." But wasn't the alleged need for role models and a critical mass of "persons of color" a key justification for "diversity"? Describing a colleague as a "good Black scientist" is another microaggression. But such a categorization merely reflects the race-consciousness and bean counting that the campus diversity enforcers insist upon.

Color blindness constitutes an entire microaggression "Theme" in the "Tool," *pace* Martin Luther King Jr. Beware of saying, "When I look at you, I don't see color" or "There is only one race, the human race." Doing so, according to the "Tool," denies "the individual as a racial/cultural being." Never mind that diversity ideologues reject the genetic basis of racial categories and proclaim that race is merely a "social construct." The nondiverse world is under orders both to deny that race exists and to "acknowledge race," in Tool-parlance, regarding Persons of Color.

Other microaggressions provided a glimpse into the future. It may have seemed like a stretch in 2015 to label as a microaggression "being forced to choose Male or Female when completing basic forms." By 2018, however, the movement to discredit binary, biological sex distinctions had accelerated to the point that many institutions could expect media denunciation if they did not allow their members to choose from an array of "gender" possibilities and combinations.

The ultimate question raised by the "Fostering Inclusive Excellence" seminar was: Are there any grown-ups left on campus, at least in administrative offices? And the answer is: no. The most disturbing aspect of the exercise is that it was initiated by the president's office without outside provocation. Had Napolitano not come up with these antibias trainings, no one would have noticed their absence. Instead, she promulgated *sua sponte* an initiative deeply ignorant about how seriously most professors—at least in the sciences—take their responsibilities to build up a faculty of accomplishment and research prowess. We have come to expect such ignorance from coddled, self-engrossed students. Now it turns out that those students may be the least of the university's problems.

5

ARE WE ALL UNCONSCIOUS RACISTS?

Few academic ideas have been as eagerly absorbed into public discourse in recent years as "implicit bias." Embraced by a president, a would-be president, and the nation's top law-enforcement official, the implicit-bias conceit has launched a movement to remove the concept of individual agency from the law and spawned a multimillion-dollar consulting industry. The statistical basis on which it rests is now crumbling, but don't expect its influence to wane anytime soon.

Implicit bias purports to answer the question: Why do racial disparities persist in household income, job status, and incarceration rates, when explicit racism has, by all measures, greatly diminished over the last half-century? The reason, according to implicit-bias researchers, lies deep in our brains, outside the reach of conscious thought. We may consciously embrace racial equality, but almost all of us harbor unconscious biases favoring whites over blacks, the proponents claim. And those unconscious biases, which the implicit-bias project purports to measure scientifically, drive the discriminatory behavior that, in turn, results in racial inequality.

The need to plumb the unconscious to explain ongoing racial gaps arises for one reason: It is taboo in universities and mainstream society to acknowledge intergroup differences in interests, abilities, cultural values, or family structure that might produce socioeconomic disparities.

The implicit-bias idea burst onto the academic scene in 1998 with the rollout of a psychological instrument called the Implicit Association Test (IAT). Created by social psychologists Anthony Greenwald and Mahzarin Banaji, with funding from the National Science Foundation and National Institute of Mental Health, the IAT was announced as a breakthrough in prejudice studies: "The pervasiveness of prejudice, affecting 90 to 95 percent of people, was demonstrated today . . . by psychologists who developed a new tool that measures the unconscious roots of prejudice," read the press release.

The race IAT (there are nonrace varieties) displays a series of black faces and white faces on a computer; the test subject must sort them quickly by race into two categories, represented by the "i" and "e" keys on the keyboard. Next, the subject sorts "good" or "positive" words like "pleasant," and "bad" or "negative" words like "death," into good and bad categories, represented by those same two computer keys. The sorting tasks are then intermingled: faces and words appear at random on the screen, and the test-taker has to sort them with the "i" and "e" keys. Next, the sorting protocol is reversed. If, before, a black face was to be sorted using the same key as the key for a "bad" word, now a black face is sorted with the same key as a "good" word and a white face sorted with the reverse key. If a subject takes longer sorting black faces using the computer key associated with a "good" word than he does sorting white faces using the computer key associated with a "good" word, the IAT deems the subject a bearer of implicit bias. The IAT ranks the subject's degree of implicit bias based on the differences in milliseconds with which he accomplishes the different sorting tasks; at the end of the test, he finds out whether he has a strong, moderate, or weak "preference" for blacks or for whites. A majority of test-takers (including many blacks) are rated as showing a preference for white faces. Additional IATs sort pictures of women, the elderly, the disabled, and other purportedly disfavored groups.

Greenwald and Banaji did not pioneer such response-time studies; psychologists already used response-time methodology to measure how closely concepts are associated in memory. And the idea that automatic cognitive processes and associations help us navigate daily life is also widely accepted in psychology. But Greenwald and Banaji, now at the University of Washington and Harvard University, respectively, pushed the response-time technique and the implicit-cognition idea into charged political territory. Not only did they confidently assert that any differences in sorting times for black and white faces flow from unconscious prejudice against blacks; they also claimed that such unconscious prejudice, as measured by the IAT, predicts discriminatory behavior. It is "clearly . . . established that automatic race preference predicts discrimination," they wrote in their 2013 bestseller *Blindspot,* which popularized the IAT. And in the final link of their causal chain, they hypothesized that this unconscious predilection to discriminate is a cause of racial disparities: "It is reasonable to conclude not only that implicit bias is a cause of Black disadvantage but also that it plausibly plays a greater role than does explicit bias in explaining the discrimination that contributes to Black disadvantage."

The implicit-bias conceit spread like wildfire. President Barack Obama denounced "unconscious" biases against minorities and females in science in 2016. NBC anchor Lester Holt asked Hillary Clinton during a September 2016 presidential debate whether "police are implicitly biased against black people." Clinton answered: "Lester, I think implicit bias is a problem for everyone, not just police." Then–FBI director James Comey claimed in a 2015 speech that "much research" points to the "widespread existence of unconscious bias." "Many people in our white-majority culture," Comey said, "react differently to a white face than a black face." The Obama Justice Department packed off all federal law-enforcement agents to implicit-bias training. Clinton promised to help fund it for local police departments, many of which had already begun the training following the 2014 Ferguson, Missouri, police shooting of Michael Brown.

A parade of journalists confessed their IAT-revealed preferences, including Malcolm Gladwell in his acclaimed book *Blink.* Corporate diversity trainers retooled themselves as purveyors of the new "science of bias." And the legal academy started building the case that the concept of intentionality in the law was scientifically obtuse. Leading the charge was Jerry Kang, a UCLA law professor in the school's critical race studies program who became UCLA's fantastically paid vice chancellor for equity, diversity, and inclusion in 2015 (starting salary: $354,900, now up to $444,000). "The law has an obligation to respond to changes in scientific knowledge," Kang said in a 2015 lecture. "Federal anti-discrimination law has been fixated on, and obsessed with, conscious intent." But the new "behavioral realism," as the movement to incorporate IAT-inspired concepts into the law calls itself, shows that we "discriminate without the intent and awareness to discriminate." If we look only for conscious intent, we will "necessarily be blind to a whole bunch of real harm that is painful and consequential," he concluded. Kang has pitched behavioral realism to law firms, corporations, judges, and government agencies.[1]

A battle is underway regarding the admissibility of IAT research in employment-discrimination lawsuits: Plaintiffs' attorneys regularly offer Anthony Greenwald as an expert witness; the defense tries to disqualify him. Greenwald has survived some defense challenges but has lost others. Kang is philosophical: "It might not matter if Tony's expert testimony is kicked out now," he said in his 2015 lecture—in ten years, everyone will know that our brains harbor hidden biases. And if that alleged knowledge becomes legally actionable, then every personnel decision can be challenged as the product of implicit bias. The only way to guarantee equality of opportunity would be to mandate equality of results through quotas, observes the University of Pennsylvania's Philip Tetlock, a critic of the most sweeping IAT claims.

The potential reach of the behavioral-realism movement, which George Soros's Open Society Foundation is underwriting, goes far beyond employment-discrimination litigation. Some employers are using the IAT to screen potential workers, diversity consultant Howard Ross says. More and more college administrations require members of faculty-search committees to take the IAT to confront their hidden biases against minority and female candidates. Promotion committees at many corporations undergo the IAT. UCLA's law school strongly encourages incoming law students to take the test to confront their implicit prejudice against fellow students; the University of Virginia might incorporate the IAT into its curriculum. Kang has argued for FCC regulation of how the news media portray minorities, to lessen implicit prejudice. If threats to fair treatment "lie in every mind," as Kang and Banaji argued in a 2006 *California Law Review* article, then the scope for government intervention in private transactions to overcome those threats is almost limitless.

But though proponents refer to IAT research as "science"—or, in Kang's words, "remarkable," "jaw-dropping" science—their claims about its social significance leapfrogged ahead of scientific validation. There is hardly an aspect of IAT doctrine that is not now under methodological challenge.

Any social-psychological instrument must pass two tests to be considered accurate: reliability and validity. A psychological instrument is reliable if the same test subject, taking the test at different times, achieves roughly the same score each time. But IAT bias scores have a lower rate of consistency than is deemed acceptable for use in the real world—a subject could be rated with a high degree of implicit bias on one taking of the IAT and a low or moderate degree the next time around. A recent estimate puts the reliability of the race IAT at half of what is considered usable. No evidence exists, in other words, that the IAT reliably measures anything stable in the test-taker.

But the fiercest disputes concern the IAT's validity. A psychological instrument is deemed "valid" if it actually measures what it claims to be measuring—in this case, implicit bias and, by extension, discriminatory behavior. If the IAT were valid, a high implicit-bias score would predict discriminatory behavior, as Greenwald and Banaji asserted from the start. It turns out, however, that IAT scores have almost no connection to what ludicrously counts as "discriminatory behavior" in IAT research—trivial nuances of body language during a mock interview in a college psychology laboratory, say, or a hypothetical choice to donate to children in Colombian, rather than South African, slums. Oceans of ink have been spilled debating the statistical strength of the correlation between IAT scores and lab-induced "discriminatory behavior" on the part of college students paid to take the test. The actual content of those "discriminatory behaviors" gets mentioned only in passing, if at all, and no one notes how remote those behaviors are from the discrimination that we should be worried about.

Even if we accept at face value that the placement of one's chair in a mock lab interview or decisions in a prisoner's-dilemma game are significant "discriminatory behaviors," the statistical connection between IAT scores and those actions is negligible. A 2009 meta-analysis of 122 IAT studies by Greenwald, Banaji, and two management professors found that IAT scores accounted for only 5.5 percent of the variation in laboratory-induced "discrimination." Even that low score was arrived at by questionable methods, as Jesse Singal discussed in a masterful review of the IAT literature in *New York* magazine. A team of IAT skeptics—Fred Oswald of Rice University, Gregory Mitchell of the University of Virginia law school, Hart Blanton of the University of Connecticut, James Jaccard of New York University, and Philip Tetlock—noticed that Greenwald and his coauthors had counted opposite behaviors as validating the IAT. If test subjects scored high on implicit bias via the IAT but demonstrated better behavior toward out-group members (such as blacks) than toward in-group members, that was a validation of the IAT on the theory that the subjects were over-compensating for their implicit bias. But studies that found a correlation between a high implicit-bias score and discriminatory behavior toward out-group members also validated the IAT. In other words: heads, I win; tails, I win.

Greenwald and Banaji now admit that the IAT does not predict biased behavior. The psychometric problems associated with the race IAT "render [it] problematic to use to classify persons as likely to engage in discrimination," they wrote in 2015, just two years after their sweeping claims in *Blindspot*. The IAT should not be used, for example, to select a bias-free jury, maintains Greenwald. "We do not regard the IAT as diagnosing something that inevitably results in racist or prejudicial behavior," he told *The Chronicle of Higher Education* in January 2017. Their fallback position: Though the IAT does not predict individual biased behavior, it predicts discrimination and disadvantage in the aggregate. "Statistically small effects" can have "societally large effects," they have argued. If a society has higher levels of implicit bias against blacks as measured on the IAT, it will allegedly have higher levels of discriminatory behavior. Hart Blanton, one of the skeptics, dismisses this argument. If you don't know what an instrument means on an individual level, you don't know what it means in the aggregate, he told *New York*'s Singal. In fairness to Greenwald and Banaji, it is true that a cholesterol score, say, is more accurate at predicting heart attacks the larger the sample of subjects. But too much debate exists about what the IAT actually measures for much confidence about large-scale effects.

Initially, most of the psychology profession accepted the startling claim that one's predilection to discriminate in real life is revealed by the microsecond speed with which one sorts images. But possible alternative meanings of a "pro-white" IAT score are now beginning to emerge. Older test-takers may have cognitive difficulty with the shifting instructions of the IAT. Objective correlations between group membership and socioeconomic outcomes may lead to differences in sorting times, as could greater familiarity with one ethnic-racial group compared with another. These alternative meanings should have been ruled out before the world learned that a new "scientific" test had revealed the ubiquity of prejudice.

The most recent meta-analysis deals another blow to the conventional IAT narrative. This study, not yet formally published, looked at whether changes in implicit bias allegedly measured by the IAT led to changes in "discriminatory behavior"—defined as the usual artificial lab conduct. While small changes in IAT scores can be induced in a lab setting through various psychological priming techniques, they do not produce changes in behavior, the study found.

The analyses' seven authors propose a radical possibility that would halt the implicit-bias crusade in its tracks: "perhaps automatically retrieved associations really are causally inert"—that is, they have no relationship to how we act in the real world. Instead of "acting as a 'cognitive monster' that inevitably leads to bias-consistent thought and behavior," the researchers propose, "automatically retrieved associations could reflect the residual 'scar' of concepts that are frequently paired together within the social environment." If this is true, they write, there would need to be a "reevaluation of some of the central assumptions that drive implicit bias research." That is an understatement.

Among the study's authors are Brian Nosek of the University of Virginia and Calvin Lai of Washington University in St. Louis. Both have collaborated with Greenwald and Banaji in furthering the dominant IAT narrative; Nosek was Banaji's student and helped put the IAT on the web. It is a testament to their scientific integrity that they have gone where the data have led them. (Greenwald warned me in advance about their meta-analysis: "There has been a recent rash of popular press critique based on a privately circulated 'research report' that has not been accepted by any journal, and has been heavily criticized by editor and reviewers of the one journal to which I know it was submitted," he wrote in an email. But the Nosek, Lai, et al., study was not "privately circulated"; it is available on the web, as part of the open-science initiative that Nosek helped found.)

The fractious debate around the IAT has been carried out exclusively at the micro-level, with hundreds of articles burrowing deep into complicated statistical models to assess minute differences in experimental reaction times. Meanwhile, outside the purview of these debates, two salient features of the world go unnoticed by the participants: the pervasiveness of racial preferences and the behavior that lies behind socioeconomic disparities.

One would have difficulty finding an elite institution today that does not pressure its managers to hire and promote as many blacks and Hispanics as possible. Nearly 90 percent of Fortune 500 companies have some sort of diversity infrastructure, according to corporate diversity trainer Howard Ross. The federal Equal Employment Opportunity Commission requires every business with a hundred or more employees to report the racial composition of its workforce. Employers know that empty boxes for blacks and other "underrepresented minorities" can trigger governmental review.

Some companies tie manager compensation to the achievement of "diversity," as Roger Clegg documented before the US Civil Rights Commission in 2006. "If people miss their diversity and inclusion goals, it hurts their bonuses," Miles White, the CEO of Abbott Laboratories, said in a 2002 interview. Since then, the diversity pressure has only intensified. Google's "objectives and key results" for managers include increased diversity. Walmart and other big corporations require law firms to put minority attorneys on the legal teams that represent them. "We are terminating a firm right now strictly because of their inability to grasp our diversity expectations," Walmart's general counsel announced in 2005. Any reporter seeking a surefire story idea can propose tallying up the minorities in a particular firm or profession; Silicon Valley has become the favorite subject of bean-counting "exposés," though Hollywood and the entertainment industry are also targets of choice, especially in the #MeToo era (see chapter 9). Organizations will do everything possible to avoid such negative publicity.

In colleges, the mandate to hire more minority (and female) candidates hangs over almost all faculty recruiting. Deans have canceled faculty-search results and ordered the hiring committee to go back to the drawing board if the finalists are not sufficiently "diverse." As previously discussed, [every selective college today admits black and Hispanic students with much weaker academic qualifications than those of white and Asian students], as any high school senior knows. At the University of Michigan, an Asian with the same GPA and SAT scores as the median black admit had zero chance in 2005 of admission; a white with those same scores had a 1-percent chance of admission. At Arizona State University, a white with the same academic credentials as the average black admit had a 2-percent chance of admission in 2006; that average black had a 96-percent chance of admission. The preferences continue into graduate and professional schools. From 2013 to 2016, medical schools nationally admitted 57 percent of black applicants with low MCATs of 24 to 26 but only 8 percent of whites and 6 percent of Asians with those same low scores, as Claremont McKenna College's Frederick Lynch reported in *The New York Times*.[2] The reason for these racial preferences is administrators' burning desire to engineer a campus with a "critical mass" of black and Hispanic faces.

Similar pressures exist in the government and nonprofit sectors. In the New York Police Department, blacks and Hispanics are promoted ahead of whites for positions to which promotion is discretionary, as opposed to being determined by an objective exam. In the 1990s, blacks and Hispanics became detectives almost five years earlier than whites and took half the time as whites did to be appointed to deputy inspector or deputy chief.

And yet, we are to believe that alleged millisecond associations between blacks and negative terms are a more powerful determinant of who gets admitted, hired, and promoted than these often-explicit and heavy-handed preferences. If a competitively qualified black female PhD in computer engineering walks into Google, say, we are to believe that a recruiter will unconsciously find reasons not to hire her, so as to bring on an inferior white male. The scenario is preposterous on its face—in fact, such a candidate would be snapped up in an instant by every tech firm and academic department across the country. The same is true for competitively qualified black lawyers, accountants, and portfolio managers.

If such discrimination is so ubiquitous, there should be victims aplenty that the proponents of implicit bias can point to. They cannot.

I twice asked Anthony Greenwald via email if he was aware of qualified candidates in faculty searches anywhere who were overlooked or rejected because of skin color. He ignored the question. I twice asked Jerry Kang's special assistant for equity, diversity, and inclusion via email if Vice Chancellor Kang was aware of faculty candidates for hire or promotion at UCLA or elsewhere who were overlooked because of implicit bias. Kang's assistant ignored the question. Howard Ross has been a prominent corporate diversity trainer for thirty years, with clients that include hundreds of Fortune 500 companies, Harvard and Stanford medical schools, and two dozen other colleges and universities. I asked him in a phone interview if he was aware of the most qualified candidate for a business or academic position not getting hired or promoted because of bias. Ross merely said that there was a "ton of research that demonstrates that it happens all the time," without providing examples.

PricewaterhouseCoopers has spearheaded an economy-wide diversity initiative, dubbed the CEO Action for Diversity & Inclusion™. Nearly two hundred CEOs have signed a pledge to send their employees to implicit-bias training; in the case of PricewaterhouseCoopers, that means packing off fifty thousand employees to the trainers. Any organization spending a large sum of money on a problem would presumably have a firm evidentiary basis that the problem exists. Megan DiSciullo is a spokesman for the CEO Action for Diversity & Inclusion and a member of PricewaterhouseCoopers's human resources department. I asked her if she was aware of candidates who should have been hired at PwC but weren't because of implicit bias. Our telephone exchange went as follows:

> **DiSciullo:** I'm not aware of someone not getting a job because of bias.
>
> **Me:** But are your managers making suboptimal decisions because of bias?
>
> **DiSciullo:** The coalition as a group recognizes that everyone has unconscious bias; we are committed to training our managers to be better.
>
> **Me:** Your managers are not making optimal decisions because of bias?
>
> **DiSciullo:** Everyone has unconscious bias. I'm not saying that anyone is not being hired or promoted, but it's part of the workplace.
>
> **Me:** In what way? People are being treated differently?
>
> **DiSciullo:** People have bias, but it manifests itself differently. I think you have an agenda, which I am trying to unpack. The facts are clear that people have biases and that they could bring them to the workplace. Corporations recognize that fact and want to build the most inclusive workplace.
>
> **Me:** You base the statement that everyone has biases on what?
>
> **DiSciullo:** On science and on the *Harvard Business Review*.

Other signatories to the CEO Action for Diversity & Inclusion include Cisco, Qualcomm, KPMG, Accenture, HP, Procter & Gamble, and New York Life, several of which are on the steering committee. These companies either failed to respond to preliminary requests for an interview about the CEO Action for Diversity & Inclusion or went silent when asked if they knew of implicit bias infecting hiring and promotion decisions. Obviously, such reticence may be motivated by a fear of litigation. But it is also likely that there are no known victims of implicit bias.

(The insistence that implicit bias routinely denies competitively qualified minority candidates jobs and promotions also requires overlooking the relentless pressure to take race into account in employment and admissions decisions) I asked Greenwald if implicit bias overrides these institutional pressures to hire and promote by race. He evaded the question. "'Override' is the wrong word," he wrote back. "Implicit biases function as filters on perception and judgment, operating outside of awareness and often rendering perception and judgment invalid." In response to a follow-up question, he denied that those institutional pressures were all that strong, as evidenced by the fact that many diversity programs produced no "beneficial effect." Another explanation for the persistent lack of proportional representation in the workplace, however, is that there are not proportional numbers of qualified minorities in the hiring pipeline.

Diversity trainers invoke behavioral economics to explain why explicit diversity mandates don't override implicit bias. This field, popularized by the work of cognitive psychologist Daniel Kahneman, has shown that people often fail to use information in rational ways. "We now know that most decisions are visceral and emotional," said Ross, in response to my incredulity that a university physics department would not leap at a competitively qualified black PhD candidate. Joelle Emerson, a high-profile diversity trainer in Silicon Valley, claims that because companies are "not purely rational actors," they will as a group discriminate against the most qualified candidate. "People will be left out of entire industries," she said. "People from stereotyped groups have a harder time getting hired and promoted."[3]

But incentives can overcome the flaws in rational analysis identified by behavioral economics. The incentive for race-conscious employment decisions is so strong that the burden of proof is on those who maintain that implicit bias will override it. The fact is that blacks on the academic market and in many other fields enjoy a huge hiring advantage.

Yet they are still not proportionally represented in the workplace, despite decades of trying to engineer "diversity." You can read through hundreds of implicit-bias studies and never come across the primary reason: the academic skills gap. Given the gap's size, anything resembling proportional representation can be achieved only through massive hiring preferences.

From 1996 to 2015, the average difference between the mean black score on the math SAT and the mean white score was 0.92 standard deviation, reports a February 2017 Brookings Institution study. The average black score on the math SAT was 428 in 2015; the average white score was 534, and the average Asian score was 598. The racial gaps were particularly great at the tails of the distribution. Among top scorers—those scoring between 750 and 800—60 percent were Asian, 33 percent were white, and 2 percent were black. At the lowest end—scores between 300 and 350—6 percent were Asian, 21 percent were white, and 35 percent were black. If the SATs were redesigned to increase score variance—that is, to spread out the scores across a greater range by adding more hard questions and more easy questions—the racial gaps would widen.

The usual poverty explanations for the SAT gap don't hold up. In 1997, white students from households with incomes of $10,000 or less scored better than black students from households with incomes of $80,000 to $100,000[4]. In 2015, students with family incomes of $0 to $20,000 (a category that includes all racial groups) had a higher average math SAT score (455) than the average math SAT score of black students from all income levels (435). At the University of California, race predicts SAT scores better than class. Proponents of racial preferences routinely claim that the SATs are culturally biased and do not measure actual cognitive skills. If that were the case, blacks would do better in college than their SAT scores would predict. As discussed in chapter 2, blacks do worse. Further, the math test is not amenable to the "cultural-bias" criticism (unless one believes that math is itself biased). Low scores reflect an actual difficulty with math. In 2016, 54 percent of black elementary and high school students in California, for example, did not meet the state's math standards, compared with 21 percent of white students and 11 percent of Asian students. The chancellor of the California Community Colleges system proposed in July 2017 that intermediate algebra be removed from graduation requirements for associate's degrees because blacks and Hispanics have such a hard time passing the course. Math difficulties are the greatest reason that, in California, only 35 percent of black students earn their associate's degrees, compared with 54 percent of whites and 65 percent of Asians.

The math SAT and algebra require abstract quantitative reasoning. The math achievement gap will most affect hiring in fields with advanced quantitative requirements. In 2016, 1 percent of all PhDs in computer science went to blacks, or 17 out of 1,659 PhDs, according to the Computing Research Association's annual Taulbee Survey. Three blacks received a PhD in computer engineering, or 3.4 percent of the total. Blacks earned 0.7 percent of master's degrees in computer science and 3 percent of undergraduate degrees in computer science. Yet the biggest Silicon Valley firms are wedded to the idea that their own implicit bias is responsible for the racial (and gender) composition of their workforce. A member of Google's "People Analytics" (i.e., HR) department, Brian Welle, lectures widely about implicit bias and the IAT; Google declined to let me interview him or a People Analytics colleague.

A host of other professions beyond the sciences draw on the analytic skills required by algebra and the math SAT. Business management and consulting, for example, call for logic and conceptual flexibility. Anyone in medicine, including nursing, should be able to master basic algebra. These professions should not be tainted with the implicit-bias charge when they are hiring from the same finite pool of competitively qualified blacks.

The SAT's verbal sections show the same 100-point test-score gap between whites and blacks as the math section. *Pace* the critics, that is not an artifact of cultural bias: The average black twelfth-grader reads at the level of the average white eighth-grader. In California in 2016, 44 percent of black students through the high school grades did not meet state standards in English language arts and literacy, compared with 16 percent of white students and 11 percent of Asian students.[5]

Like the SAT, the LSAT also measures reading comprehension and verbal reasoning. It has a greater test-score gap than the SAT: 1.06 standard deviations between average black and white scores in 2014. If the LSAT test-score gap were the result of cultural bias, the LSAT would underpredict black performance in law school. It does not. The (majority of black law students cluster in the bottom tenth of their class, thanks to racial preferences in admissions) as mentioned in chapter 2. The median black law school GPA is at the sixth percentile of the median white GPA, meaning that 94 percent of whites do better than the median black. This achievement gap cannot be chalked up to implicit bias on the part of law school professors. The overwhelming majority of law school exams are still graded blind, meaning that the identity of the test-taker is concealed from the grader. The bar exam is also graded blind. If blacks were discriminated against in law school by professors, they should do better on the bar exam than their GPAs would predict. They do not. A 1998 study by the Law School Admissions Council found that 22 percent of black test-takers never pass the bar examination after five attempts, compared with 3 percent of white test-takers. Yet the relatively low number of blacks among law firm partners is routinely attributed—by the firms themselves—to hiring and promotion committee bias. In fact, corporate law firms hire blacks at rates that exceed their representation among law school graduates. But because the preferences in their favor are so large—the law school GPAs of black associates are at least a standard deviation below those of white associates—black attrition from corporate firms is high. By the time the partnership decision rolls around, few black associates remain at their firms to be promoted, as UCLA's Richard Sander has shown.

Implicit-bias researchers do not discuss the cognitive skills gap. I asked Greenwald if gaps in academic preparedness should also be considered in explaining socioeconomic disparities. He responded simply by offering up more wellsprings of bias: "There are sources of unintended disparities other than implicit bias (esp. institutional discrimination and in-group favoritism)." But a 2014 study for the Federal Reserve Bank of Chicago by economist Bhashkar Mazumder found that differences in cognitive skills measured by the Armed Forces Qualification Test account for most of the black–white difference in intergenerational mobility. Blacks and whites with the same score on the AFQT have similar rates of upward and downward mobility. The AFQT should overpredict upward mobility for blacks if bias were holding them back; it does not.

The iron grip of the implicit-bias concept on the corporate world will merely result in a loss of efficiency as workers are again trundled off to this latest iteration of diversity training and are further pressured to take race into account in personnel decisions. Most ominously for productivity, signatories to the CEO Action for Diversity & Inclusion have pledged to encourage more conversations among their employees about race, even though a recent report found that 70 percent of employees are not comfortable discussing race relations at work—understandably, given the potential tensions created by diversity preferences and the oversaturation of race talk in American life. Procter & Gamble is on the steering committee of the CEO Action for Diversity & Inclusion. You would think that its managers would have better things to do than lead bull sessions about racial microaggressions, in light of the company's lackluster growth over the last decade and the ongoing fight for control of its board.

But it is in law enforcement that the mania for implicit-bias training exacts its most serious cost. Police officers unquestionably need more hands-on tactical training to avoid ending up in a position that requires the use of force. Officers need tools for keeping their cool in highly charged, hostile encounters. They should practice de-escalating confrontations and gaining voluntary compliance. Some officers pay out of their own pocket for tactical training, since their departments offer too little of it. But now there will be less time and departmental money available for the necessary skills upgrades because precious training resources are being diverted to the implicit-bias industry. And that wasteful training is being carried out in the name of a problem that does not even exist: bias-driven police killings of black men.

Joshua Correll, a psychologist at the University of Colorado, has been studying police shoot/don't shoot decisions for years. His experiments require officers to react to rapidly changing images of potential targets on a computer screen. He has found that officers are no more likely to shoot an unarmed black target than an unarmed white one. Officers are slightly quicker to identify an armed black target as armed than an armed white target, and slower to identify an unarmed black target as unarmed than an unarmed white target. But the faster cognitive processing speeds for stereotype-congruent targets (i.e., armed blacks and unarmed whites) do not result in officers shooting unarmed black targets at a higher rate than unarmed white ones.

Correll's conclusions were confirmed in 2016 with the release of four studies that found either no antiblack bias in police shootings or a bias that favored blacks. Three of the studies—by Roland Fryer, Ted Miller, and the Center for Policing Equity—reviewed data on actual police use of force; a fourth put officers in a more sophisticated life-size video simulator than the computers that Correll uses.[6] That study, led by the University of Washington's Lois James, found that officers waited significantly longer before shooting an armed black target than an armed white target and were three times less likely to shoot an unarmed black target than an unarmed white target. James hypothesized that officers were second-guessing themselves when confronting black suspects because of the current climate around race and policing.

Both experimental and data-based research, in other words, dispel the claim that police officers are killing blacks out of implicit bias. That has not stopped the implicit-bias juggernaut, however. Police departments across the country are subjecting their officers to implicit-bias training at considerable cost; any controversial shooting invariably triggers a pledge to bring in the bias consultants. The New York Police Department will now start requiring recruits and officers already on the job to attend a full-day seminar in implicit bias, time that could be better spent practicing tactical and communication skills.

All the IAT-inspired lecturing cannot change the reality that drives police activity: the incidence of crime. And that is a topic about which implicit-bias trainers have little to say, as I discovered while observing a three-day training program in Chesterfield, Missouri, in May 2016.

About three dozen officers and supervisors had come to this green suburb of St. Louis from as far away as Montana, Virginia, North Carolina, Michigan, and Kentucky for a "train-the-trainer" session offered by the premier antibias outfit in the field. Lori Fridell has been lecturing to police departments about bias-based policing since the "driving while black" notion emerged in the 1990s. But the implicit-bias idea has boosted her business enormously, as has the Black Lives Matter movement. In 2016, Fridell was fielding a call a day from police departments, courts, and other parts of the criminal-justice system. The Obama Justice Department funded her organization's implicit-bias trainings for police departments that it considered particularly troubled. Other agencies pay their own way.

A day and a half into the three-day Chesterfield training, the attendees had been informed that the Michael Brown shooting was a function of implicit bias (even though Brown had tried to grab the officer's gun and had assaulted him) and that the overrepresentation of blacks in prison was because blacks get longer sentences than whites for the same crime (in fact, sentences are equal, once criminal history is taken into account). The attendees had learned about the IAT; they had watched a video of singer Susan Boyle's victory in the television show *Britain's Got Talent*; they had viewed photos of a hot babe on a motorcycle and a female executive with a briefcase; they had written down stereotypes about the "unhoused"—not activities directly related, say, to serving a felony warrant safely.

The theme of these exercises was that everyone carries around stereotypes, and that to be human is to be biased. In the case of police officers, the two trainers explained, those biases could put an officer's life in jeopardy if he discounts a potential threat from a white female or a senior citizen because it is counter-stereotypical. But those implicit biases are also killing black men, said trainer Sandra Brown, a retired Palo Alto police public-affairs lieutenant.

Brown described a study by Stanford psychologist Jennifer Eberhardt in which Stanford students in a psych lab were shown a blurry object on a computer screen. The students were quicker to identify it correctly as a gun if they had been shown an image of a black face right beforehand. (Greenwald and Banaji also invoke this study.) "Black men are dying because we see the gun too quickly," Brown said—never mind that the aforementioned research on police shootings shows that black men are not dying because police officers "see the gun too quickly." Why might such a priming function occur? Eberhardt and her coauthors, of course, attributed it to irrational stereotype. But another explanation comes to mind: Blacks are objectively more associated with crime. The Chesterfield training only tiptoed up to this topic.

It is "partially factual," Brown said, that "people of color" are disproportionately involved in street crime. Actually, it is fully factual; street crime today is almost exclusively the province of "people of color." In New York City, for example, blacks and Hispanics committed 98 percent of all shootings in 2016; whites, who, at 34 percent of the population, are the city's largest racial group, committed less than 2 percent of all shootings.[7] Those figures come from the victims of, and witnesses to, those shootings. These disparities are repeated in cities across the country. If you're hit in a drive-by shooting, the odds are overwhelming that your assailant will be black or Hispanic—and that you will be, too, since blacks and Hispanics are usually the victims of such crimes. If the public associates blacks with violent street crime, it is the tragic facts that lead to that association.

Yes, a police action should not be based on a "stereotype," as Brown rightly admonished. But crime is the overwhelming determinant of policing today, and to pretend that implicit bias drives policing distracts from the challenges that officers face. By day two, the audience was interjecting some social and political reality back into the training. "Are there any studies about black and white officer shootings?" asked a black officer. "No one's outraged if I shoot a black, but if a white officer does, it will be pandemonium." Another local officer said that he worried about the violence in the black community: "It's so disproportionate. When black people are shot by other blacks, it doesn't make the news. There were over a dozen people shot in a theater the other day. I worry about that disparity."

Then an officer from Chesterfield raised the most pressing concern in the Black Lives Matter era: depolicing. Seventy-five percent of the apprehended shoplifters in the Chesterfield mall were black, he said. (Chesterfield's black population was 2.6 percent in 2010.) "We struggle with depolicing; it's difficult to tell officers to enforce the shoplifting laws when they will be confronted with the implicit bias issue." That is the dilemma facing officers today: If they enforce the law, they will generate the racially disproportionate stop-and-arrest statistics that fuel specious implicit-bias charges. But it is the reality of crime, not bias, which results in those disproportions.

The trainers had nothing to offer to resolve this problem. "It's hard to answer these tough questions," Brown said. Her partner, Scott Wong, also from the Palo Alto Police Department, gamely tried to bring the discussion back to the official topic. "You need a passion for this; you have to believe in implicit bias and how it affects officers." But while many officers could do with a courtesy tune-up, they are overwhelmingly not making bad decisions based on invidious stereotypes. What they are doing, on a daily basis, is trying to deal with the breakdown of family and bourgeois norms in inner-city areas that leads to so many young black men gang-banging in the streets. Joshua Correll has found that officers' neurological threat response is more pronounced when confronting black suspects. Might that be because black males have made up 42 percent of all cop-killers over the last decade,[8] though they are only 6 percent of the national population? Or because the individuals involved in the daily drive-by shootings in American cities are overwhelmingly black? Until those realities of crime change, any allegedly "stereotypical" associations between blacks and crime in the public mind will remain justified and psychologically unavoidable. Those crime rates will also affect the pool of job candidates without a criminal record, further reducing the likelihood of proportional representation in the workplace.

The Chesterfield training did offer several profound pieces of advice: "Make every day the day you try to change someone's perceptions" of the police, Brown said. She urged officers to get out of their cars and talk to civilians: "They need to know us; people are afraid to talk to us as human beings." However sage this message, though, it should not be necessary to contract with a pricey implicit-bias trainer to convey it.

The implicit-bias crusade is agenda-driven social science. Banaji seems to see herself on a crusade. In an email to *New York's* Jesse Singal, she attacked both the credentials and the motives of the academics who have subjected the IAT narrative to critical scrutiny: "I don't read commentaries from non-experts," she wrote (those "non-experts" are overwhelmingly credentialed psychologists, like herself). "It scares people (fortunately, a negligible minority) that learning about our minds may lead people to change their behavior so that their behavior may be more in line with their ideals and aspirations." The critics should explore with their "psychotherapists or church leaders" their alleged obsession with the race IAT, she suggested. Kang has accused critics of holding a "tournament of merit" vision of society and of having financial reasons for IAT skepticism. (Of course, the fact that Banaji and Kang hire themselves out as IB trainers, for "non-trivial . . . fees," as Kang puts it about himself, and that Greenwald serves as a paid expert witness in discrimination lawsuits, does not lead Kang to impute financial reasons for such pro-IAT advocacy.)

A thought experiment is in order: If American blacks acted *en masse* like Asian Americans for ten years in all things relevant to economic success—if they had similar rates of school attendance, paying attention in class, doing homework and studying for exams, staying away from crime, persisting in a job, and avoiding out-of-wedlock childbearing—and we *still* saw racial differences in income, professional status, and incarceration rates, then it would be well justified to seek an explanation in unconscious prejudice. But as long as the behavioral disparities remain so great, the minute distinctions of the IAT are a sideshow. America has an appalling history of racism and brutal subjugation, and we should always be vigilant against any recurrence of that history. But the most influential sectors of our economy today practice preferences in favor of blacks. The main obstacles to racial equality at present lie not in implicit bias but in culture and behavior.

. . .

CONJURING DISRESPECT

The attempt to find implicit bias in policing has come to this: the difference between an officer saying "uh" and saying "that, that's." According to a team of Stanford University researchers headed by psychology professor Jennifer Eberhardt, police officers in Oakland, California, use one of those verbal tics more often with white drivers and the other more often with black drivers. If you can guess which tic conveys "respect" and which "disrespect," you may have a career ahead of you in the exploding field of bias psychology.

In June 2017, the team of nine psychologists, linguists, and computer scientists released a paper purporting to show that Oakland police treat black drivers less respectfully than white ones. The study, published in the *Proceedings of the National Academy of Sciences,* elicited a huzzah from the press.

The Washington Post, The New York Times, and *Science,* among many other outlets, gave it prominent play. "Police officers are significantly less respectful and consistently ruder toward black motorists during routine traffic stops than they are toward white drivers," gloated *The New York Times.*

Reading the coverage, one expected reports of cops cursing at black drivers, say, or peremptorily ordering them around, or using the N-word. Instead, the most "disrespectful" officer utterance that the researchers presented was: "Steve, can I see that driver's license again? It, it's showing suspended. Is that—that's you?" The second most "disrespectful" was: "All right, my man. Do me a favor. Just keep your hands on the steering wheel real quick."

The researchers themselves undoubtedly expected more dramatic results. Undaunted by the lackluster findings, they packaged them in the conventional bias narrative anyway, opening their study by invoking the "onslaught of incidents" involving officers' use of force with black suspects that have "rocked" the nation. A cofounder of the Black Lives Matter movement helpfully commented in the *San Francisco Chronicle* that the study goes beyond individual racism to highlight a "systemic set of practices that has impacts on people's lives."

The study is worth examining in some detail as an example of the enormous scientific machinery being brought to bear on a problem of ever-diminishing scope, whether in police departments, on campus, or in American society generally. The most cutting-edge research designs, computer algorithms, and statistical tools, such as Fisher's exact tests, Cronbach's alpha, and Kernel density estimation, are now deployed in the hunt for crippling white racism, while a more pressing problem—inner-city dysfunction—gets minimal academic attention.

The Oakland Police Department gave Eberhardt virtually unlimited access to its policing data as part of a federal consent decree governing the department's operations. Her first study of the department—on racial profiling in police stops—managed to run nearly four hundred pages without ever disclosing black and white crime rates in Oakland. (*Hint*: They are vastly disparate.)

This latest study analyzed officer body-camera footage from 981 car stops that Oakland officers made during April 2014. Blacks were 682 of the drivers in those stops, whites 299. The resulting officer-driver conversations yielded 36,738 discrete officer utterances. In the first phase of the study, college students rated 414 of those officer utterances (1.1 percent of the total) for levels of respect. The students were shown what, if anything, the driver said immediately preceding each officer statement but were not shown any more of the earlier interaction between officer and driver. They were not told the race of the driver or officer or anything else about the stop. The students rated police utterances to white drivers as somewhat more respectful than those to black drivers, though the officers were equally "formal," as the researchers defined it, with drivers of both races.

In the second phase of the study, the linguisticians tried to tease out which features of the 414 officer utterances had generated the student ratings. They came up with twenty-two categories of speech that seemed most determinative. On the positive scale were, *inter alia,* officer apologies, the use of surnames, the use of "um" and "uh" (known in linguistics as "filled pauses"), use of the word "just," and what is referred to as "giving agency" (saying "you can," "you may," or "you could"). The eight negative categories included asking a question, "asking for agency" (phrases such as "do me a favor," "allow me," "may I," "should I"), "disfluency" (a repeated word such as "that, that"), informal titles ("bro," "my man"), first names, and, most disrespectful, the phrase "hands on the wheel." If some of those distinctions seem arbitrary—"could I" is disrespectful, "you could" is respectful; "um" is respectful," a word repetition is not—they are. More important, they are minute and innocuous. The twenty-two categories each received a score allegedly capturing their degree of respect or disrespect, with apologizing at the top of the respect scale and "hands on the wheel" at the bottom. There were no categories for swear words or even for unsoftened commands, presumably because officers never engaged in those forms of speech.

Finally, in phase three, the researchers turned their computers loose on all 36,738 officer utterances, using the twenty-two-category rating system. They found that officers' utterances toward white drivers scored somewhat higher in respect than utterances toward black drivers, even after controlling for whether the stop resulted in a search, citation, arrest, or warning. (The sample size for white arrests and searches was quite small, however: one arrest and two searches; black drivers were fifteen times more likely to be arrested than whites.) Black officers scored the same as white officers in respect toward black and white drivers. White drivers were 57 percent more likely than black drivers to hear something from the top 10 percent of the respect categories, and black drivers were 61 percent more likely to hear something from the bottom 10 percent of the disrespect categories.

There is plenty to criticize in the study's methodology and assumptions. Doing so, however, risks implying that the substantive claims are significant. They are not. Nevertheless, if it were the case that we should worry about whether an officer says, "you can" (good) or "can I" (bad) to black drivers, the study leaves out critical components of officer-civilian interactions. The most disrespectful phrase in the disrespect scale is "hands on the wheel." Black drivers are 29 percent more likely to hear those words than white drivers. Why might an officer ask a driver to put his hands on the wheel? Perhaps because the driver was not complying with an officer's initial requests or was otherwise belligerent. Yet nothing about driver behavior is included in phase three's regression analyses—not drivers' words, demeanor, or actions.

Moreover, given crime rates in Oakland, a black driver is far more likely than a white driver to be on parole or probation, a fact that will show up when an officer runs his plates or his license. In 2013, blacks committed 83 percent of homicides, attempted homicides, robberies, assaults with firearms, and assaults with weapons other than firearms in Oakland, according to Oakland PD data shared with former *San Francisco Chronicle* columnist Chip Johnson, even though blacks are only 28 percent of Oakland's population. Whites were 1 percent of robbery suspects, 1 percent of firearm assault suspects, and an even lower percent of homicide suspects, even though they are about 34 percent of the city's population. (The roadways draw on a population beyond Oakland, but Oakland's crime disparities are repeated in neighboring towns.) Being on parole or probation could contribute to an officer's hands-on-the-wheel request, but drivers' criminal history is not included in the study's models.

The authors claim to have controlled for the severity of any underlying offense that may have triggered the stop, but they do not show whether offense severity differed between blacks and whites. The proportion of male drivers in the black sample was higher than in the white sample, which will also skew the results toward a more crime-prone population. Males were 67 percent of ail black drivers, but only 59 percent of white drivers.

The study's much-cited statistic that black drivers are about 60 percent more likely to hear a phrase from the bottom 10 percent of the disrespect scale is entirely accounted for by the "hands on the wheel" phrase, since there are only eight items on the disrespect list. The next two items on the disrespect list are first names and informal titles. Whites were 4 percent more likely to have a first name used with them, and blacks were 65 percent more likely to have an informal title used with them, by far the greatest discrepancy on the eight-item disrespect scale. An officer who uses "my man" or "bro" with a black driver in Oakland is likely trying to establish rapport through the use of street vernacular, hardly an invidious impulse; black officers were as likely to use such informal titles as white officers. The white drivers stopped were, on average, three years older than the black drivers. Though age had a greater effect on respect and formality than race in the regression models, the study did not test the connection between age and race. Given the socioeconomic profile of the Bay Area's white population, class differences, too, could explain why officers are less likely to use "man" and "bro" with white drivers.

Whether a young black male in Oakland would feel affirmatively disrespected by "my man" is nowhere demonstrated. Eberhardt claimed in an email exchange that black and white DMV patrons in a replication effort also rated utterances from the study's phase one as "more respectful" toward white drivers, from which she concluded that "the use of urban vernacular by officers is not seen as more respectful by black citizens." The question is, however: Are such street terms affirmatively experienced as *disrespectful*?

None of these methodological objections really matters, though, because the substantive results are so innocuous. Consider again the most disrespectful utterance provided by the researchers: "Steve, can I see that driver's license again? It, it's showing suspended. Is that—that's you?" In no possible universe with any minimal connection to common sense should that utterance be deemed disrespectful. Why does it get that rating? A first name is used, which is the second most disrespectful item on the researchers' disrespect scale. "Can I see" is "asking for agency," the fifth most disrespectful thing an officer can say. Worse, "can I see" is part of a question, and questions are the eighth most disrespectful term on the list. If "Can I see that driver's license?" is now deemed racially disrespectful, it's hard to see how police officers can do their jobs.

More demerits follow from "It, it's showing." The repeated "it" counts as a "disfluency," fourth on the disrespect scale. The chance that a driver is even aware of such verbal tics is almost zero. The chance that he would distinguish a disfluency from a so-called filled pause ("um" or "uh") and experience the one as disrespectful and the other as respectful is less than zero. The word "suspended" generates another strike because it is "negative." Again, it is hard to see how officers can conduct traffic stops if such "negative words" are off-limits. The final sentence also racks up two demerits: "Is that—that's you?" is a disfluency *and* a question. The question may have been asked to soften the fact that the driver is operating with a suspended license.

This is madness. In their franker moments, the researchers all but admit that their study makes a mountain of a molehill. "To be clear," Dan Jurafsky, a linguistics and computer science professor told *Science,* "these were well-behaved officers." The "differences are subtle," Eberhardt said to *Science.* The language used with blacks was not "really disrespectful," she added. No kidding. But the authors cannot resist pumping up their results to fit the conventional policing narrative. "We have found that police officers' interactions with blacks tend to be more fraught," they write at the end. They have found no such thing. Even if the professors had actually measured drivers' reactions to the 36,738 officer utterances, rather than simply running those utterances through a computer algorithm, a *de minimis* difference on the respect scale is not tantamount to a finding of "fraughtness." Nevertheless, Eberhardt repeated the "fraughtness" claim in numerous interviews. The study goes on to conclude that "we now have a method of quantifying these troubled interactions." But the authors also did not measure whether the interactions were "troubled" from the driver's perspective. Their method recalls campus-rape surveys that never ask alleged victims if *they* think they have been raped—a topic for another chapter.

The authors titled their study "Language from police body camera footage shows racial disparities in officer respect." A more accurate title would have been: "Language from police body camera footage shows that officers treat all drivers courteously but are more colloquial with young black drivers."

In 2015, the last year for which full data are available, Oakland's violent-crime rate was nearly four times the national average: 1,442 violent crimes per 100,000 residents, compared with 372 violent crimes per 100,000 residents nationwide. Oakland's violent crime rate was fourteen times higher than Palo Alto's and twice as high as San Francisco's. If police training starts insisting that officers refer to everyone as "Mr." and "Ms." and scrupulously avoid street appellations, there would be no loss. But it is the disparity in criminal offending and victimization that should concern race researchers, not whether police officers are more likely to repeat words or use "my man" with black drivers.

■ ■ ■

PART II
GENDER

6

THE CAMPUS RAPE MYTH

It's a lonely job, working the phones at a college rape crisis center. Day after day, you wait for the casualties to show up from the campus rape epidemic—but few victims call. Could this mean that the crisis is overblown? No: It means, according to the campus sexual-assault industry, that the abuse of coeds is worse than anyone had ever imagined. It means that consultants and counselors need more funding to persuade student rape victims to break the silence of their suffering.

The campus rape movement highlights the current condition of radical feminism, from its self-indulgent bathos to its embrace of ever more vulnerable female victimhood. But the movement is an even more important barometer of academia itself. In a striking historical irony, the baby boomers who dismantled the university's intellectual architecture in favor of unbridled sex and protest have now bureaucratized both. While social-justice administrators coordinate antirape rallies, in the dorm next door, freshman counselors organize games of Sex Jeopardy and pass out tips for condom and dental dam use. The academic bureaucracy is roomy enough to include both the dour antimale feminism of the college rape movement and the promiscuous hookup culture of student life. The only thing that doesn't fit into the university's new commitments is serious scholarly purpose.

The campus rape industry's central tenet is that one fifth to one quarter of all college girls will be raped or be the targets of attempted rape by the end of their college years (completed rapes outnumbering attempted rapes by a ratio of about three to two). The girls' assailants are not terrifying strangers grabbing them in dark alleys but the guys sitting next to them in class or at the cafeteria.

This claim, first published in *Ms.* magazine in 1985, took the universities by storm. By the early 1990s, campus rape centers and twenty-four-hour hotlines were opening across the country, aided by tens of millions of dollars of federal funding. Victimhood rituals sprang up: first the Take Back the Night rallies, in which alleged rape victims reveal their stories to gathered crowds of candle-holding supporters; then the Clothesline Project, in which T-shirts made by self-proclaimed rape survivors are strung on campus, while recorded sounds of gongs and drums mark minute-by-minute casualties of the "rape culture." A special rhetoric emerged: Victims' family and friends were "co-survivors"; "survivors" existed in a larger "community of survivors."

An army of salesmen took to the road, selling advice to administrators on how to structure sexual-assault procedures and lecturing freshmen on the "undetected rapists" in their midst. Rape bureaucrats exchanged notes at such gatherings as the Inter Ivy Sexual Assault Conferences and the New England College Sexual Assault Network. Organizations like One in Four and Men Can Stop Rape tried to persuade college boys to redefine their masculinity away from the "rape culture." The college rape infrastructure ballooned. Harvard University, for example, recently created an Office for Sexual and Gender-Based Dispute Resolution, to go along with a heavily staffed Office of Sexual Assault Prevention and Response and over fifty Title IX coordinators.

If the one-in-five to one-in-four statistic is correct, campus rape represents a crime wave of unprecedented proportions. No crime, much less one as serious as rape, has a victimization rate remotely approaching 20 percent or 25 percent, even over many years. In 2016, the violent crime rate in Detroit, the most violent city in America, was 2,000 murders, rapes, robberies, and aggravated assaults per 100,000 inhabitants—a rate of 2 percent.[1] The one-in-five to one-in-four statistic would mean that every year, hundreds of thousands of young women graduate who have suffered the most terrifying assault, short of murder, that a woman can experience. Such a crime wave would require nothing less than a state of emergency—Take Back the Night rallies and twenty-four-hour hotlines would hardly be adequate to counter this tsunami of sexual violence. Admissions policies letting in thousands of vicious criminals would require a complete revision, perhaps banning boys entirely. The nation's 11.5 million female undergrads would need to take the most stringent safety precautions.

None of this crisis response occurs, of course. To the contrary, every year the stampede of girls trying to get into the most selective colleges grows more frenzied, driving admissions rates to historic lows. Girls now constitute a large majority of students on college campuses. Harvard received a record number of applications for the Class of 2021, for an acceptance rate of 5.2 percent. Highly educated mothers in New York City pay $200 an hour to prep their female tots for nursery school admissions tests, all in the hope of winning a spot for their little darlings in the Ivy League thirteen years later. Yet we are to believe that these ambitious mothers are deliberately packing off their daughters to a hellhole of sexual predation.

Are they that callous? No, some part of them understands that the rape epidemic doesn't exist. During the 1980s, feminist researchers committed to the rape-culture theory had discovered that asking women directly if they had been raped yielded disappointing results— very few women said that they had been. So *Ms.* commissioned University of Arizona public health professor Mary Koss to develop a different way of measuring the prevalence of rape. Rather than asking female students about rape per se, Koss asked them if they had experienced actions that she then classified as rape. Koss's method produced the 25 percent rate, which *Ms.* then published.

Koss's study had serious flaws. Her survey instrument was highly ambiguous, as University of California at Berkeley social-welfare professor Neil Gilbert has pointed out. But the most powerful refutation of Koss's research came from her own subjects: 73 percent of the women whom she characterized as rape victims said that they hadn't been raped. Further—though it is inconceivable that a raped woman

would voluntarily have sex again with the fiend who attacked her—
42 percent of Koss's supposed victims had intercourse again with their
alleged assailants.

All subsequent feminist rape studies have resulted in this discrepancy between the researchers' conclusions and the subjects' own views.
A 2006 survey of sorority girls at the University of Virginia found that
only 23 percent of the subjects whom the survey characterized as rape
victims felt that they had been raped—a result that the university's
director of Sexual and Domestic Violence Services deemed "discour-
aging."[2] Equally unhelpful was a 2000 campus rape study conducted
under the aegis of the Department of Justice. Sixty-five percent of what
the feminist researchers called "completed rape" victims and three-
quarters of "attempted rape" victims said that they did not think that
their experiences were "serious enough to report." The "victims" in the
study, moreover, "generally did not state that their victimization resulted in physical or emotional injuries," report the researchers.[3]

A 2015 sexual-assault survey conducted at Harvard and twenty-six
other colleges, and led by the Association of American Universities
(AAU), declared that 16 percent of Harvard female seniors had experienced nonconsensual sexual penetration during their time at college, and nearly 40 percent had experienced nonconsensual sexual
contact.[4] Yet the vast majority of survey respondents on all campuses
whom the AAU researchers classified as sexual-assault victims never
reported their alleged assaults to their colleges' rape hotlines, sexual-
assault resource centers, or Title IX offices, much less to campus or
city police. And the overwhelming reason that the alleged victims did
not report is that they did not think that what happened to them was
that serious. At Harvard, over 69 percent of female respondents who
checked the box for penetration by use of force did not report the incident to any authority. Most of those nonreporters—65 percent—did
not think that their experience was serious enough to report. This outcome is inconceivable in the case of real rape. No woman who has
actually been raped would think that the rape was not serious enough
to report.

The rate of nonreporting climbs as the sexual-assault categories ginned up by the AAU grow ever more distant from the common understanding of rape. Over 78 percent of Harvard female respondents who checked the box for penetration due to "incapacitation" did not report. Three-quarters of them said that what happened to them was not serious enough to report. Over 92 percent of Harvard female respondents who said that they were the victim of sexual touching by force did not report; over 81 percent said that what happened to them was not serious enough to report. Over 93 percent of respondents who had been sexually touched due to incapacitation did not report. Over 80 percent of them did not think it serious enough to report. The picture is identical at every other college in the survey.

And college administrators overwhelmingly think that the alleged sex crimes on their campus are not serious enough to warrant an arrest. Stanford University reports 33 rapes in 2016, a catastrophic level of violence, if true.[5] Yet in none of those cases was there an arrest, even though the alleged rapist was almost certainly known to the accuser. Indeed, if parents actually acted on administrators' rape rhetoric and started home-schooling their college-aged daughters as a protective measure, those administrators would turn on a dime and affirm the obvious: that their colleges are blessedly violence-free zones.

Just as a reality check, consider an actual student-related rape: In 2006, Labrente Robinson and Jacoby Robinson broke into the Philadelphia home of a Temple University student and a Temple graduate, and anally, vaginally, and orally penetrated the women, including with a gun.[6] The chance that the victims would not consider this event "serious enough to report," or physically and emotionally injurious, is exactly nil.

And consider how colleges respond to credible rape cases: They go into emergency mode. In August 2012, a rape was reported in Harvard Yard, sending shock waves throughout the campus. Police cruisers idled around college buildings; uniformed and plainclothes officers came out in force. Students were advised not to walk alone. A member of the undergraduate council called for the closing of Harvard Yard. "I thought Cambridge wasn't a dangerous area," a freshman told the student newspaper. "It was Harvard—it was supposed to be safe, academic."[7] (Apparently, she hadn't read the copious materials from Harvard's sexual-assault bureaucracy insisting that campus rape was everywhere.) In 2015, a University of Virginia freshman was abducted from a local mall, raped, and murdered. Though a suspect was already in custody and the abduction had happened off campus, university administrators beefed up campus lighting and security cameras anyway. Nervous students walked in groups or took buses and cabs.[8]

According to the advocates, such sexual violence is virtually a daily occurrence on campuses. Yet such intense security precautions are rare, and only follow reports of what is commonly understood as rape. Drunken coeds continue to troop eagerly into frat-house parties at UVA and elsewhere. Either the sisterhood fails to inform and protect its own or these girls know that whatever sex they encounter at those parties will be a far cry from rape.

In short, believing in the campus rape epidemic depends on ignoring women's own interpretations of their experiences—supposedly the most grievous sin in the feminist political code.

But none of the weaknesses in the research has had the slightest drag on the campus rape movement, because the movement is political, not empirical. In a rape culture, which "condones physical and emotional terrorism against women as a norm," sexual assault will wind up underreported, argued the director of Yale's Sexual Harassment and Assault Resources and Education Center in a newsletter.[9] You don't need evidence for the rape culture; you simply know that it exists. But if you do need evidence, the underreporting of rape is the best proof there is.

Campus rape researchers may feel that they know better than female students themselves about the students' sexual experiences, but the students are voting with their feet and staying away in droves from the massive rape apparatus built up since the *Ms.* article. Referring to rape hotlines, rape consultant Brett Sokolow lamented: "The problem is, on so many of our campuses, very few people ever call. And mostly, we've resigned ourselves to the under-utilization of these resources."[10]

The federal Clery Act requires colleges to report the number of crimes affecting their students. From 2005 to 2016, campuses got safer. Total crimes, including burglary and crimes of violence, dropped 43.5 percent from 2005 to 2016. Such increased safety contradicts the dominant narrative and is therefore ignored. When it comes to sex crimes, both the federal government and local campuses regularly fiddle with the categorization of campus sex crimes to get the numbers up. In 2014, federal authorities changed the reporting category of "Sex offenses—Non-forcible" to the inherently vague "Fondling." Voilà! The reports increased 6,000 percent, from 59 non-forcible sex offenses in 2013 to 3,614 fondling incidents in 2016. Even with this more expansive classification, and the efforts of campus authorities to come up with even more categories of sex offenses, the total number of Clery sex offense reports in 2016 was 10,297. Corroboration is not required; a defendant can be cleared and the accusation against him will still be entered into the Clery tally. Those 10,297 reports include all alleged improprieties against males, females, graduates, and undergraduates at 6,500 institutions. By comparison, if the one-in-five figure of campus assaults were correct, there would be between 300,000 and 400,000 sexual assaults on female undergraduates alone each year. In 2017, the American Association of University Women complained that rape numbers were still too low. Among college campuses (including branch campuses of a central institution) with enrollments of 250 students or more, 73 percent reported 0 rapes in 2015—a wholly unacceptable "picture," as the AAUW put it.

Those meager allegations are higher than the numbers reported in the 2000s, however, thanks to a controversial directive from the Education Department's Office of Civil Rights in 2011. That guidance, known as a "Dear Colleague Letter," warned every college and university in the country that unless they weakened their already-inadequate due-process protections in campus rape tribunals, they would lose federal funding. Colleges had to adopt a preponderance-of-evidence standard of proof for finding guilt, for example—meaning just 50.5 percent certainty that the offense had occurred—and allow accusers to appeal acquittals of the defendant. The message was clear: Get your rape reports up or face federal investigation. Colleges took the Dear Colleague Letter and ran with it, adding even flimsier categories of sexual impropriety; eliminating the greatest of all Anglo-Saxon truth-finding mechanisms—the right of cross examination; and doing everything they could to encourage accusations. The resulting procedures were "frequently so unfair as to be truly shocking," wrote Harvard law professors Jeannie Suk Gersen, Janet Halley, Elizabeth Bartholet, and Nancy Gertner in an August 2017 white paper filed with the Office of Civil Rights.[11] (In September 2017, President Trump's Education secretary Betsy DeVos rescinded the preponderance-of-evidence requirement, but nearly all colleges have promised to continue using it—making clear that their compliance with the directive has hardly been involuntary.)

You might think that having few reports of sexual assault a year would be a point of pride; in fact, it's a source of gall for administrators. *The Harvard Crimson* reported in 2016 that "some University officials do not consider a high level of reported rapes as a wholly negative statistic." That is an understatement. Yale's associate general counsel and vice president were clearly on the defensive when asked by the Yale alumni magazine back in 2004 about Harvard's higher numbers of reported assaults; the reporter might as well have been needling them about a Harvard-Yale football rout. Harvard must have double-counted or included incidents not required by federal law, groused the officials.

Even after the 2011 Dear Colleague Letter, the persistent scarcity of reported sexual assaults means that the females who do report them must be treated like rare treasures. New York University's Wellness Exchange counsels people to "believe unconditionally" in sexual-assault charges because "only 2 percent of reported rapes are false reports" (a ubiquitous claim that dates from radical feminist Susan Brownmiller's 1975 tract *Against Our Will*). As Stuart Taylor and K. C. Johnson point out in their book *Until Proven Innocent,* however, the rate of false reports may be closer to 50 percent. Title IX investigators are usually trained in "victim-centered practices," which reverse the presumption of innocence and treat the male as guilty unless overwhelming evidence unavoidably demands the opposite conclusion. Even the Association of Title IX Administrators warned in 2017 that "victim-centered" had come to signify "victim-favoring," and that students were being expelled from school on uncertain evidence. The equally influential concept of "trauma-informed" analysis holds that the more unreliable and incoherent a rape complainant is, the more she should be believed, noted Harvard law professor Janet Halley in 2015.[12]

Just how powerful is the "believe unconditionally" credo? David Lisak, a retired University of Massachusetts psychology professor who lectures extensively on the antirape college circuit, acknowledged to a hall of Rutgers students in November 2008 that the "Duke case," in which a black stripper falsely accused three white Duke lacrosse players of rape in 2006, had "raised the issue of false allegations." But Lisak didn't want to talk about the Duke case, he said. "I don't know what happened at Duke. No one knows." Actually, we do know what happened at Duke: The prosecutor ignored clearly exculpatory evidence and alibis that cleared the defendants, and was later disbarred for his misconduct. But to the campus rape industry, a lying plaintiff remains a victim of the patriarchy, and the accused remain forever under suspicion.

So what reality does lie behind the campus rape industry? A booze-fueled hookup culture of one-night, or sometimes just partial-night, stands. Students in the 1960s demanded that college administrators stop setting rules for fraternization. "We're adults," the students shouted. "We can manage our own lives. If we want to have members of the opposite sex in our rooms at any hour of the day or night, that's our right." The colleges meekly complied and opened a Pandora's box of boorish behavior that gets cruder each year. Do the boys, riding the testosterone wave, act thuggishly toward the girls? Yes! Do the girls try to match their insensitivity? Indisputably.

College girls drink themselves into near or actual oblivion before and during parties. That drinking is often goal-oriented, suggests University of Virginia graduate Karin Agness: It frees the drinker from responsibility and "provides an excuse for engaging in behavior that she ordinarily wouldn't." A Columbia University security official marveled at the scene at homecomings: "The women are shit-faced, saying, 'Let's get as drunk as we can,' while the men are hovering over them."[13] As anticipated, the night can include a meaningless sexual encounter with a guy whom the girl may not even know. This less-than-romantic denouement produces the "roll and scream: you roll over the next morning so horrified at what you find next to you that you scream," a Duke coed reports in Laura Sessions Stepp's book *Un-hooked*. To the extent that they're remembered at all, these are the couplings that are occasionally transformed into "rape"—though far less often than the campus rape industry wishes.

The magazine *Saturday Night: Untold Stories of Sexual Assault at Harvard*, produced until recently by Harvard's Office of Sexual Assault Prevention and Response, provides a first-person account of such a coupling:

> What can I tell you about being raped? Very little. I remember drinking with some girlfriends and then heading to a party in the house that some seniors were throwing. I'm told that I walked in and within 5 minutes was making out with one of the guys who lived there, who I'd talked to some in the dining hall but never really hung out with. I may have initiated it. I don't remember arriving at the party; I dimly remember waking up at some point in the early morning in this guy's room. I remember him walking me back to my room. I couldn't have made it alone; I still had too much alcohol in my system to even stand up straight. I made myself vulnerable and even now it's hard to think that someone here who I have talked and laughed with could be cold-hearted enough to take advantage of that vulnerability. I'd rather, sometimes, take half the blame than believe that a profound evil can exist in mankind. But it's easy for me to say, that, of the two of us, I'm the only one who still has nightmares, found myself panicking and detaching during sex for many months afterwards, and spent more time looking into the abyss than any one person should.
>
> The inequalities of the consequences of the night, the actions taken unintentionally or not, have changed the course of only one of our lives, irrevocably and profoundly.

Now perhaps the male willfully exploited the narrator's self-inflicted incapacitation; if so, he deserves censure for taking advantage of a female in distress. But to hold the narrator completely without responsibility requires stripping women of volition and moral agency. Though the Harvard victim does not remember her actions, it's highly unlikely that she passed out upon arriving at the party and was dragged away like roadkill while other students looked on. Rather, she probably participated voluntarily in the usual prelude to intercourse, and probably even in intercourse itself, however woozily.

Even if the Harvard victim's drunkenness cancels any responsibility that she might share for the interaction's finale, is she equally without responsibility for all of her behavior up to that point, including getting so drunk that she can't remember anything? Campus rape ideology holds that inebriation strips women of responsibility for their actions but preserves males' responsibility not only for their own actions but for their partners' as well. Thus do men again become the guardians of female well-being.

As for the story's melodrama, perhaps the narrator's life really has been "irrevocably" changed, for which one sympathizes. One can't help observing, however, that the effect of this "profound evil" on at least her sex life appears to have been minimal—she found herself "detaching" during sex for "many months afterwards," but sex she most certainly had. Real rape victims, however, can fear physical intimacy for years, along with suffering a host of other terrors. We don't know if the narrator's "looking into the abyss" led her to reconsider getting plastered before parties and initiating sexual contact with casual acquaintances. But if a Harvard student doesn't understand that getting very drunk and becoming physically involved with a boy at a hookup party carries a serious probability of intercourse, she's at the wrong university, if she should be at college at all.

Or take a case at Washington and Lee University. After a late-night party filled with the usual heavy drinking, the female accuser, Jane Doe, told her male companion: "I usually don't have sex with someone I meet on the first night, but you are a really interesting guy." Jane Doe began kissing John Doe, took off her clothes, and led John Doe to his bed, where she took off his clothes. They had intercourse. This was on February 8, 2014. (Jane later denied using that pickup line on the ground that she often had sex with someone she had just met.) The next day, Jane Doe told a friend that she had had sex with John Doe and that she had "had a good time last night." Over the next month, Jane and John Doe exchanged flirty texts and had intercourse again. Jane Doe attended several more parties at John Doe's fraternity. At one of them, Jane observed John kissing another female and left the party early, upset. John developed a publicly known relationship with that other female. Jane started psychological therapy after seeing John's name on a list of applicants for a study-abroad program that she had also applied to. She told one of her therapists that she had "enjoyed the sexual intercourse" with John Doe, but was advised that her actions and positive feelings during their first sexual encounter "didn't negate that it was sexual assault." She told another therapist that "she had a strong physical reaction" to seeing John's name on the study-abroad list. Jane had also been working at a women's clinic and attending lectures on sexual assault. During one of those talks, Washington and Lee's Title IX officer informed the audience of the emerging consensus that "regret equals rape." After Jane Doe learned that John had been accepted to her study-abroad program, she decided to initiate her campus's sexual-assault machinery against him. A travesty of a proceeding followed, in which the Title IX officer rejected John Doe's request to consult a lawyer with the Dantesque warning that "a lawyer can't help you here."[14] The school expelled him.

A large number of complicating factors makes such stories far more problematic cases than the term "rape" usually implies. Unlike the campus rape industry, most students are well aware of those complicating factors, which is why there are so few rape charges brought for college sex. Equally telling, alleged campus rapes have a noticeable tendency to fall apart when subjected to traditional police investigations. In 2014, the federal government started requiring that campuses disclose "unfounded"—that is, false or baseless—crime reports in their annual Clery Act criminal statistics. Colleges agonized over whether to identify the unfounded crimes by category, and many colleges did not. Harvard, to its credit, did classify the unfounded crimes by category. The results show why the issue was so difficult for the rape bureaucracy. The only unfounded crimes that Harvard reported were rapes—six of them. By contrast, none of the 492 property crimes reported to Harvard law enforcement in 2014 were found to be baseless. And those six unfounded rapes represented all of the rapes reported to the Harvard police in 2014—not one survived law-enforcement investigation, even though they were presumably the strongest cases out there. The other twenty-seven "rapes" listed by Harvard on its Clery Act form were reported instead to Harvard's various non-law-enforcement sexual-assault resource centers, none of which has the authority to "unfound" a crime report. Harvard has yet to initiate a proceeding against any false accuser for violation of its honor code, presumably on the feminist theory that there are no false rape reports.

In 2014, consultant Brett Sokolow provided another window into the promiscuous couplings that the feminist-industrial complex converts into campus rape. In an open letter to higher education, he described a series of trumped-up charges with which his firm had been involved[15]:

> —A female student had spread rumors by social media that she had been raped by a male student. She then admitted to investigators that she had consented to their drunken hook-up. When asked why she had called the encounter rape, she replied: "You know, because we were drunk. It wasn't rape, it was just rapey rape." She dismissed the idea that publicly charging her companion with rape would injure his reputation: "Everyone knows it wasn't really a rape, we just call it that when we're drunk or high."

> —A female student was caught by her boyfriend while cheating on him with another male student. She then filed a complaint of assault against that second male. The morning after their sexual encounter they had exchanged texts:

> **He:** *How do I compare with your boyfriend?*

> **She:** *You were great*

> **He:** *So you got off?*

> **She:** *Yes, especially when I was on top*

He: *We should do it again, soon*

She: *Hehe*

—A female student charged non-consensual oral intercourse. Her texts to the male both before and after positively referred to their experience, stating that she enjoys swallowing and "dirty boys who cum in [her] mouth."

—Two students had a long-term sexual relationship. They broke up and the male started sleeping with another girl. His former girlfriend then retroactively charged him with sexual assault, despite the lack of any previous expression of dismay on her part.

These incidents almost certainly ended up in their school's Clery Act reports.

If the rape industrialists are so sure that foreseeable and seemingly co-operative drunken sex amounts to rape, there are some obvious steps that they could take to prevent it. Above all, they could persuade girls not to put themselves into situations whose likely outcome is intercourse. Specifically: Don't get drunk, don't get into bed with a guy, and don't take off your clothes or allow them to be removed. Once you're in that situation, the rape activists could say, it's going to be hard to halt the proceedings, for lots of complex emotional reasons. Were this advice heeded, the campus "rape" epidemic would be wiped out overnight.

But suggest to a rape bureaucrat that female students should behave with greater sexual restraint as a preventive measure, and you might as well be saying that the girls should enter a convent or don the burka. "I am uncomfortable with the idea," emailed Hillary Wing-Richards, a psychology professor at James Madison University in Virginia who ran the school's Women's Resource Center and Office of Sexual Assault Prevention. "This indicates that if [female students] are raped it could be their fault—it is never their fault—and how one dresses does not invite rape or violence. . . . I would never allow my staff or myself to send the message it is the victim's fault due to their dress or lack of restraint in any way." Putting on a tight tank top doesn't, of course, lead to what the bureaucrats call "rape." But taking *off* that tank top does increase the risk of sexual intercourse that will be later regretted, especially when the tank-topper has been intently drinking rum and Cokes all evening. (In February 2018, a federal magistrate recommended that James Madison University reimburse a male student's $849,231.25 legal costs spent fighting an unconstitutional and unjustified expulsion for sexual assault.)[16]

The baby boomers who demanded the dismantling of all campus rules governing the relations between the sexes now sit in dean's offices and student-counseling services. They cannot explicitly repudiate their revolution, even on pragmatic grounds. Instead, they have responded to the fallout of the college sexual revolution with bizarre and anachronistic legalism. Campuses have created a bureaucratic infrastructure for responding to postcoital second thoughts more complex than that required to adjudicate maritime commerce claims in Renaissance Venice.

Procedures available to "victims" for bringing their complaints include "structured meetings" with deans, voluntary mediation with a trained professional, or formal adjudications before sexual assault boards. These options mutate constantly; the manuals describing them run for dozens of pages.

Out in the real world, people who regret a sexual coupling must work it out on their own; no counterpart exists outside academia for this superstructure of hearings, mediations, and negotiated settlements. If you've actually been raped, you go to criminal court—but the overwhelming majority of campus "rape" cases that take up administration time and resources would get thrown out of court in a twinkling, which is why they're almost never prosecuted. Indeed, if the campus rape industry really believes that these hookup encounters are rape, it is unconscionable to leave them to flimsy academic procedures. "Universities are equipped to handle plagiarism, not rape," observes University of Pennsylvania history professor Alan Charles Kors. "Sexual-assault charges, if true, are so serious as to belong only in the criminal system."[17]

Risk-management consultants travel the country to help colleges craft legal rules for student sexual congress. These rules presume that an activity originating in inchoate desire, whose nuances have taxed the expressive powers of poets, artists, and philosophers for centuries, can be reduced to a species of commercial code. The process of crafting these rules combines a voyeuristic prurience and a seeming cluelessness about sex. "It is fun," wrote Alan D. Berkowitz, one of the pioneers in the campus rape lecture circuit, in 2002, "to ask students how they know if someone is sexually interested in them." (Fun for whom? one must ask.) Continued Berkowitz: "Many of the responses rely on guesswork and inference to determine sexual intent." Such signaling mechanisms, dating from the dawn of the human race, are no longer acceptable on the rape-sensitized campus. "In fact," explains our consultant, "sexual intent can only be determined by clear and unambiguous communication about what is desired."[18] So much for seduction and romance; bring in the MBAs and lawyers.

The campus sex-management industry locks in its livelihood by introducing a specious clarity to what is inherently mysterious and an equally specious complexity to what is straightforward. Both the pseudo-clarity and pseudo-complexity work in a woman's favor, of course. "If one partner puts a condom on the other, does that signify that they are consenting to intercourse?" asked Berkowitz. Short of guiding the thus-sheathed instrumentality to port, it's hard to imagine a clearer signal of consent. But perhaps a girl who has just so outfitted her partner will decide after the fact that she has been "raped"—so better to declare the action, as Berkowitz does, "inherently ambiguous." A rape case at Occidental College, discussed in chapter 7, presents a near-identical situation.

The university is sneaking back in its *in loco parentis* oversight of student sexual relations, but it has replaced the moral content of that regulation with supposedly neutral legal procedure. The generation that got rid of parietal rules has re-created a form of bedroom oversight as pervasive as Bentham's Panopticon.

But the post-1960s university is nothing if not capacious. It has institutionalized every strand of adolescent-inspired rebellion familiar since student sit-in days. The campus rape industry may decry ubiquitous male predation, but a campus sex industry puts bureaucratic clout behind the message that students should have recreational sex at every opportunity.

Consider one school event, which saw New York University's professional "sexpert" set up her wares in the light-filled atrium of the Kimmel Student Center. Along with the usual baskets of lubricated condoms, female condoms, and dental dams (a lesbian-inspired latex innovation for "safe" oral sex), Alyssa LaFosse, looking thoroughly professional in a neatly coiffed bun, also provided brightly colored instructional sheets on such important topics as "How to Female Ejaculate" ("First take some time to get aroused. Lube up your fingers and let them do the walking") and "Masturbation Tips for Girls" ("Draw a circle around your clitoris with your index finger"). In a heroic effort at inclusiveness, she also provided a pamphlet called "Exploring Your Options: Abstinence," but a reader could be forgiven for thinking that he had mistakenly grabbed the menu of activities at a West Village bathhouse. NYU's officially approved "abstinence options" included "outercourse, mutual masturbation, pornography, and sex toys such as vibrators, dildos, and a paddle." Ever the responsible parent-surrogate, NYU recommended that "abstinence" practitioners cover their sex toys "with a condom if they are to be inserted in the mouth, anus, or vagina."

The students passing LaFosse's table showed a greater interest in the free Hershey's Kisses than in the latex accessories and informational sheets; very occasionally, someone would grab a condom. No one brought "questions about sexuality or sexual health" to LaFosse, despite the university's official invitation to do so. NYU was not about to be daunted in its mission of promoting better sex, however. So it also offered workshops on orgasms—"how to achieve that (sometimes elusive) state"—and "Sex Toys for Safer Sex" ("an evening with rubber, silicone, and vibrating toys") in residence halls and various student clubs.

Brown University's Student Services helps students answer the compelling question: "How can I bring sex toys into my relationship?" Brown categorizes sex toys by function ("Some sex toys are meant to be used more gently, while others are used for sexual acts involving dominance and submission . . . such as restraints, blindfolds, and whips") and offers the usual safe-sex caveats ("If sharing sex toys, such as dildos, butt plugs, or vibrators, use condoms and dental dams").[19] Oberlin College's Sexual Information Center has offered sex toy sales.[20] The 2017 Harvard Sex Week, underwritten by such bureaucratic principalities as the Office of Sexual Assault Prevention and Response, Sexual Health and Relationship Counselors, and the Office of BGLTQ Student Life, presented a workshop in "Sex Toys 101: Feel those Good Vibrations."[21]

By now, universities have traveled so far from their original task of immersing students in the greatest intellectual and artistic creations of humanity that criticizing any particular detour seems arbitrary. Still, the question presents itself: Why, exactly, are the schools promoting orgasms instead of Michelangelo's Campidoglio or Pushkin's *Eugene Onegin*? Are students already so saturated with knowledge of Renaissance humanism or the evolution of constitutional democracy, say, that colleges can happily reroute resources to matters readily available on porn websites?

Columbia University's Go Ask Alice! website illustrates the dilemma posed by a college's simultaneous advocacy of "healthy sexuality" and of the "rape is everywhere" ideology. Go Ask Alice! is run by Columbia's Health Services; it addresses both nonsexual health queries and such burning topics as: "Sex with four friends—Mutual?" and "Kinky Sex." In one post, titled "I'm sure I was drunk, but I'm not sure if I had sex," Alice takes up the classic hookup scenario: a girl who has no recollection of whether she had intercourse during a drunken encounter and now wonders if she's pregnant. Alice's initial reaction is pure free-love toleration: "Depending upon your relationship with your partner, you may want to ask what happened. Understandably, this might feel awkward and embarrassing, but the conversation might . . . help you to understand what happened and what steps you might decide to take." Absent that pesky worry about insemination, there would presumably be no compelling reason to engage in something as "awkward and embarrassing" as a post-roll-in-the-hay conversation.

But then a shadow passes over the horizon: the date-rape threat. "On a darker note," continues Alice, "it's possible your experience may have been non-consensual, considering that you were drunk and don't remember exactly what happened." Alice recommends a call to Columbia's Rape Crisis/Anti-Violence Support Center (officially dedicated to "speaking our truths about sexual violence").[22] Alice's advice shows the incoherence of the contemporary university's multiple stances toward college sex. It's hard to speak your truths about sexual violence when your involvement with your potential date-rapist is so tenuous that it's awkward to speak to *him*. And the support center can't know whether the encounter was consensual. But Alice declines to condemn the behavior that both got the girl into her predicament and erased her memory of it.

The only lesson that Alice offers is that the girl might—purely as an optional matter—want to think about how alcohol affected her. As for rethinking whether she should be getting into bed with someone whom, Alice presumes, she would be reluctant to contact the next day, well, that never comes up. Members of the multifaceted campus sex bureaucracy never seem to consider the possibility that the libertinism that one administrative branch champions, and the sex that another branch portrays as rape, may be inextricably linked.

Modern feminists defined the right to be promiscuous as a cornerstone of female equality. Understandably, they now hesitate to acknowledge that sex is a more complicated force than was foreseen. Rather than recognizing that no-consequences sex may be a contradiction in terms, however, the campus rape industry claims that what it calls campus rape is about not sex but rather politics—the male desire to subordinate women.

This characterization may well describe the psychopathic violence of stranger rape. But it is inapt for the sexual contacts that undergraduate men, happily released from older constraints, seek. The guys who push themselves on women at keggers are after one thing only, and it's not a reinstatement of the patriarchy.

One group on campus isn't fully buying the politics of the campus "rape" movement, however: students. To the despair of rape industrialists everywhere, many students have held on to the view that women usually have considerable power to determine whether a campus social event ends with intercourse.

"Promiscuity" is a word that you will never see in the pages of a campus rape center publication; it is equally repugnant to the sexual liberationist strand of feminism and to the Catharine MacKinnonite "all-sex-is-rape" strand. But it's an idea that won't go away among the student lumpen proletariat. Students refer to "sororistutes"—those wild and crazy Greek women so often featured in spring-break soft-porn videos. And they persist in seeing a connection between promiscuity and the alleged campus rape epidemic. A Rutgers University freshman noted that he knows women who claim to have been sexually assaulted, but adds: "They don't have the best reputation. Sometimes it's hard to believe that kind of stuff."[23]

Rape consultant Lisak faced a similar problem in one of his sessions: an auditorium of Rutgers students who kept treating women as moral agents. He might have sensed the trouble ahead when in response to a photo array of what Lisak calls "undetected rapists," a girl asked: "Why are there only white men? Am I blind?" It went downhill from there. Lisak did his best to send a tremor of fear through the audience with the news that "rape happens with terrifying frequency. I'm not talking of someone who comes onto campus but students, Rutgers students, who prowl for victims in bars, parties, wherever alcohol is being consumed." He then played a dramatized interview with a student "rapist" at a fraternity that had deliberately set aside a room for raping girls during parties, according to Lisak. The students weren't convinced. "I don't understand why these parties don't become infamous among girls," wondered one. Another asked: "Are you saying that the frat brothers decided that this room would be used for committing sexual assault, or was it just: 'Maybe I'll get lucky, and if I do, I'll go there'?" And then someone asked the most dangerous question of all: "Shouldn't the victim have had a little bit of education beforehand? We all know the dangers of parties. The victim had miscalculations on her part; alcohol can lead to things."

You can read thousands of pages of rape crisis center hysteria without coming across such bracing common sense.

Some student rebels are going one step further: organizing in favor of sexual restraint. Such campus groups as the Love and Fidelity Network and the True Love Revolution advocate an alternative to the rampant regret sex of the hookup scene: wait until marriage. Their message would do more to return a modicum of manners to campus male—and female—behavior than endless harangues about the rape culture ever could.

ROLLING STONE'S UNIVERSITY OF VIRGINIA GANG RAPE FICTION AND THE REAL WORLD

Skepticism should have greeted *Rolling Stone*'s now-infamous 2014 story about gang rape at the University of Virginia, which collapsed once Charlottesville police got involved. The story was patently the product of a delusional mind, depicting a level of grotesque violence that is unheard of on college campuses. According to the magazine's almost sole source—the victim, a freshman called "Jackie" in the story—she was escorted into a pitch-black room in the Phi Kappa Psi fraternity during a party on September 28, 2012. A huge male student immediately tackled her and sent her crashing through a glass table. A group of eight males then punched and gagged her, while one shouted: "Grab its motherfucking leg." She is sexually assaulted for hours, including with a beer bottle when one of the frat brothers was unable to get an erection.

Afterward, bloodied and shaking, Jackie seeks help from her best friends. They tell her not to report the rape, however, because it will reflect badly on the University of Virginia and damage their own hopes of joining a Greek house and being admitted to high-prestige frat parties. The campus administrators responded just as callously, according to Jackie, allegedly conceding that they suppress rape incidents to protect the University of Virginia's reputation.

If such a tale bore any relation to reality, parents would have demanded the creation of single-sex schools where their daughters could study in safety. And yet the *Rolling Stone* story was greeted with triumphant elation by the campus rape industry and with reluctant credulity even by conservative academics and journalists. Finally, we were told, we were seeing the ugly reality behind the fantastical statistics about college rape. The University of Virginia went into a paroxysm of self-flagellation; its president suspended all activities of its fraternities and sororities.

The demolition of the University of Virginia gang rape hoax drove a stake through *Rolling Stone*'s credibility. Its reporter, Sabrina Rubin Erdely, ignored almost every journalistic canon, failing even to seek out Jackie's alleged assailants in order to get their side of the story. It turned out that those assailants didn't exist.

The *Rolling Stone* fiction was treated as truth, however, because feminists have convinced a large swath of society that we live in a "rape culture," where women are perpetual victims and men are assailants in waiting. Indeed, so strong is the feminist lock on our culture that the Charlottesville police chief was unwilling to close the case, even though nothing was left of it.

■ ■ ■

7

NEO-VICTORIANISM ON CAMPUS

Sexual liberation is having a nervous breakdown on college campuses. Campus feminists are reimporting selective portions of a traditional sexual code that they have long scorned, in the name of ending the purported epidemic of campus rape. They are once again making males the guardians of female safety and are portraying females as fainting, helpless victims of the untrammeled male libido. While the campus feminists are not yet calling for an assistant dean to be present at their drunken couplings, they have created the next best thing: the opportunity to replay every grope and caress before a tribunal of voyeuristic administrators.

The ultimate result of the feminists' crusade may be the same as if they were explicitly calling for a return to sexual modesty: a sharp decrease in casual, drunken sex.

Let us recall the norms that the sexual revolution contemptuously swept away in the 1960s. Males and females were assumed on average to have different needs regarding sex: The omnivorous male sex drive would leap at all available targets, whereas females were more selective, associating sex with love and commitment. The male was expected to channel his desire for sex through the rituals of courtship and a proposal of marriage. A high premium was placed on female chastity and great significance accorded its loss; males, by contrast, were given a virtual free pass to play the sexual field to the extent that they could find or purchase a willing partner. The default setting for premarital sex was "no," at least for females. Girls could opt out of that default—and many did. But placing the default at "no" meant that a female didn't have to justify her decision not to have sex with particular reasons each time a male importuned her; individual sexual restraint was backed up by collective values. On campuses, administrators enforced these norms through visitation rules designed to prevent student couplings.

The sexual revolution threw these arrangements aside. From now on, males and females would meet as equals on the sexual battlefield. The ideal of female modesty, the liberationists declared, was simply a cover for sexism. Chivalry was punished; females were assumed to desire sex as voraciously as males; they required no elaborate courtship rituals to engage in it and would presumably experience no pang of thwarted attachment after a one-night stand. The default for premarital sex was now "yes," rather than "no"; opting out of that default required an individualized explanation that could no longer rely on the fact that such things are simply not done. In colleges, the authorities should get out of the way and leave students free to navigate coital relations as they see fit.

Four decades later, the liberationist regime is disintegrating before our eyes. The new order is emerging as a bizarre hybrid of liberationist and traditionalist values. It carefully preserves the prerogative of no-strings-attached sex while cabining it with legalistic caveats that allow females to revert at will to a stance of offended virtue. Consider the sexual consent policy of California's Claremont McKenna College, shared almost verbatim with other schools such as Occidental College in Los Angeles. Paragraphs long, consisting of multiple sections and subsections, and embedded within an even wordier forty-four-page document on harassment and sexual misconduct, Claremont's sexual consent rules resemble nothing so much as a multi-lawyer-drafted contract for the sale and delivery of widgets, complete with definitions, the obligations of "all" (as opposed to "both") parties, and the preconditions for default. "Effective consent consists of an affirmative, conscious decision by each participant to engage in mutually agreed upon (and the conditions of) sexual activity," the authorities declare awkwardly. The policy goes on to elaborate at great length upon each of the "essential elements of Consent"—"Informed and reciprocal," "Freely and actively given," "Mutually understandable," "Not indefinite," "Not unlimited." "All parties must demonstrate a clear and mutual understanding of the nature and scope of the act to which they are consenting"—think: signing a mortgage—"and a willingness to do the same thing, at the same time, in the same way," declare Claremont's sex bureaucrats. Never mind that sex is the realm of the irrational and inarticulate, fraught with ambivalence, fear, longing, and shame. Doing something that you are not certain about does not make it rape, it makes it sex.

The policy's assumption of transparent contractual intention may be laughably out of touch with reality. But its agenda is serious: to rehabilitate the "no" default for premarital sex, despite a backdrop of permissiveness. In fact, the policy goes even further into the realm of Victorian sex roles than simply a presumption of female modesty. Females are now considered so helpless and passive that they should not even be assumed to have the strength or capacity to say "no." "Withdrawal of Consent can be an expressed 'no' or can be based on an outward demonstration that conveys that an individual is hesitant, confused, uncertain, or is no longer a mutual participant," announce Claremont's sexocrats.

Good luck litigating that clause in a campus sex tribunal. The female can allege that the male should have known that she was "confused" because of what she didn't do. The male will respond that he didn't notice any particular nonactivity on her part. Resolving this evidentiary dispute would not be helped by bedside cameras—the logical next step in campus rape hysteria. Pressure sensors would be needed as well to detect asymmetries in touch.

With or without cameras, adjudicating college sex in the neo-Victorian era requires a degree of prurience that should be repugnant to any self-respecting university. A campus sex investigator named Djuna Perkins described the enterprise to National Public Radio in 2014: "It will sometimes boil down to details like who turned who around, or [whether] she lifted up her body so [another student] could pull down her pants. There have been plenty of cases that I've done when the accused student says, 'What do you mean? [The accuser] was moaning with pleasure. He was raising his body, clutching my back, exhibiting all signs that sounded like this was a pleasurable event.'"[1]

Rather than shrinking from this Peeping Tom role, college administrators are enthusiastically drafting new sex rules that require even more minute analysis of drunken couplings. Harvard, also assuming that delicate coeds cannot summon the will to say "no," now allows females unfettered discretion after the fact to allege that they were sexually assaulted by conduct they silently regarded as "undesirable."

We have come very far from the mud-drenched orgies of Woodstock. Feminists in the neo-Victorian era are demanding that written material that allegedly evokes nonconsensual sex be prefaced by warnings regarding its threatening content, so that female readers can avoid fits of vapors and fainting—the phenomenon now famously known as "trigger warnings." Early in 2014, Wellesley College students petitioned for the removal of a statue of a sleepwalking, underwear-clad middle-aged man, whose installation on college grounds immediately caused "apprehension, fear, and triggering thoughts regarding sexual assault" among many students, according to the petition.[2] Ohio State University underwent a four-year investigation by the US Department of Education for its crude marching-band culture, even though the only assault that female band members may have experienced was on their sensibilities.[3] Many girls, we belatedly rediscover, don't enjoy bawdy sexual humor as much as boys do.

It turns out that when you decouple the sex drive from restraint and prudence, it takes armies of elected officials, bureaucrats, and consultants to protect females from "undesirable" behavior. In 2014, Virginia's then-governor Terry McAuliffe set up a task force on campus sexual violence comprising up to thirty top state officials and representatives from law enforcement and higher education. Connecticut has required colleges to form sexual-assault response teams, on the model, presumably, of active-shooter response teams. California has enacted a law mandating that colleges receiving state funds require students to be in "affirmative, conscious and voluntary agreement" in order to engage in sexual activity, agreement that is "ongoing throughout a sexual activity and that can be revoked at any time." Gloria Steinem and a gender studies professor from New York's Stony Brook University explained in a 2014 *New York Times* op-ed: The California law "redefines that gray area" between "yes" and "no." "Silence is not consent; it is the absence of consent. Only an explicit 'yes' can be considered consent."[4] In other words, California's statute, like many existing campus policies, moved the sexual default for female students back to "no." The next year, 2015, New York state required all private colleges in the state to adopt a uniform definition of affirmative consent.

A case from Occidental College illustrates the neo-Victorian ethos perfectly. The freshman complainant, Jane Doe (a pseudonym), began her weekend drinking binge on Friday, September 6, 2013. She attended a dance party in the dorm room of John Doe, another freshman whom she had just met, and woke up the next morning with a hangover. She soon began "pregaming" again—that is, drinking before an event at which one expects to drink further. Jane drank before a daytime soccer game and continued during the evening, repeatedly swigging from a bottle of orange juice and vodka that she had prepared. Around midnight, she went to a second party in John Doe's dorm room, still drinking vodka. John, too, had been drinking all day. Jane removed her shirt while dancing with John and engaged in heavy petting on his bed, sitting on top of him and grinding her hips. Jane's friends tried to shepherd her home, but before she left John's room, she gave him her cell phone number so that they could coordinate their planned sexual tryst.

When she arrived at her own dorm room, John texted her: "The second that you're away from them, come back." Jane responded: "Okay do you have a condom." John replied: "Yes." Jane texted back: "Good give me two minutes." John texted: "Knock when you're here."[5]

Before leaving her dorm room, Jane texted a friend from back home: "I'mgoingtohave sex now." Jane walked down to John's room at approximately 1 AM, knocked on his door, went in, took off her earrings, got undressed, performed oral sex, and had sexual intercourse with him. When an acquaintance knocked on John's door to check up on her, Jane three times called out: "Yeah, I'm fine."[6] Shortly before 2 AM, Jane dressed herself and returned to her room. On her way there, she texted her friends vapid messages, complete with smiley faces, none of which mentioned assault. She then walked to a different dorm, where she sat on the lap of another male student whom she had met the night before, talking and joking. The next day, she texted John, asking if she had left her earrings and belt in his room and asked to come by to pick them up.

Now someone who asks a male if he has a condom, who conspires with him to have sex, who announces to a friend that she intends to have sex, who voluntarily goes to his dorm room in order to have sex, who has sex through no coercion or force on the male's part, is as voluntary and responsible an agent in that sex act as the male. Any male on the receiving end of such behavior, who is asked if he has a condom before a planned sex act, is going to assume rightly that he is facing a willing and consenting partner. And yet Occidental, put under investigation by the Obama administration for ignoring sexual violence (a baseless charge), found John guilty of assault and expelled him. Though Jane's actions and statements seemed to indicate that she consented to sexual intercourse, John should have known that she was too incapacitated to consent, the adjudicators concluded.

This finding once again makes the male the sole guardian of female safety. John and Jane were both drunk. They both agreed to have sex. Neither of them remembered the actual moment of intercourse afterward (though Jane remembers the oral sex). Yet John is viewed as the primary mover in that sex act, and the only member of the pair obligated to evaluate the mental capacities of his partner. Jane, however, could be deemed equally guilty of having sex with a partner who was too drunk to consent. In the neo-Victorian worldview, however, females have no responsibility for their own behavior, while the male is responsible not only for himself but for his partner as well. (John Doe has sued Occidental College for the expulsion; no judgment has been reached.)

Pace the feminists, the Occidental case is emblematic not of "rape culture" but of the emotional fallout from sexual liberation. Jane was a virgin before her tryst with John. She only decided to report her intercourse to the Occidental authorities, after prompting from her college advisers, when she realized how much it had affected her psychologically. She saw that John "wasn't fazed by what happened at all" and appeared to attend classes without difficulty, whereas she found herself distracted and unable to concentrate. She should not have to risk the discomfort of seeing him, she concluded, and thus, Occidental should expel him.

Jane's reactions are understandable, if hardly grounds for expulsion. While there are thankfully few actual rape victims on college campuses, there are thousands of girls feeling taken advantage of by partners who walk away from casual sex with no apparent sense of thwarted attachment. What campus feminists call "post-traumatic stress disorder" and fear of getting "raped" again is often rather a female's quite natural embarrassment at reencountering a sex partner whom she barely knew and with whom she has no continuing relationship. Girls losing their virginity are at particular risk of being emotionally ambushed by drunken hookup couplings. Though sexual liberation has stripped virginity and its loss of any formally recognized significance, the lived experience can be more momentous than girls are prepared for.

The conservative response to campus rape hysteria has been only partially helpful. The main line of attack has been to say: "Yes, campus rape is a grave problem. But because rape is so serious an offense, all such charges should be tried in criminal court, not in flimsy college tribunals." As both a legal and a strategic move, this position is unimpeachable. The due-process deficiencies of campus rape tribunals have been glaring. As of early 2018, seventy-nine judges had issued rulings against schools' rape trial procedures. Criticism of college tribunals for denying due process to the accused was "valid," said Supreme Court Justice Ruth Bader Ginsburg in a February 2018 interview.[7] Nor would campus definitions of illegal sexual behavior, such as whether it was "undesirable" from the female's point of view, pass muster in a court of law.

Requiring that every campus rape allegation be sent to the criminal-justice system would end the campus rape movement overnight. Very few alleged campus rape cases are brought to the police because the accuser and her counselors know that most cases wouldn't have a chance in court. Occidental College professor Caroline Heldman, a leader in the campus rape movement, asserted during a debate that campus rape cases should not be taken to criminal trial because juries are steeped in rape culture—i.e., they cannot be trusted to convict. (I was her debate opponent.) Remarkably, Heldman also argued that the preponderance-of-evidence standard for rape findings was too *high*. Apparently requiring that the fact-finder have a negligible 50.5-percent certainty that a rape occurred does not guarantee enough convictions. So conservatives are right to call the rape hysterics' bluff by arguing: If you believe that this is rape, treat it as such by seeking a criminal conviction.

But conservatives are making two errors. The first is to agree that campus rape is a significant problem, en route to calling for its adjudication in court. If campus rape were the epidemic that the activists allege, there would be no need for campus or governmental rape tribunals because colleges would have emptied of females years ago.

Conservatives' second error is a tone of occasional exasperation at the burgeoning sex regulations for taking the fun out of college sex. In fact, this is the only upside to the whole sordid situation.

To be sure, the new campus sex regime puts boys in danger of trumped-up assault charges heard before kangaroo courts. But the solution is not more complex procedural protections cobbled over a sordid culture; the solution is to reject that culture entirely. Just as girls can avoid the risk of what the feminists call "rape" by not getting drunk and getting into bed with a guy whom they barely know, boys, too, can radically reduce the risk of a rape accusation by themselves not getting drunk and having sex with a girl whom they barely know. Mothers worried that their college-bound sons will be hauled before a biased campus sex tribunal by a vindictive female should tell them: "Wait. Find a girlfriend and smother her with affection and respect. Write her love letters in the middle of the night. Escort her home after a date and then go home yourself." If one-sided litigation risk results in boys taking a vow of restraint until graduation, there is simply no loss whatsoever to society and only gain to individual character. Such efforts at self-control were made before, and can be made again.

Unlike the overregulation of natural gas production, say, which results in less of a valuable commodity, there is no cost to an overregulation-induced decrease in campus sex. Society has no interest in preserving the collegiate bacchanal. Should college fornication become a rare event preceded by contract signing and notarization, maybe students would actually do some studying instead. At present, many students drink through the entire weekend without worrying about any academic repercussions. Maybe colleges should focus on the transmission of real knowledge instead of wasting faculty and administrator time drafting cringingly lurid consensual and nonconsensual sex scenarios, as Yale did in 2013. Colleges might send the message that they expect students to learn the periodic table, read the Greek tragedies, and understand the evolution of constitutional government. Parents might get some value out of their extortionate tuition payments, and boys might catch up to girls' graduation rates.

There are no sympathetic victims in the campus sex wars. While few boys are guilty of what most people understand as rape, many are guilty of acting as boorishly as they can get away with. Sexual liberation and radical feminism unleashed the current mess by misunderstanding male and female nature. Feminists may now be unwittingly accomplishing what they would never allow conservatives to do: restoring sexual decorum.

8

THE FAINTING COUCH AT COLUMBIA

In February 2015, Columbia University—currently tied for fifth most-distinguished US academic institution in the *U.S. News & World Report* rankings—announced that all its students, undergraduate and graduate alike, would have to enroll in a "Sexual Respect and Community Citizenship Initiative." This "new, required programming," the Columbia bureaucracy explained, was designed to explore "the link between sexual respect and membership in the Columbia community."[1]

Columbia's students were given a menu of "participation options." They could watch a minimum of two preselected videos about "rape culture" and gender identity and write a "reflection" about what they had learned. They could attend film screenings about sexual assault and masculinity and engage in a monitored discussion afterward. They could create a "work of art" about the "relationship between sexual respect and University community membership." Or, if they "identif[ied] as survivors, co-survivors, allies, or individuals who have experienced forms of secondary trauma," they could attend workshops on "Finding Keys to Resiliency."

Options in the "Finding Keys to Resiliency" module included a "mindfulness workshop" on "cultivating nonjudgmental awareness and being more present for their experience." If attending the book launch for *SLUT: A Play and Guidebook for Combating Sexism* got you too agitated about female oppression, you could unwind at a "knitting circle."

To help students organize their required "reflections" on the vid-eos, Columbia provided a set of questions suggestive of a New Age encounter session: "Kalin (a speaker in a video) shares his 'why' for passion around prevention education. What is his why? If you have a passion for prevention, 'what is your why?'" Another prompt suggested: "Reflect on the idea of manhood as discussed in this talk. What is the interaction of the constructs of manhood and power dynamics?"

The Columbia administrators were careful to avoid any possible mis-understanding that they themselves had failed to "cultivate nonjudg-mental awareness" when it comes to college sex. One of the films on offer, *The Line: A Personal Exploration About Sexual Assault & Consent*, is "told through a 'sex-positive' lens," according to Columbia's promo-tional materials.

But Columbia's "nonjudgmentalism" extends only so far. There was *no* give-and-take about participation in the Sexual Respect and Com-munity Citizenship Initiative. The materials announced that it was "essential to arrive on time and participate" in the film screenings and discussions; late arrivals would not be admitted. Attendance at all events would be taken and passed on to the authorities. (This is a far stricter standard than Columbia applies to mere academic classes, where attendance policies are at the professor's discretion.) Students who failed to log the requisite sexual-respect hours and complete the requisite sexual-respect assignments could be blocked from register-ing for academic coursework—or from graduating.

The rollout, which hit just as students were taking midterms, was a shambles. The computer portals for registering often didn't work; many students couldn't find participation options that were still open and that fit into their class schedule or that weren't restricted to specific groups such as the "LGBTQ community." Despite the administra-tion's admonitions, some Columbia students decided that studying or researching their dissertation took priority over proctored discussions on "how gender affects relationships." And so they neglected to do their sexual-respect assignments before the deadline ran out.

Columbia soon lowered the boom. In July 2015, it started notify-ing the recalcitrant students that they were no longer in "good administrative standing." Such a declaration is no small matter. Columbia treats a loss of administrative standing as seriously as an academic default; failure to repair one's administrative standing can lead to dismissal. By July, however, the options remaining to laggard students for demonstrating "sexual respect" had shrunk. No longer could a student view a webinar on "Transgender Sexuality and Trauma" or attend Momma's Hip Hop Kitchen to satisfy the requirement. By then, in order to restore his administrative standing, the non-sexually-respectful student could only watch a recorded TED Talk and write a "reflection" on his experience.

One of those recalcitrant students was a PhD candidate doing serious archival research on a central figure in Western civilization. A number of his liberal graduate-student colleagues were also in trouble for not taking part in the initiative. "Even they felt the requirement was quite infantilizing and they had better things to do with their time, like actual academic work and teaching undergraduates," he said. That Columbia would elevate this "burdensome distraction" to the level of actual academic responsibilities, he noted, is "yet more proof that universities have lost their bearings entirely."[2]

But the initiative signaled something more worrisome than just Columbia's distorted priorities, according to this refusenik. "People like me might be losing the right simply to be silent, to be left alone," he observed. "The initiative implies that agreement with an ideological code of sexual ethics is actually required for attendance at this institution." In keeping with its "sex-positive" focus, the sexual-respect initiative never challenged the regime of drunken hookup sex. Instead, it simply assigned wildly asymmetrical responsibilities and liabilities within that regime, consistent with the current practice of college administrations everywhere.

One of the initiative's videos portrays two females drinking frenetically at a series of dance clubs; a male disengages one of them and escorts her to her dorm room where he has sex with her, allegedly nonconsensually because she is too woozy from the boatloads of booze she consumed to offer proper consent. The moral of the video is that bystanders should intervene if they think that someone is too drunk to agree to sex with a stranger. Fair enough, but several additional interpretations also come to mind. First, that university administrations should perform an "intervention" on the entire booze-fueled hookup scene. Second, that females almost always have control over whether they end up in a mentally compromised state and should therefore be careful to avoid such a condition. This second reading is unthinkable in today's university, however.

If Columbia felt compelled to take on the issue of "sexual respect," it could have done so in a way that actually had intellectual value, had it remembered that its primary mission is to fill the empty noggins of the young with at least passing knowledge of mankind's greatest works. Civilization has grappled for thousands of years with the challenge of ordering the relationship between the sexes and has come up with more sophisticated solutions than forcing males to watch videos on escaping the "man box." Reading Baldassare Castiglione's *Book of the Courtier* and Edmund Spenser's *The Faerie Queene* would offer students an elegant take on sexual respect, albeit one grounded in the now-taboo virtues of chivalry and chastity. If "relevance" is necessary, Mozart's *Don Giovanni* might provide an example of "bystander intervention," as when Don Giovanni's aristocratic peers try to hustle the peasant girl Zerlina away from his clutches.

Mozart and his librettist, Lorenzo Da Ponte, however, were unblinkered about the male sex drive, something about which contemporary feminists can't make up their minds. To recognize the specific hungers of the specifically male libido puts one dangerously close to acknowledging biological differences between the sexes. And it is precisely the force of the male sex drive that makes the norms of courtship and modesty so important for carving out a zone of freedom and civility for females.

Feminists, by contrast, are inclined to reduce the male libido to a political power play that has more to do with keeping females out of the boardroom than getting them into the bedroom. If gender "power dynamics" are really what lead men to aggressively seek sex, then a lecture from a TED "anti-sexism educator" might be relevant. But if, in fact, men pursue sex because they want to have sex, then a different set of strategies is called for.

Naturally, the Columbia initiative embraces the conceit that college campuses are filled with shell-shocked female victims of rape culture who might collapse at any minute from the trauma of college experience. It is for them, explains Columbia, that the "Finding Keys to Resiliency" module was designed. The "Finding Keys to Resiliency" option allows "individuals who identify as survivors" and their "allies" to "incorporate wellness and healing into their day-to-day lives . . . from trauma-focused therapy to healing circles, from dance and movement to yoga and mind/body work." If, however, you are a religiously conservative student who believes that premarital intercourse is immoral (a few such closeted throwbacks still exist), you are out of luck. There is no module for you.

Predictably, the sexual-respect initiative created more trauma for Columbia's wilting coeds, but not always in the expected ways. One "survivor" was forced to wait forty-five minutes outside her "survivors-only" workshop, only to be told that the workshop had been canceled. "Sitting there waiting with no word caused me to panic," she told the *Columbia Daily Spectator*. The university had failed to provide her with a Victorian fainting couch.

The sexual-respect initiative was undoubtedly triggered, to borrow a phrase, by Columbia's most famous self-identified survivor: Emma Sulkowicz, otherwise known as the "mattress girl." Sulkowicz belatedly claimed that she had been raped by a fellow student with whom she had been having intermittent casual sex. When Columbia, after a lengthy investigation, failed to find her alleged rapist guilty and expel him, she started carrying around a dormitory mattress in protest. This yearlong stunt, for which Columbia granted her academic credit, earned Sulkowicz rapturous accolades from the campus-rape industry and inspired scores of student imitators at other campuses. (Sulkowicz carried the mattress to her graduation and has since become a performance artist.)

If anyone needed the qualification of being a "self-identified" survivor, it is Sulkowicz. After her alleged rape, she emailed her alleged rapist, begging to get together again. Two days after the incident, Sulkowicz texted him: "Also I feel like we need to have some real time where we can talk about life and thingz because we still haven't really had a paul-emma chill sesh since summmmmerrrr." A week later, she suggested that they hang out together: "I want to see yoyououoyou." Two months later, she texted: "I love you Paul. Where are you?!?!?!?!"[3]

It took Sulkowicz six months to decide that she had been raped. Columbia was indubitably right not to find her sexual partner guilty, but it lost the public-relations battle anyway over its alleged mistreatment of rape "survivors." Thus, Columbia's burgeoning campus-rape boondoggles, including the "Sexual Violence Response" unit and the "Special Adviser to the President for Sexual Assault Prevention and Response." This special adviser, a self-described decades-long "social-justice advocate," was soon elevated to executive vice president, heading a new Office of Community Life. From there, she designed the sexual-respect initiative.

I asked the Columbia administration how many students had lost their good standing as a result of not participating in the sexual-respect initiative. The chief of staff for the Office of University Life would only respond that "because it was a University requirement, there was a high compliance rate with the program." That may, sadly, be true. Columbia, after all, has power on its side. Even the most obstreperous comments about the mandate on the *Columbia Daily Spectator* student-newspaper website were calling for civil disobedience within the confines of the initiative: "Make sure to record every word spoken. If just one feminist gets out of line: walk out, claim you were traumatized by a trigger and file a grievance. . . . Demand to take your class with men, because women trigger your false rape accusation."

The bitter humor of this "advice" reveals the absurdity of the entire enterprise. Such non-compliance would not mean that sanity and scholarship are holding their own on college campuses. It merely means that force is for now still necessary to snuff out the last vestiges of serious learning.

9

POLICING SEXUAL DESIRE: THE #METOO MOVEMENT'S IMPOSSIBLE PREMISE

In fall 2017, Hollywood mogul Harvey Weinstein was credibly accused of ugly and possibly criminal sexual predation toward a succession of actresses. The media and university feminists greeted the revelation as a long-awaited instantiation of the "rape culture" conceit. Unlike in drunken campus hookups, the workplace power disparities in this case were real and large, and Weinstein's interactions clearly nonconsensual. Soon, leading males in entertainment, the press, and politics were exposed as harassers and forced to apologize, in many cases losing their jobs.

The resulting #MeToo movement, formed to out other workplace predators, inevitably adopted the epistemology of the campus rape movement. "Overly broad definitions of what constitutes sexual misconduct are now being legitimized in the work place," observes Kimberly C. Lau, partner of Warshaw Burstein LLP. While the #MeToo incidents covered a broad continuum of behavior—from alleged rape, at one extreme, to an unwanted touch or kiss, at the other—the advocates usually ignored such distinctions: All men are guilty and deserve condemnation. Hollywood star Matt Damon discovered how reactionary the new dispensation had become when he faced outrage from feminist actresses and advocates for making the most banal of observations: "There's a difference between, you know, patting someone on the butt and rape or child molestation, right? Both of those behaviors need to be confronted and eradicated without question, but they shouldn't be conflated, right?"[1]

The #MeToo movement will accelerate academic feminism's conquest of mainstream discourse. The *New York Times*'s "gender editor," a position created in fall 2017, penned an op-ed later that year that mimics the confusions around sex that we've seen on campus.

Gender editor Jessica Bennett had unforced sex with a thirty-year-old acquaintance when she was nineteen because "saying 'yes' [was] easier than saying 'no,'" as the op-ed's title put it. She allowed the encounter to proceed out of "some combination of fear (that I wasn't as mature as he thought), shame (that I had let it get this far), and guilt (would I hurt his feelings?)." Naturally, Bennett attributes her passivity and embarrassment at that moment to "dangerously outdated gender norms." It is the patriarchy, she claims, that makes "even seemingly straightforward ideas about sex—such as, you know, whether we want to engage in it or not—feel utterly complex."[2]

Actually, it is not the patriarchy that makes sexual decisions "utterly complex"; it is sex itself, inherently subject to "fear," "shame," and "guilt." Sexual seduction is carried on through ambiguity and indirection; exposing that ambiguity to light, naming what may or may not be going on, is uncomfortable and risks denial and rejection. "[D]angerously outdated gender norms" are not what make it difficult to say no to sexual advances; *contemporary* gender norms have confused these already fraught situations.

Traditional mores, as this book has argued, set the default for premarital sex at "no." This norm recognized the different sexual priorities of males and females and the difficulties of bargaining with the male libido. Sexual liberation changed that default for premarital sex to "yes." A "no" now has to be extricated *in media res*. A contributor to the website Total Sorority Move described an instance of drunken college coitus several years ago that, like Bennett's op-ed, limns the resulting state of affairs. Contributor Veronica Ruckh agreed to sex simply because stopping it would have involved providing reasons. "We have sex with guys, because sometimes it's just easier to do it than to have the argument about not doing it," observed Ruckh. She quotes other females who have been defeated by the "yes" default for sex: "To be honest, it would have been awkward to say no, so I just did it." "Sometimes you have to have lunch with girls you don't want to have lunch with, and sometimes you have to have sex with boys you don't want to have sex with."

This situation would have been unthinkable sixty years ago. Then, there was no cultural compulsion to have "sex with boys you don't want to have sex with." The assumption was that of course you would not, and that assumption gave females power to control the outcome. Now, however, females have to go mano a mano with male lust in a realm of potential embarrassment and uncertainty. The male sex drive will win in many of those cases.

Feminists cannot acknowledge the divide between men and women when it comes to sex and sensibility. Doing so would violate what Harvard psychologist Steven Pinker calls the blank slate doctrine, a foundation stone of modern liberalism. One of that doctrine's core tenets is that differences between men and women have nothing to do with biology but are socially constructed. Ignoring biology, feminists recast difficult sexual interactions in terms of power and politics. Sexual harassment, real or imagined, is portrayed as an effort to subordinate females. Actually, sexual harassment is usually just about sex, even if differential power is used to obtain it.

There is nothing inconsistent or hypocritical about liberal male icons championing feminist issues like abortion or equal pay while also putting heavy-handed or offensive moves on females. Charlie Rose, Matt Lauer, and Harvey Weinstein (all #MeToo casualties) would all undoubtedly be thrilled to have a female president, since they would thereby be routing Red State misogyny. For now, however, they want access to private parts. (In another installment of the *Times*'s #MeToo series, male models claimed to have been sexually harassed by fashion photographers Bruce Weber and Mario Testino. "'I felt helpless,'" read the front-page headline.[3] According to the feminist interpretation of sexual harassment, these males are themselves victims of the patriarchy, the target of a political power play to subordinate men. The simpler explanation is: They were targets, if their claims are correct, of overreaching sexual desire, like most female victims.)

Treating the untamed male libido as a political problem calls forth a legal remedy, manifested by the highly technical "affirmative consent" rules for sex on college campuses. But law is less effective than informal norms in regulating behavior, especially in a post-liberation environment that has stripped females of the protections of modesty and restraint. Traditional culture tried to civilize the male libido by celebrating the virtues of gentlemanliness and respect. Under a traditional concept of propriety, masturbating in front of a female acquaintance (as the comedian Louis C.K. was wont to do) would have been unthinkable, a violation of the lady's modesty and the gentleman's dignity. Now, however, with "ladies" and "gentlemen" banished from our social universe, and even from language, such behavior is apparently no longer unthinkable. Most men would not feel themselves harassed if a female acquaintance masturbated in front of them; they might even consider themselves to be lucky dogs. That women recoil from this same behavior reveals a fundamental divide between male and female experiences of the body and sex.

Feminists' tic of blaming males for every female behavior that contradicts their ideal of gender equality undercuts that very claim of equality. Naturally, Jessica Bennett trots out the feminist trope that it is the patriarchy that makes females want to "attract male desire." Women are apparently the helpless dupes of the fashion and cosmetics industries, and have been brainwashed into spending hundreds of billions of dollars a year in order to be noticed by men. That brainwashing extends to highly paid movie stars as well. The *Times*'s gender team produced an online series called "The New Red Carpet" to combat gender stereotyping and harassment in Hollywood. Before the 2018 Golden Globe Awards, team member Bonnie Wertheim informed readers that stars' dresses during such awards ceremonies "are not a reflection of their own style." Rather, the "red carpet industrial complex" forces those gowns on otherwise self-effacing and reclusive actresses in order to reinforce the "widely held perception that women's bodies are available for public consumption."[4] (The "red carpet industrial complex" exerted its dastardly power to the bitter end. Though the female stars at the Golden Globes wore black outfits as a #MeToo protest, those outfits just happened to include bare shoulders, plunging necklines, slit skirts, and stiletto heels.)

But if women are so vulnerable to advertising and manipulation, why should we be bootstrapping them into positions of economic and political authority? In fact, the fashion and cosmetics industries respond to consumer demand; it is women who, irrespective of the alleged patriarchy, try to attract male desire. And they are not averse to exploiting their sex appeal in order to get ahead. An internationally famous opera conductor stopped visiting the dressing rooms of female soloists unaccompanied after two singers made passes, but women in the orchestra and other singers continue to throw themselves at him, according to an assistant. Many of Arturo Toscanini's affairs were instigated by the singers in question, including Geraldine Farrar and Lotte Lehmann; career advancement may not have been an unhoped-for consequence of those liaisons. And regarding Hollywood, today and historically, is it so unimaginable that actresses have used sex as currency to gain access to roles, when an entire body of literature documents the phenomenon?

If the #MeToo movement only eradicates exploitative sexual demands in the workplace, it will have been a force for good. Its likely results, however, will be to unleash a new wave of gender quotas throughout the economy and to mystify further the actual differences between males and females. *Pace* the feminists, Western culture is in fact the least patriarchal society in human history; rather than being forced to veil, females can parade themselves in as scantily clad a manner as they choose; pop culture stars flaunt their promiscuity. There is not a single mainstream institution that is not trying to hire and promote as many females as possible. And yet females are apparently still so beaten down by sexism that the *Times*'s gender editor asks rhetorically if females should even be deemed able to consent to sex, since "cultural expectations" make it awkward to say no. How long will it be before feminists demand the return of chaperones?

. . .

Hollywood and the media are already showing the #MeToo quota effect. It's no coincidence that the *Today* show now has two female anchors. The Academy of Motion Picture Arts and Sciences has pledged to double its female and minority members by 2020. Actress Natalie Portman's sneer in presenting the best director prize at the 2018 Golden Globe movie awards—"And here are the all-male nominees"—will become the standard response to any perceived lack of "diversity" in entertainment. The *Wall Street Journal*'s pop music critic, Jim Fusilli, for example, groused that females were underrepresented among Grammy award nominees. "There is no Grammy category comprised entirely of women," he complained. "No groups led by women are among the nominees in the Best Contemporary Instrumental, Best Jazz Instrumental, Best Large Jazz Ensemble and Best Contemporary Christian Music album categories."[5] How many female-headed groups exist in those categories and how good are they? That question is sexist. Six female music industry executives then accused the Recording Academy's board of trustees and leadership of suffering from "inclusion issues across all demographics." In response, management has penitently promised to overcome the "unconscious biases that impede female advancement" in the music industry.[6] The National Hispanic Media Coalition protested the 2018 Academy Awards lunch because of the paucity of Hispanic Oscar nominations. Even before the Hispanic protest, Hollywood execs were experiencing quota fatigue, given the pressures from feminist, LGBTQ, and disability activists to hire by identity category.

The prospect of left-wing entertainment moguls having to sacrifice their box-office judgment to identity politics is an unalloyed pleasure and of little consequence to society at large. But bean counting won't be limited to Hollywood. Corporate diversity trainers already sense a windfall from #MeToo. Requests from organizations wanting to "explore further the intersection of power with diversity dimensions and inclusion" have recently increased, according to a "client success" manager at a major diversity-consulting firm. A rival Silicon Valley–based consultancy, Paradigm, sent around an email celebrating Oprah Winfrey's #MeToo speech at the 2018 Golden Globes and reminding potential clients of "how much work needs to be done" regarding "inclusion." "I absolutely think the broader cultural conversation is motivating organizations to take a more serious look at their cultures," says Paradigm's leader, Joelle Emerson.[7] Corporate boardrooms, executive suites, and management structures will be scoured for gender and race imbalances. The advocacy group 50/50 by 2020, which argues for equal male and female representation in business, has recently received several new commitments from organizations pledging to achieve gender parity by the year 2020.

The art world will be hard hit. After harassment allegations surfaced against a publisher of the contemporary-art magazine *Artforum,* the *Los Angeles Times* published a gender tally of art museum directorships. Females hold 48 percent of them—not a promising start for a diversity crusader. There is a silver lining, however: Only three women run museums with annual budgets of more than $15 million, and they're paid less than their male counterparts. It doesn't matter if director salaries are commensurate with experience and credentials; sexism is assumed, and impossible to rebut.

Two months before the explosion of #MeToo, New York mayor Bill de Blasio anticipated the coming pressures on museum management. The city's culture funding would henceforth be contingent on the diversity of an arts organization's employees and board members, he announced. *The New York Times* helpfully pointed out that the Metropolitan Museum of Art, Carnegie Hall, and the American Museum of Natural History are led "largely by white male executives and power brokers from Wall Street, real estate and other industries." Have those "white male executives" preserved the cultural patrimony bestowed by visionary collectors of the past? Did those "white male executives" generously donate millions of dollars to the institutions they serve? Who cares? *The Times* put a picture of conductor Andris Nelsons—a white man—performing at Carnegie Hall on the front page as a damning illustration of the problem.

What hangs on the walls of art museums and galleries is an equally inviting bean-counting target. In a sample of nearly seventy institutions analyzed by the *Art Newspaper,* females had solo shows only 27 percent of the time from 2007 to 2013. Female artists have graced the cover of *Artforum* only 18 percent of the time since the magazine's inception. That is about to change. "The art world is misogynist," *Artforum*'s new editor-in-chief David Velasco told the *Los Angeles Times.* "Art history is misogynist. Also, racist, classist, transphobic, able-ist, homophobic. I will not accept this. . . . Intersectional feminism is an ethics near and dear to so many on our staff."[8] The history of art that Velasco so derides has produced crushing beauty and profound insight into human nature. That is irrelevant to the coming crusade.

Individual artists will now be subjected to #MeToo litmus tests. Phony sexual-harassment charges against contemporary painter Chuck Close led the National Gallery of Art in Washington to postpone indefinitely an upcoming exhibition. Museums will try to inoculate themselves against such purges by bulking up in advance on "diversity" acquisitions. They'll need to expand the definition of who belongs in a museum by bringing in female artists and people of color, Tom Eccles, the executive director of the Center for Curatorial Studies at Bard College, told *The New York Times.*[9]

Orchestra conductors will be evaluated based on their gender and race, especially after harassment allegations surfaced against Metropolitan Opera conductor James Levine (those allegations involved gay sex but will be leveraged for feminist purposes) and against Royal Philharmonic Orchestra conductor Charles Dutoit. Orchestra boards will pay penance for their own inadequate diversity by a mad rush on female conductors, whose numbers are minuscule. It was already difficult two years ago to land a US conducting position for a universally esteemed white male conductor, reports his agent. Now it would be nearly impossible, the agent believes, adding wistfully: "If I had a trans conductor, I would be rich."[10]

New Yorker music critic Alex Ross triggered outrage against the Chicago Symphony Orchestra and the Philadelphia Orchestra when he tweeted in February 2018 that they had programmed no female composers in their upcoming season. It is ludicrous to suggest that these institutions are discriminating against female composers. That same month, CSO conductor Riccardo Muti brought Jennifer Higdon's *Low Brass Concerto* to Carnegie Hall, a piece commissioned by the Chicago, Philadelphia, and Baltimore orchestras. But Ross and his followers demand affirmative programming quotas. The fact is that over most of music history, the greatest composers have been male. At a time of diminishing classical music audiences, it is reckless to wield identity politics against our most important and precious musical institutions.

The economics field has also been hit with #MeToo diversity pressures. A panel at the annual American Economic Association meeting in January 2018 charged that gender discrimination was pervasive in economics, an argument that fit into the "larger national examination of bias and abuse toward women in the work force," *The New York Times* reminded readers. If females are underrepresented on economics faculties, it is because of such insurmountable barriers as the percentage of male economists cited in leading college textbooks: 90 percent. Were there comparable female economists who could have been cited for the relevant proposition instead? Unlikely, but in any case, we don't need to know. Is it possible to pursue intellectual inquiry out of love, rather than because you're following someone of your own gender or race? Apparently not. *The Times* bemoaned the "shrinking pipeline of women in economics departments": while females made up 33 percent of first-year PhD students in 2016, only 13 percent of full-tenured professors were females in 2016. But it takes decades for graduating cohorts to work their way through the system; when those tenured economics professors were students, their cohort was much less than 33 percent female.

Economist Deirdre McCloskey rejects the idea that competitively qualified females are being excluded: "There is nothing like discrimination on the part of hiring committees," she says.[11] Self-selection may come into play, however, she adds, since economics is a "macho field" that pays relatively little attention to the impact of females' family roles on the timing of a scholarly career. Modern-day economics has grown

increasingly math-based. The percentage of males who score in the up-
per range of the math SATs (scoring 700 or more on an 800-point
scale) is nearly twice as high as the percentage of female high-scorers.
Males outperform females on the macroeconomics and microeconom-
ics AP exams. Males are also more competitive than females, economist Johanna Mollerstrom and others have shown. Such facts have a
clear bearing on the composition of a "macho," quantitative field like
economics, but they are not allowed to be mentioned in any discussion of "diversity."

Stanford's business school is claiming surprise at a recent whistle-
blower study showing that it favors females over males in awarding financial aid. The chance that such a practice was inadvertent is zero.
But such female preferences in business and economics programs will
only accelerate to combat an alleged culture of bias. Dow Jones, publisher of *The Wall Street Journal,* has instituted a year-long program in
leadership development, IGNITE, to create a "truly diverse and inclusive senior leadership team." Participants will receive executive spon-
sorship, coaching, and personality assessments, something that many
aspiring top managers might value. Participation is limited to women,
however, as part of Dow Jones's campaign to reach 40 percent female
executive leadership quickly. Such efforts are undoubtedly underway at
many major news outfits and have only redoubled in urgency.

Silicon Valley is a #MeToo diversity bonanza waiting to happen. It's
not for nothing that the Mountain View headquarters of Google is
referred to as the "Google campus"; the culture of the Silicon Valley
behemoth is an echo chamber of shrill academic victimology. Managers and employees reflexively label dissenters from left-wing orthodoxy misogynists and racists, as revealed in the lawsuit filed in
January 2018 against Google by James Damore. (See chapter 1.)
"Punching Nazis" is celebrated on Google chat boards.[12] It is assumed
that the lack of proportional representation of female, black, and Hispanic engineers at the company is due to implicit bias on the part of
every other type of engineer.

In February 2018, a panel at the American Association for the

Advancement of Science's annual meeting addressed the "cultural and institutional practices" that suppress female and underrepresented minority "voices" in STEM fields (science, technology, engineering, and mathematics). But as we'll see, those "voices" have already been the target of hundreds of millions of dollars from government, foundations, businesses, and schools pouring into gender- and race-exclusive math and science programs. The results of such efforts, such as the Latinas in Tech initiative, run by the National Center for Women & Information Technology, or the overhyped Girls Who Code program, have been modest.

It is curious that the #MeToo movement is concerned only with gender representation in particular occupational categories. For instance, most HVAC and refrigeration installers and mechanics are men, yet there is little outcry about getting more girls into vocational training for these jobs. Similarly, virtually all workers in the carting, moving, trucking, and mining industries are males, but female underrepresentation in these high-injury and high-fatality occupations has not sparked celebrity outrage.

As the #MeToo moment swells the demand for ever more draconian diversity mandates, a finding in a 2017 Pew Research Center poll on workplace equity is worth noting: The perception of bias is directly proportional to the number of years the perceiver has spent in an American university. Females in STEM businesses who have a postgraduate degree are more than three times as likely as STEM females without a college degree to say that their gender has impeded their success. It is doubtful that those highly educated female STEM workers are actually more subject to chauvinism than their less-educated counterparts. Their workplaces are likely composed of other highly educated products of the academy, marinated for years in an environment dominated by feminist thinking. Those are also the workplaces most subject to external pressures to achieve gender parity. All the incentives run in the opposite direction: away from chauvinism and toward favoring females over males at every possible opportunity. The persistent claim of gender bias is ideological, not empirical. But after

#MeToo extends the reach of academic feminism, it will have an even more disruptive effect.

FROM 1970S HIGH THEORY TO TRANSGENDER BATHROOMS ON CAMPUS

Academic theory leapt again from the university to the real world with the Obama administration's 2016 ruling that public schools must allow boys, bearing their full complement of male genitals, to use girls' bathrooms and locker rooms if they declare themselves female.

For two decades, a growing constellation of gender studies, queer studies, and women's studies departments had been beavering away at propositions that would have struck many people outside academia as surprising—such as that biological sex and "gender" are mere ideological constructs imposed by a Eurocentric, heteronormative power structure. Even though skeptical journalists have regularly dived into the murky swamp of academic theory and returned bearing nuggets of impenetrable jargon and even stranger ideas, the public and most politicians have shrugged off such academic abominations, if they have taken note at all. (Senator Marco Rubio's deplorable jab at "philosophy majors" during his 2016 presidential run demonstrated how clueless your typical politician is about the real problems in academia.)

But a pipeline now channels left-wing academic theorizing into the highest reaches of government and the media. The products of the narcissistic academy graduate and bring their high-theory indoctrination with them into the federal and state bureaucracies and into newsrooms. Even the judiciary is affected. The opinion of the federal district court striking down California's Proposition 8 (declaring that marriage was an institution uniting men and women), for example, was steeped in the women's studies notion that marriage originated as a way to impose a subordinate "gender" role on females.

The most notable aspect of this latest public eruption of academic theory is how quickly the new academically driven moral consensus was formed. The current wave of nonacademic transgender activism began in the spring of 2015, when *The New York Times* ran a full-page editorial declaring the oppression of the transgendered one of our most pressing civil rights struggles. *The Times* then followed up with a series of news stories documenting the plight of the "trans community."[13] Now, a few years later, any parent with qualms about having his twelve-year-old daughter share a locker room with a fourteen-year-old boy is branded as the equivalent of someone advocating a return to whites-only water fountains. An issue that didn't even exist a short time ago is now completely settled in the minds of the cultural elite; anyone who opposes the new regime is simply an atavistic, benighted bigot. (In February 2017, Trump's Education and Justice Departments rescinded the Obama transgender bathroom rule on the ground that it went beyond the scope of Title IX and had not complied with administrative rule-making procedure.)

How short are the memories of the politically righteous! In the 1970s, Judge Ruth Bader Ginsburg pooh-poohed as sheer demagoguery the idea that the Equal Rights Amendment would require co-ed bathrooms, her implicit assumption being that such an arrangement would, of course, be preposterous. In 1991, the Michigan Women's Festival expelled a transsexual woman on the ground that she was, in biological fact, a male. The First International Conference on Crossdressing, Sex, and Gender at California State University at Northridge in 1995 maintained separate bathroom facilities for males and females, causing a protest by trans activists. Gay-rights activist and historian Martin Duberman stormed out of a gender-theory presentation. Now those early advocates for gay and women's rights would be lumped into the same category as segregationists.

There are several corollary takeaways to the present day. First, we have learned that the trans movement trumps feminism, just as Europe's reaction to the mass Muslim sexual assaults of New Year's Eve, 2015, revealed that multiculturalism trumps feminism. Given the constant caterwauling about "rape culture" by campus feminists, one would have thought that feminists would have opposed allowing males' use of facilities frequented by unclothed or otherwise vulnerable females. But apparently, the claim that college campuses are awash in serial "rapists" waxes and wanes in salience, depending on context. It now becomes merely another sign of redneck bigotry to suggest that a heterosexual male (i.e., a rapist in waiting) or a sexual pervert may take advantage of the new trans rules. Wellesley and Smith Colleges have twisted themselves into knots deciding whether the "trans" category trumps the favored status of females. They concluded that being trans cancels the disability of being male and, in fact, elevates the trans "female" to the highest rank on the victim totem pole.

Second, we have learned that all academic high theory bears watching. The conceptual roots of gender theory lie in 1970s-era deconstruction and poststructuralism, with their pretense to having obliterated the traditional categories of Western epistemology and metaphysics. From Jacques Derrida's purported "deconstruction" of the privileging of the spoken word over the written sign, and of presence over absence, it turned out to be not so big a step to the alleged dismantling of the biological difference between male and female.

Third, we notice that *all* colleges matter when it comes to the generation of corrosive high theory—not just the Ivy League. The University of Iowa, for example, jump-started the field of queer studies in 1994 with a conference on queerness.

Finally, we see that narcissistic students are now coequal drivers with their professors when it comes to rapidly evolving victim theory. By one count, there are now 117 categories of gender identity, many of those developed by students struggling to find some last way to be transgressive in an environment where their every self-involved claim of victimhood is met with tender attention and apologies from the campus diversity bureaucracy. How those 117 categories will play out for public policy remains to be seen.

The ultimate agenda here, however, is to destroy any last shred of female modesty that might stand in the way of the total normalization of casual promiscuity, in obedience to the sexual-liberation movement of the 1960s. Many girls are embarrassed to be seen naked by other *girls*. Now, however, they are being told to swallow their inhibitions if a boy is in their bathroom or locker room. This can be achieved only by adopting a stance of utter indifference to the powerful, primal taboos around nakedness and sex—in other words, to adopt the sad sexual crudeness of the stars of *Sex and the City* or of Lena Dunham. And according to progressive elites, any parent or school official who disagrees is standing in the way of moral progress. One shrinks to contemplate what the academy is cooking up next.

■ ■ ■

PART III
THE
BUREAUCRACY

10

MULTICULTI U.

In 2012, as the University of California reeled from one piece of bad budget news to another—California was still recovering from the 2008 financial crisis—a veteran political columnist sounded an alarm. Cuts in state funding were jeopardizing the university's mission of preserving the "cultural legacy essential to any great society," Peter Schrag warned in *The Sacramento Bee*:

> Would we know who we are without knowing our common history and culture, without knowing Madison and Jefferson and Melville and Dickinson and Hawthorne; without Shakespeare, Milton and Chaucer; without Dante and Cervantes; without Charlotte Brontë and Jane Austen; without Goethe and Molière; without Confucius, Buddha, Gandhi and Martin Luther King, Jr.; without Mozart, Rembrandt and Michelangelo; without the Old Testament; without the Gospels; without Plato and Aristotle, without Homer and Sophocles and Euripides, without Tolstoy and Dostoyevsky; without Gabriel García Márquez and Toni Morrison?

Schrag's appeal to the value of humanistic study was unimpeachable. It just happened to be laughably ignorant about the condition of such study at the University of California. Stingy state taxpayers aren't endangering the transmission of great literature, philosophy, and art; the university itself is. No UC administrator would dare to invoke

Schrag's list of mostly white, mostly male thinkers as an essential element of a UC education; no UC campus has sought to ensure that its undergraduates get any exposure to even one of Schrag's seminal thinkers (with the possible exception of Toni Morrison), much less to America's founding ideas or history (see chapter 13).

Schrag isn't the only Californian ignorant about UC's priorities. The public is told that the university needs more state money—its current budget is $34 billion—to stay competitive in the sciences but not that the greatest threat to scientific excellence comes from the university's obsession with "diversity" hiring. The public knows about tuition increases but not about the unstoppable growth in the university's bureaucracy. Taxpayers may have heard about larger class sizes but not about the sacrosanct status of faculty teaching loads. Before the public decides how much more money to pour into the system, it needs a far better understanding of how UC spends the large sums it already commands. The surrender of this once-great university system to the diversity delusion is a story repeated at schools across America.

The first University of California campus opened in Berkeley in 1873, fulfilling a mandate of California's 1849 constitution that the state establish a public university for the "promotion of literature, the arts and sciences." Expectations for this new endeavor were high; Governor Henry Haight had predicted that the campus would "soon become a great light-house of education and learning on this Coast, and a pride and glory" of the state.

He was right. Over the next 140 years, as nine more campuses were added, the university would prove an engine for economic growth and a source of human progress. UC owns more research patents than any other university system in the country. Its engineers helped achieve California's mid-century dominance in aerospace and electronics; its agronomists aided the state's fecund farms and vineyards. The nuclear technology developed by UC scientists and their students secured America's Cold War preeminence (while provoking one of the country's most cataclysmic student protest movements). UC's physical infrastructure is a precious asset in its own right. Anyone can wander its trellised gardens and groves of native and exotic trees, or browse its library stacks and superb research collections.

But by the early 1960s, UC was already exhibiting many of the problems that afflict it today. The bureaucracy had mushroomed, both at the flagship Berkeley campus and at the Office of the President, the central administrative unit that oversees the entire UC system. Nathan Glazer, who taught sociology at Berkeley at the time, wrote in *Commentary* in 1965: "Everyone—arriving faculty members, arriving deans, visiting authorities—is astonished by the size" of the two administrations. Glazer noted the emergence of a new professional class: full-time college administrators who specialized in student affairs, had never taught, and had little contact with the faculty.

The result of this bureaucratic explosion reminded Glazer of the federal government: "Organization piled upon organization, reaching to a mysterious empyrean height."

At Berkeley, as federal research money flooded into the campus, the faculty were losing interest in undergraduate teaching, observed Clark Kerr, UC's president and a former Berkeley chancellor. (Kerr once famously quipped that a chancellor's job was to provide "parking for the faculty, sex for the students, and athletics for the alumni.")[1] Back in the 1930s, responsibility for introductory freshman courses had been the highest honor that a Berkeley professor could receive, Kerr wrote in his memoirs; thirty years later, the faculty shunted off such obligations whenever possible to teaching assistants, who, by 1964, made up nearly half the Berkeley teaching corps.

Most presciently, Kerr noted that Berkeley had split into two parts: Berkeley One, an important academic institution with a continuous lineage back to the nineteenth century; and Berkeley Two, a recent political upstart centered on the antiwar, antiauthority Free Speech Movement that had occupied Sproul Plaza in 1964. Berkeley Two was as connected to the city's left-wing political class and to its growing colony of "street people" as it was to the traditional academic life of the campus. In fact, the two Berkeleys had few points of overlap.

Today, echoing Kerr, we can say that there are two Universities of California: UC One, a still-serious university system centered on the sciences (though with representatives throughout the disciplines) and UC Two, a profoundly unserious institution dedicated to the all-consuming crusade against phantom racism and sexism. Unlike Berkeley Two in Kerr's Day, UC Two reaches to the topmost echelon of the university, where it poses a real threat to the integrity of its high-achieving counterpart.

It's impossible to overstate the extent to which the diversity ideology has encroached upon UC's collective psyche and mission. No administrator, no regent, no academic dean or chair can open his mouth for long without professing fealty to diversity. It is the one constant in every university endeavor; it impinges on hiring, distorts the curriculum, and sucks up vast amounts of faculty time and taxpayer resources. The university's budget problems over the last decade have not touched it. In September 2012, for instance, in the midst of California's then-budget crisis, as the university system faced the threat of another $250 million in state funding cuts on top of the $1 billion lost since 2007, UC San Diego hired its first vice chancellor for equity, diversity, and inclusion, who would pull in a starting salary of $250,000, plus a re-location allowance of $60,000, a temporary housing allowance of $13,500, and the reimbursement of all moving expenses. (A pricey but appropriately "diverse" female-owned executive search firm had found this latest diversity accretion.) This new diversocrat position would augment UC San Diego's already massive diversity apparatus, which included the Chancellor's Diversity Office; the associate vice chancellor for faculty equity; the assistant vice chancellor for diversity; the faculty equity advisers; the graduate diversity coordinators; the staff diversity liaison; the undergraduate student diversity liaison; the graduate student diversity liaison; the chief diversity officer; the director of development for diversity initiatives; the Office of Academic Diversity and Equal Opportunity; the Committee on Gender Identity and Sexual Orientation Issues; the Committee on the Status of Women; the Campus Council on Climate, Culture, and Inclusion; the Diversity Council; and the directors of the Cross-Cultural Center, the Lesbian Gay Bisexual Transgender Resource Center, and the Women's Center.

The previous year, UCLA named a professional bureaucrat with a master's degree in student-affairs administration as its first assistant dean for "campus climate," tasked with "maintaining the campus as a safe, welcoming, respectful place," in the words of UCLA's assistant vice chancellor and dean of students.[2] The year before that, UC San Francisco appointed its first vice chancellor of diversity and outreach—with a starting salary of $270,000—to create a "diverse and inclusive environment," in the words of UC San Francisco chancellor Susan Desmond-Hellmann.[3] Each of these new posts was wildly redundant with the armies of diversity functionaries already larding UC's bloated bureaucracy. In 2015, in an improved budgeting climate, UCLA appointed Jerry Kang, whom we met in chapter 5, as its first and royally remunerated chancellor for equity, diversity, and inclusion.

UC Two's worldview rests on the belief that certain racial and ethnic groups face ongoing bias, both in America and throughout the university. UCLA encapsulated this conviction in 2010, in a "Principle of Community" (one of eight) approved by the Chancellor's Advisory Group on Diversity (since renamed the UCLA Council on Diversity and Inclusion, in the usual churn of rebranding to which such bodies are subject). Principle Eight reads: "We acknowledge that modern societies carry historical and divisive biases based on race, ethnicity, gender, age, disability, sexual orientation and religion, and we seek to promote awareness and understanding through education and research and to mediate and resolve conflicts that arise from these biases in our communities."[4]

The idea that a salient—if not the most salient—feature of "modern societies" is their "divisive biases" is ludicrously unhistorical. No culture has been more blandly indifferent than modern Western society to the individual and group characteristics that can still lead to death and warfare elsewhere. There is also no place that more actively celebrates the characteristics that still handicap people outside the West than the modern American campus. Yet when UC Two's administrators and professors survey their domains, they see a landscape riven by the discrimination that it is their duty to extirpate.

Thus it was that UC San Diego's electrical and computer engineering department a few years later found itself facing a mandate from campus administrators to hire a fourth female professor. The possibility of a new hire had opened up—a rare opportunity in that budget climate—and after winnowing down hundreds of applicants, the department put forward its top candidates for on-campus interviews. Scandalously, all were male. Word came down from on high that a female applicant who hadn't even been close to making the initial cut must be interviewed. She was duly brought to campus for an interview, but she got mediocre reviews. The powers-that-be then spoke again: Her candidacy must be brought to a departmental vote. In an unprecedented assertion of secrecy, the department chair refused to disclose the vote's outcome and insisted on a second ballot. After that second vote, the authorities finally gave up and dropped her candidacy. Both vote counts remained secret.

An electrical and computer engineering professor explained what was at stake. "We pride ourselves on being the best," he said. "The faculty know that absolute ranking is critical. No one had ever considered this woman a star."[5] You would think that UC's administrators would value this fierce desire for excellence. Thanks to its commitment to hiring only "the best," San Diego's electrical and computer engineering department has made leading contributions to circuit design, digital coding, and information theory.

Maria Herrera Sobek, UC Santa Barbara's associate vice chancellor for diversity, equity, and academic policy and a professor of Chicana and Chicano studies, provided a window into how UC Two thinks about its mission. If a faculty hiring committee selects only white male finalists for an opening, the dean will suggest "bringing in some women to look them over," Sobek said. These female candidates, she noted, "may be borderline, but they are all qualified." And what do you know! "It turns out [the hiring committees] really like the candidates and hire them, even if they may not have looked so good on paper."[6] This process has "energized" the faculty to hire more women, Sobek explained. She added that diversity interventions get "more positive responses" from humanities and social-sciences professors than from scientists.

Leave aside Sobek's amusing suggestion that the faculty just happen to discover that they "really like" the diversity candidate whom the administration has forced on them. More disturbing is the subversion of the usual hiring standard from "most qualified" to "borderline but qualified." UC Two sets the hiring bar low enough to scoop in some female or minority candidates, and then declares that anyone above that bar is qualified enough to trump the most qualified candidate, if that candidate is a white or an Asian male. This is a formula for mediocrity.

Sometimes, UC Two can't manage to lower hiring standards enough to scoop in a "diverse" candidate. In that case, it simply creates a special hiring category outside the normal channels. In September 2012, after the meritocratic revolt in UC San Diego's electrical and computer engineering department, the engineering school announced that it would hire an "excellence" candidate, the school's Orwellian term for faculty who, it claims, will contribute to diversity and who, by some odd coincidence, always happen to be female or an underrepresented minority.

The physics department at UC San Diego advertised an assistant-professor position several years ago with a "specific emphasis on contributions to diversity," such as a candidate's "awareness of inequities faced by underrepresented groups." Social-justice concerns now apparently trump the quest to solve the mystery of dark energy. All five candidates on UC San Diego's short list were females,[7] leading one male candidate with a specialty in extragalactic physics to wonder why the school had even solicited applications from Asian and white men.

Every campus has throngs of diversity enforcers like Sobek. In 2010, as a $637 million cut in state funding closed some facilities temporarily and forced UC faculty and staff to take up to three and a half weeks of unpaid leave, Mark Yudof, at the time the president of the entire university system, announced the formation of a presidential Advisory Council on Campus Climate, Culture, and Inclusion. It would be supported by five working groups of faculty and administrators: the Faculty Diversity Working Group; the Diversity Structure Group; the Safety and Engagement Group; the Lesbian, Gay, Bisexual, and Transgender Group; and the Metrics and Assessment Group.

Needless to say, the new burst of committee activity replicated a long line of presidential diversity initiatives, such as the 2006 President's Task Force on Faculty Diversity and the president's annual Account-ability Sub-Report on Diversity.

These earlier efforts must have failed to eradicate the threats that large subsets of students and faculty face. Yudof promised that his new council and its satellite working groups would address, yet again, the "challenges in enhancing and sustaining a tolerant, inclusive environ-ment on each of the university's 10 campuses . . . so that every single member of the UC community feels welcome, comfortable and safe."[8] Of course, under traditional measures of safety, UC's campuses rate extremely high, but more subtle dangers apparently lurk for women and certain minorities.

In April 2012, one of Yudof's five working groups disgorged its first set of recommendations for creating a "safe" and "healthy" climate for UC's beleaguered minorities, even as the university's regents, who the-oretically govern the school, debated whether to raise tuition yet again to cover the latest budget shortfall. The Faculty Diversity Work-ing Group called for hiring quotas, which it calls "cluster hiring," and more diversity bureaucrats, among nine other measures. (California's pesky constitutional ban on taking race and gender into account in public hiring, which took effect after voters approved Proposition 209 in 1996, has had only a limited influence on UC behavior and rhetoric, as we have seen.)

You would think that an institution ostensibly dedicated to reason would have documented the widespread bias against women and mi-norities before creating such a costly apparatus for fighting that alleged epidemic. I asked Dianne Klein, the press secretary for UC's Office of the President, whether any members of the office were aware of any faculty candidates rejected by hiring committees because of their race or sex. Or perhaps the office knew of highly qualified minority or female faculty candidates simply *overlooked* in a search process because the hiring committee was insufficiently committed to diversity outreach? Klein ducked both questions: "Such personnel matters are confiden-tial and so we can't comment on your question about job candidates."

Did UC Santa Barbara's associate vice chancellor for diversity, equity, and academic policy know of such victims of faculty bias? "It's hard to prove that qualified women haven't been hired," said Sobek. But "people don't feel comfortable working with people who don't look like them and tend to hire people that look like them." Didn't the high proportion of Asian professors in UC's science departments and medical schools suggest that UC's white faculty *were* comfortable working with people who don't look like them? "Oh, Asians are discriminated against, too," replied Sobek. "They face a glass ceiling. People think that maybe Asians are not good enough to run a university." Sobek's own university, UC Santa Barbara, has an Asian chancellor (Henry Yang), but never mind.

In September 2012, even as he warned of financial ruin if voters didn't approve Governor Jerry Brown's $6 billion tax hike in November, Yudof announced yet another diversity boondoggle. The university was embarking on the nation's largest-ever survey of "campus climate," at a cost of $662,000 (enough to cover four years of tuition for more than a dozen undergraduates). The system-wide climate survey was, of course, drearily repetitive. Individual campus "climate councils" had been conducting "climate checks" for years, and an existing UC survey already asked each undergrad if he felt that his racial and ethnic group was "respected on campus."[9] Nevertheless, with the university facing a possible quarter-billion-dollar cut in state funding, Yudof and his legions of diversity councils and work groups felt that now was the moment to act on the 2007 recommendations of the little-remembered "Regents' Study Group on University Diversity (Work Team on Campus Climate)" and of the "Staff Diversity Council."

If UC One were launching a half-million-dollar survey of the incidence of bubonic plague, say, among its students, faculty, and staff, it would have assembled enough instances of infection to justify the survey. It might even have formulated a testable hypothesis regarding the main vectors of infection. But UC Two's campus-climate rhetoric promiscuously invoked the need for "safe spaces" and havens from "risk" without ever identifying either the actual victims of its unsafe climates or their tormentors. These unsavory individuals must be out

there, of course; otherwise, UC's "marginalized and vulnerable populations," as the president's office described them, wouldn't require
such costly interventions. But who were these people, and where did
they hide? Further, the presence of such bigots meant that UC's hiring and admissions policies must be seriously flawed. What did UC
intend to do about them?

UC Two's pressures on the curriculum are almost as constant as the
growth of the diversity bureaucracy. Consider Berkeley's sole curric-
ular requirement. The campus's administration and faculty can think
of only one thing that all its undergraduates need to know in order to
have received a world-class education: how racial and ethnic groups
interact in America. Every undergraduate must take a course that addresses "theoretical or analytical issues relevant to understanding race,
culture, and ethnicity in American society" and that takes "substantial account of groups drawn from at least three of the following: African Americans, indigenous peoples of the United States, Asian
Americans, Chicano/Latino Americans, and European Americans."[10]
In decades past, "progressives" would have grouped Americans in quite
different categories, such as labor, capital, and landowners, or bank-
ers, farmers, and railroad owners. Historians might have suggested
Northerners, Southerners, and Westerners, or city dwellers, suburban-
ites, and rural residents. Might the interplay of inventors, entrepre-
neurs, and industrialists, say, or of scientists, architects, and patrons,
be as fruitful a way of looking at American life as the distribution of
skin color? Not in UC Two.

Naturally, this "American Cultures" requirement, taught in courses
across approximately fifty departments and programs, is run by
Berkeley's ever-expanding Division of Equity and Inclusion. Berkeley
students have been able to fulfill the requirement with such blatantly
politicized courses as "Gender, Race, Nation, and Health," offered by
the gender and women's studies department, which provides students
with "feminist perspectives on health care disparities" while considering gender "in dynamic interaction with race, ethnicity, sexuality,
immigration status, religion, nation, age, and disability."[11] Another

possibility is "Lives of Struggle: Minorities in a Majority Culture," from the African American studies department, which examines "the many forms that the struggle of minorities can assume." It is a given that to be a member of one of the course's favored "three minority aggregates"—"African-Americans, Asian-Americans (so called), and Chicano/Latino-Americans"—means having to struggle against the oppressive white majority.

Earlier in the decade, the UCLA administration and a group of faculty restarted a campaign to require all undergraduates to take a set of courses explicitly dedicated to group identity. UCLA's existing "general-education" smorgasbord, from which students must select a number of courses in order to graduate, already contained plenty of the narcissistic identity and resentment offerings so dear to UC Two, such as "Critical Perspectives on Trauma, Gender, and Power" and "Anthropology of Gender Variance Across Cultures from Third Gender to Transgender." Yet that menu did not sufficiently guarantee exposure to race-based thinking to satisfy the UC Two power structure.

So even though UCLA's faculty had previously rejected a "diversity" general-education requirement in 2005, the administration and its faculty allies simply repackaged it under a new title, with an updated rationale. The new requirement would give meaning, they said, to that ponderous Eighth Principle of Community that the Chancellor's Advisory Group on Diversity had just approved. After the usual profligate expenditure of committee time, the faculty voted down the repackaged diversity requirement in May 2012, recognizing the burdens that any new general-education mandate puts on both students and faculty. UCLA chancellor Gene Block issued a lachrymose rebuke: "I'm deeply disappointed that the proposed new general education requirement was not approved and I'm especially disappointed for the many students who worked with such passion to make the case for a change in curriculum." As a consolation prize to UC Two, Block ordered his administrators to "bring about the intentions of the failed GE requirement proposal" anyway, in the words of UCLA's student-affairs vice chancellor.[12] And sure enough, in February 2013, the community-programs office rolled out a series of initiatives to provide "spaces for dialogue and education about diversity." Block kept pushing, however, and in April 2015, the faculty finally voted in the diversity requirement. Jerry Kang crowed that it would be an opportunity to "critically examine . . . how difference, inequality and community function."[13]

UC Two captured the admissions process long ago. As we saw in chapters 2 and 3, this has brought in many underqualified students.

Their presence generates another huge chunk of UC Two's ever-expanding bureaucracy, which devotes extensive resources to supporting "diverse" students as they try to complete their degrees. Before becoming Sonoma State University president in 2017, Judy Sakaki had long served as student services administrator in the UC system. She traveled a career path typical of the "support-services" administrator, with very little traditional academic expertise or teaching experience. She started as an outreach and retention counselor in the Educational Opportunity Program at California State University, Hayward, and then became special assistant to the president for educational equity. She moved to UC Davis as vice chancellor of the division of student affairs and eventually landed in the UC president's office, where, according to her official biography, she pursued her decades-long involvement in "issues of access and equity." As vice president for student affairs, she earned more than $255,000 a year.

Sakaki has dozens of counterparts on individual campuses. UCLA's Division of Undergraduate Education, with nary a professor in sight, is a typical support-services accretion, funded to the tune of hundreds of millions of dollars a year and stuffed with "retention" specialists and initiatives for "advancing student engagement in diversity." (The division, which labels itself UCLA's "campus-wide advocate for undergraduate education," hosts nondiversity-related programs as well, intended to demonstrate that the university really *does* care about undergraduate education, despite complaints that its main interest lies in nabbing faculty research grants.) It is now assumed that being the first member of your family to go to college requires a bureaucracy to see you through, even though thousands of beneficiaries of the first GI Bill managed to graduate without any contact from a specially dedicated associate vice provost. So did the children of Eastern European Jews who flooded into the City College of New York in the 1930s and 1940s. So do the children of Chinese laborers today who get science degrees both in China and abroad. Yet UC Two and other colleges have molded a construct, the "first-generation college student," and declared it in need of services—though it is simply a surrogate for a "student admitted with uncompetitive scores from a family culture with low social capital."

It's unclear how much these retention bureaucracies actually accomplish. What *has* improved minority graduation rates, though UC Two refuses to admit it, is Prop. 209.

The costs of all these bureaucratic functions add up. From 1998 to 2009, as the UC student population grew 33 percent and tenure-track faculty grew 25 percent, the number of senior administrators grew 125 percent, according to the Committee on Planning and Budget of UC's Academic Senate.[14] The ratio of senior managers to professors climbed from 1 to 2.1 to near-parity of 1 to 1.1. University officials argue that hospitals and research functions drive such administrative expansion. But the rate of growth of nonmedical-center administrators was also 125 percent, and more senior professionals were added outside the research and grants-management area than inside it.

It's true that UC isn't wholly responsible for its own engorgement, since government officials continue to impose frivolous mandates that produce more red tape. During the first term of his second stint as governor, for example, Jerry Brown signed a bill requiring the university to provide the opportunity for students, staff, and faculty to announce their sexual orientation and "gender identity" on all UC forms. A hurricane of committee meetings ensued to develop the proper compliance procedures.

But most of UC's bureaucratic bulk is self-generated. And expanding its own bureaucracy isn't the only way that UC Two likes to spend money. After becoming UC San Diego chancellor in 2012, Pradeep Khosla announced that every employee would get two hours of paid leave to celebrate California Native American Day, a gesture that, under the most conservative salary assumptions, could cost well over $1 million. Around the same time, the vice provost of UCLA's four ethnic studies departments announced that five professors would get paid leave to pursue "transformative interdisciplinary research" regarding "intersectional exchanges and cultural fusion"—even as the loss of faculty through attrition was resulting in more crowded classrooms and fewer course offerings. (Yes, UCLA's ethnic studies departments boast their own vice provost; the position may be UC Two's most stunning sinecure.) UCLA's Center for Labor Research and Education even tried to launch a "National Dream University," an online school exclusively for illegal aliens, where they would become involved in "social justice movements" and learn about labor organizing. Only after negative publicity from conservative media outlets did UC cancel the program, while leaving open the possibility of reconstituting it in the future. The Center continues to fund, in its words, an "immigrant rights movement grounded in justice, equity, inclusion, and power," however, by underwriting political activism by illegal aliens and their allies.

UC Two's constant accretion of trivialities makes it difficult to take its leaders' recurrent protestations of penury seriously. In January 2018, UC president Janet Napolitano complained that the nearly $9 billion in state funding that UC was slated to receive in the 2018–2019 budget was inadequate. This objection did not sit well with legislators, since a 2017 state audit had revealed that Napolitano's Office of the President had squirreled away $175 million in previously undisclosed funds by overestimating the cost of programs and keeping the surplus. Napolitano claimed that only $38 million of the fund was for truly discretionary spending and that in any case, the fund was intended to cover crucial matters such as increased support for illegal-alien students, a Sexual Violence and Sexual Assault Task Force (which received nearly $9 million from 2014 to 2016), and a presence in Mexico.

Napolitano's predecessor Yudof regularly cited the addition of a tenth campus to justify UC's need for more taxpayer support. Indeed, for an institution not known for its celebrations of capitalism, the university shows a robber-baron-like appetite for growth. The system announced plans to add a fifth law school back in 2006, notwithstanding abundant evidence that California's twenty-five existing law schools were generating more than enough lawyers to meet any conceivable future demand. Initial rationalizations for the new law school focused on its planned location—at UC Riverside, in the less affluent and allegedly law-school-deficient Inland Empire east of Los Angeles. But even that insufficient justification evaporated when movers and shakers in Orange County persuaded the regents to site the school at well-endowed UC Irvine, next door to wealthy Newport Beach. Following the opening of Irvine's law school in 2009, California's glut of lawyers and law schools has only worsened.

UC's tenth campus, UC Merced, which opened in 2005, is just as emblematic of the system's reflexive expansion, which is driven by politics and what former regent Ward Connerly calls "crony academics." Hispanic advocates and legislators pushed the idea that a costly research university in California's agricultural Central Valley was an ethnic entitlement—notwithstanding the fact that UC's existing nine research institutions were already more than the state's GDP or population could justify, according to Steve Weiner, the former executive director of the Accrediting Commission for Senior Colleges and Universities. And now that the Merced campus exists, UC's socialist ethos requires redistributing scarce resources to it from the flagship campuses, in pursuit of the chimerical goal of raising it to the caliber of Berkeley, UCLA, or UC San Diego.

Smaller-scale construction projects continue as well. UC Irvine's business school got an opulent new home in 2015, though its older facility—an arcaded sandstone bungalow nestled among eucalypti—was perfectly serviceable. The new building boasts white-noise cancellation technology, as well as Apple TV and iPads in every classroom. Like the new law school and the new UC campus, this doesn't paint a portrait of a university starved for funds.

Even UC's much-lamented rise in tuition masks a more complicated picture than is usually acknowledged. Tuition has trebled over the last decade and a half, to $12,630 in 2017. But contrary to received wisdom, tuition increases have not reduced "access." The number of students attending UC whose family income is $50,000 or less rose 61 percent from 1999 to 2009; such students made up 40 percent of enrollment in 2014.[15] Students whose families earn up to $80,000 pay no tuition at all, a tuition break that extends to qualifying undocumented students.[16]

If the university doesn't engage in internal reform, the primary victim will be UC One, that historically powerful engine of learning and progress. The most necessary reform: axing the diversity infrastructure. UC Two has yet to produce a scintilla of proof that faculty or administrator bias is holding professors or students back. Accordingly, every vice chancellor, assistant dean, and associate provost for equity, inclusion, and multicultural awareness should be fired and his staff sent home. Faculty committees dedicated to ameliorating the effects of phantom racism, sexism, and homophobia should be disbanded and the time previously wasted on such senseless pursuits redirected to the classroom. Campus climate checks, sensitivity training, annual diversity sub-reports—all should go. Hiring committees should be liberated from the thrall of diversity mandates and implicit-bias training; UC's administrators should notify department chairs that they will henceforth be treated like adults and trusted to choose the very best candidates they can find. Federal and state regulators, unfortunately, will still require the compiling of "diversity" data, but staff time dedicated to such mandates should be kept to a minimum.

UC should also start honoring California's constitution and eliminate race and gender preferences in faculty appointments and student admissions. The evidence is clear: Admitting students on the basis of skin color rather than skills hurts their chances for academic success. And by jettisoning double standards in student selection, UC can significantly shrink its support-services bureaucracy.

Unfortunately, as the next chapter will show, the diversity juggernaut is levelling not only UC One but also the teaching of the hard sciences at universities across the country.

THE IDENTITY BUREAUCRACY

In 2018, the diversity bureaucracy finally swallowed an entire college. San Diego State University named to its presidency a vice chancellor of student affairs and campus diversity, hired from the University of California, Davis. The president, Adela de la Torre, is a peerless example of the intersection of identity politics and the ballooning student-services bureaucracy. De la Torre received a PhD in agricultural and resource economics from UC Berkeley and soon began specializing in Chicano studies. Before her diversity and student affairs vice chancellorship, she chaired the UC Davis Department of Chicana/Chicano Studies.

As vice chancellor of student affairs and campus diversity at UC Davis, De la Torre had presided over a division made up of a whopping twenty-eight departments—not academic departments, but bureaucratic and identity-based ones, such as the Lesbian, Gay, Bisexual, Transgender, Queer, Intersex, Asexual Resource Center; the Center for African Diaspora Student Success; the Center for Chicanx and Latinx Student Success; the Native American Academic Student Success Center; the Middle Eastern/South Asian Student Affairs Office; the Women's Resources and Research Center; the Undocumented Student Center; Retention Initiatives; the Office of Educational Opportunity and Enrichment Services; and the Center for First-Generation Student Scholars. This gallimaufry of identity-based fiefdoms illustrates the symbiosis between an artificially segmented, identity-obsessed student body and the campus bureaucracy: The more that students carve themselves into micro-groups claiming oppressed status, the more pretext there is for new cadres of administrators to shield them from oppression (The causation runs in the opposite direction as well: The very existence of such identity-based bureaucracies encourages students to see themselves as belonging to separate tribes.)

11

HOW IDENTITY POLITICS IS HARMING THE SCIENCES

Identity politics has engulfed the humanities and social sciences on American campuses; now it is taking over the hard sciences. The STEM fields—science, technology, engineering, and math—are under attack for being insufficiently "diverse." The pressure to increase the representation of females, blacks, and Hispanics comes from the federal government, university administrators, and scientific societies themselves. That pressure is changing how science is taught and how scientific qualifications are evaluated. The results will be disastrous for scientific innovation and for American competitiveness.

A UCLA scientist reports: "All across the country the big question now in STEM is: how can we promote more women and minorities by 'changing' (i.e., lowering) the requirements we had previously set for graduate level study?"[1] Mathematical problem-solving is being deemphasized in favor of more qualitative group projects; the pace of undergraduate physics education is being slowed down so that no one gets left behind.

The National Science Foundation (NSF), a federal agency that funds university research, is consumed by diversity ideology. Progress in science, it argues, requires a "diverse STEM workforce." Programs to boost diversity in STEM pour forth from its coffers in wild abundance. As we saw in chapter 5, the NSF jump-started the implicit-bias racket by underwriting the development of the Implicit Association Test. It has continued to dump millions into implicit-bias activism. In July 2017, it awarded $1 million to the University of New Hampshire and two other institutions to develop an implicit "bias awareness intervention tool." Another $2 million that same month went to the Department of Aerospace Engineering at Texas A&M University to "remediate microaggressions and implicit biases" in engineering classrooms.[2]

The tortuously named "Inclusion across the Nation of Communities of Learners of Underrepresented Discoverers in Engineering and Science" (INCLUDES) bankrolls "fundamental research in the science of broadening participation." There is no such "science," just an enormous expenditure of resources that ducks the fundamental problems of basic skills and attitudes toward academic achievement. A typical INCLUDES grant from October 2017 directs $300,000 toward increasing Native American math involvement by incorporating "indigenous knowledge systems" into Navajo Nation Math Circles.

The INCLUDES initiative has already generated its own parasitic endeavor, Early-concept Grants for Exploratory Research (EAGER). The purpose of EAGER funding is to evaluate INCLUDES grants and to pressure actual science grantees to incorporate diversity considerations into their research. The ultimate goal of such programs is to change the culture of STEM so that "inclusion and equity" are at its very core.

Somehow, NSF-backed scientists managed to rack up more than two hundred Nobel Prizes before the agency realized that scientific progress depends on "diversity." Those "un-diverse" scientists discovered the fundamental particles of matter and unlocked the genetics of viruses. Now that academic victimology has established a beachhead at the agency, however, it remains to be seen whether the pace of such breakthroughs will continue. The NSF is conducting a half-million-dollar study of "intersectionality" in the STEM fields. "Intersectionality" refers to the increased oppression allegedly experienced by individuals who can check off several categories of victimhood—being female, black, and trans, say. The NSF study's theory is that such intersectionality lies behind the lack of diversity in STEM. Two sociologists are polling more than ten thousand scientists and engineers in nine professional organizations about the "social and cultural variables" that produce "disadvantage and marginalization" in STEM workplaces.

One of the study's directors is a University of Michigan sociologist specializing in gender and sexuality. Erin Cech has received multiple NSF grants; her latest publication is "Rugged Meritocrats: The Role of Overt Bias and the Meritocratic Ideology in Trump Supporters' Opposition to Social Justice Efforts." The other lead researcher, Tom Waidzunas, is a sociologist at Temple University; he studies the "dynamics of gender and sexuality" within STEM, as well as how "scientists come to know, and hence constitute, sexuality and sexual desire." Such politically constituted social-justice research was not likely envisioned by Congress in 1950 when it created the NSF to "promote the progress of science."

The National Institutes of Health are another diversity-obsessed federal science funder. Medical schools receive NIH training grants to support postdoctoral education for physicians pursuing a research career in such fields as oncology and cardiology. The NIH threatens to yank any training grant when it comes up for renewal if it has not supported a sufficient number of "underrepresented minorities" (URMs). One problem: There is often no black or Hispanic MDs to evaluate for inclusion in the training grant. If there *is* a potential URM candidate, the principal investigators will pore over his file multiple times in the hope of persuading themselves that he is adequately qualified. Meantime, the patently qualified Indian doctor goes to the bottom of the candidate pile. For now, medical schools can claim Argentinians and the sons of Ghanaian plantation owners as underrepresented minorities, but if NIH bean counters become more scrupulous in their "diversity metrics," this aspect of biomedical research will reach an impasse.

The diversity mania also determines the way medical research is carried out. The NIH has onerous requirements that government-sponsored clinical trials include the same proportion of female and minority patients as is found in the medical school's "catchment area" (its geographic zone of study). If some of these populations drop out of medical trials at disproportionate rates or are difficult to recruit, too bad. If these URM and female-enrollment quotas are not met, the medical school must "invest the appropriate effort to correct under-accrual," in the words of the NIH guidelines.

The "appropriate effort" can cost a fortune. Schools such as the Mayo Clinic, located in overwhelmingly white areas, must still meet a diversity quota, which they can fulfill by partnering with a medical school in Tennessee, say. Lung cancer and coronary-artery disease afflict adults. If a particular immigrant group in a research trial's catchment area contains a disproportionate share of young people compared with the aging white population, that immigrant group will be less susceptible to those adult diseases. Nevertheless, cancer and heart disease drug researchers must recruit from that community in numbers proportionate to its share of the overall population.

Accrediting bodies reinforce the diversity compulsion. The Accreditation Council for Graduate Medical Education requires that medical schools maintain detailed diversity metrics on their efforts to interview and hire URM faculty. Medical school search committees go through lengthy implicit-bias training sessions and expend enormous amounts of effort looking for something that they often know *a priori* doesn't exist: qualified URM faculty candidates. The very definition of diversity used by academic review panels is becoming ever more exacting. A 2015 panel assessing the academic strength of San Diego State University's biology department complained that the faculty, though relatively representative of traditional "underserved groups," nevertheless failed to mirror the "diversity of peoples in Southern California."[3] The use of a school's immediate surroundings as a demographic benchmark for its faculty is a significant escalation of the war between the diversocrats and academic standards. Naturally, the accrediting panel made no effort to ascertain whether those Southern California peoples—including Hmong, Salvadorans, and Somalis—are netting PhDs in biology and are applying to SDSU's biology department in numbers proportional to their Southern California population.

Many private foundations fund only gender- and race-exclusive science training; others that do fund basic research, such as the Howard Hughes Medical Initiative, nevertheless divert considerable resources to diversity. The major scientific societies push the idea that implicit bias is impeding the careers of otherwise competitive scientists. In February 2018, Erin Cech presented preliminary findings from the NSF intersectionality study at the American Association for the Advancement of Science's annual meeting; naturally, those results showed "systemic anti-LGBTQ bias within STEM industry and academia." Another AAAS session addressed how the "hierarchical nature" of science exacerbates gender bias and stereotypes, and called for the "equal representation of women" across STEM.

STEM departments are creating their own internal diversity enforcers. The engineering school at the University of California, Los Angeles, minted its first associate dean of diversity and inclusion in 2017, despite already being subject to enormous pressures from the vice chancellor for equity, diversity, and inclusion and other deans. "One of my jobs," the new engineering diversocrat, Scott Brandenberg, told UCLA's student newspaper, is "to avoid implicit bias in the hiring process."[4]

The science-diversity charade wastes extraordinary amounts of time and money that could be going into basic research and its real-world application. If that were its only consequence, the cost would be high enough. But identity politics are now altering the standards for scientific competence and the way future scientists are trained. "Diversity" is now often an explicit job qualification in the STEM fields. A current job listing for a lecturer in biology at the University of Massachusetts, Amherst, announces that because diversity is "critical to the university's goals of achieving excellence in all areas," the biology department "holistically" assesses applicants and "favorably considers experiences overcoming barriers"—experiences assumed to be universal among underrepresented minorities. The University of Georgia is seeking a lecturer in biochemistry and molecular biology who will be expected to support the college's goals of "creating and sustaining a diverse and inclusive learning environment."

Entry requirements for graduate education are being revised. The American Astronomical Society has recommended that PhD programs in astronomy eliminate the requirement that applicants take the Graduate Record Exam (GRE) in physics, since it has a disparate impact on females and underrepresented minorities and allegedly does not predict future research output. Harvard and other departments have complied, even though an objective test like the GRE can spotlight talent from less prestigious schools. The National Science Foundation's Graduate Research Fellowship Program has dropped all science GREs for applicants in all fields.

Expectations are changing at the undergraduate level, as well. Oxford University extended the time on its undergraduate math and computer science exams last year, hoping to increase the number of female high-scorers; results were modest. Expect test-time extensions nevertheless to spread to the United States.

Medical school administrators urge admissions committees to look beyond the Medical College Admission Test scores of black and Hispanic student applicants and employ "holistic review" in order to engineer a diverse class. The result is a vast gap in entering qualifications, as we saw in chapter 5. This achievement gap does not close over the course of medical school, but the URM students who do complete their medical training will be fanatically sought after anyway. Adding to medical schools' diversity woes is the fact that the number of male URM student applicants has been declining in recent years, making it even harder to find qualified candidates.

Racial preferences in medical school programs are sometimes justified on the basis that minorities want doctors who "look like them." Arguably, however, minority patients with serious illnesses want the same thing as anyone else: subject mastery.

The push for gender proportionality in medical education and research is not quite as quixotic as the crusade for URM proportionality, but it, too, distorts decision-making. Two-thirds of the applicants for oncology fellowships at a prestigious medical school are male. Half of the oncology department's fellowship picks are female, however, even though females do not cluster at the top of the applicant pool.

A network of so-called teaching and learning centers at universities across the country is seeking to make science classrooms more "inclusive" by changing pedagogy and expectations for student learning. The STEM faculty is too white, male, and heteronormative, according to these centers, making it hard for females, blacks, Hispanics, and the LGBTQ population to learn. STEM professors should adopt "culturally sensitive pedagogies"[5] that are more "open- than closed-ended," and more "reflective than prescriptive," recommends the Association of American Colleges and Universities. At the University of Michigan, the Women in Science and Engineering program (WISE) collaborates with the Center for Learning and Teaching to develop "deliberately inclusive and equitable approaches to syllabus design, writing assignments, grading, and discussion." Yale has created a special undergraduate laboratory course, with funding from the Howard Hughes Medical Institute, that aims to enhance URM students' "feelings of identifying as a scientist." It does so by being "non-prescriptive" in what students research; they develop their own research questions. But "feelings" are only going to get you so far without mastery of the building blocks of scientific knowledge.

Mastering those building blocks involves the memorization of facts, among other skills. Assessing student knowledge of those facts can produce disparate results. The solution is to change the test, or, ideally, eliminate it. Medical school professors have been encouraged to write student exams that are less "fact-based," even though knowledge of pathophysiology and the working of drugs, say, entails knowing facts.

Grading on a curve is another vilified practice for those interested in building "inclusive" STEM classrooms. The only surprising aspect of that vilification is that it acknowledges one of the most self-defeating aspects of black and Hispanic culture: the stigma against "acting white." Underrepresented minorities may "reject competitiveness as an academic motivator," explains a 2015 UCLA report on the undergraduate academic-achievement gap. Instead, underrepresented minorities "draw strength in peer acceptance, nurturance, and cooperation." *Translation*: Instead of pulling all-nighters studying for a linear algebra exam, they may be inclined to hang out in the Afro-Am or LatinX center. This rejection of academic competitiveness is a "coping mechanism," says the UCLA report, that allows individuals to "devalue" things that threaten their sense of well-being, such as high academic expectations. A grading curve contributes to academic competition by objectively ranking students. As a result, URMs will be further alienated and will further withhold their academic efforts. The solution, according to diversity proponents, is to throw out the curve and grade students on whether they have achieved the expected learning outcomes. This sounds unobjectionable, but in practice a curve is the only reliable defense against raging grade inflation.

An introductory chemistry course at UC Berkeley exemplifies "culturally sensitive pedagogy." Its creators described the course in a January 2018 webinar for STEM teachers, sponsored by the University of California's STEM Faculty Learning Community. A primary goal of the course, according to teachers Erin Palmer and Sabriya Rosemund, is to disrupt the "racialized and gendered construct of scientific brilliance," which defines "good science" as getting all the right answers. The course maintains instead that "all students are scientifically brilliant." Science is a practice of collective sense-making that calls forth "inclusive ways" of being brilliant. As applied, these principles mean that students work in groups arranging data cards in the proper sequence to represent chemical processes, among other tasks. Chemical terms of art are avoided wherever possible to accommodate students' different academic backgrounds. The instructors hold the teams "accountable to group thinking"; a team can't question an instructor unless it has arrived collectively at the question and poses it in "we" language.

Progressive pedagogy has long embraced the idea that students should work exclusively in groups as a way to model collectivist democracy. This political agenda is simply a pretext for masking individual differences in achievement that might reinforce group stereotypes. Here, the rationale for group organization is that students are modeling "collective chemical practice." The group design "makes space for students to recognize themselves as competent thinkers and doers of chemistry." *Are* they competent thinkers and doers of chemistry? It's hard to say. The course's grading is idiosyncratic, and thus not comparable with other introductory chemistry courses. The final grade is based on homework (notoriously easy to crib), a final exam (which the teachers wish they could ditch), and an informal presentation to friends or family about the chemistry of compounds. Use of slang or a language other than English in this presentation is encouraged. One such effort featured a photo of the character Joey from the TV sitcom *Friends* dressed in several layers of unmatched clothes to suggest the relationship between positive and negative charges. The teachers have done no follow-up evaluation to see how students performed in their subsequent courses, nor have they determined whether the attrition rate of URMs is lower than in traditional chemistry classes. What they do know is that students showed a positive shift in *believing* that they were good at science. Scientific self-esteem is apparently now an academic goal.

STEM industry leaders are fully on board the diversity juggernaut, having absorbed academic identity politics. The giant Silicon Valley companies offer gender- and race-exclusive mentoring programs and give special consideration to females and URMs in hiring and promotions. Managers go through the same costly implicit-bias training as faculty committees. The discrimination lawsuit filed by James Damore, the computer engineer fired by Google in August 2017 (see chapter 1), reveals a workplace culture at the Silicon Valley giant infused with academic victimology. Employees denounce the advocacy of gender- and race-blind policies as a "microaggression" and the product of "racism" and "misogyny." Managers apologize for promoting males, even when females are being promoted at a higher rate. All-male research teams are mocked; employees self-righteously offer to protect Google's oppressed females and underrepresented minorities from "blinkered, pig-ignorant" conservative opinion. A manager reprimands someone for pointing out that white males are actually underrepresented at Google compared with the general population. The manager informs the errant employee that caring about facts may seem to be a trait of engineers, but "being absolutely correct is inappropriate" when it comes to "discussions of race and justice." Facts are especially inappropriate "in the context of the threat" faced by minorities and females at Google.[6] Needless to say, no female or underrepresented minority faces a threat at Google.

The idea that females and underrepresented minorities are being discriminated against in STEM is demonstrably false. A physician-scientist at a top medical school describes the environment in which he works:

> The sheer effort that is expended in complete good faith at the graduate, post-graduate, and faculty level chasing after a declining population of minority applicants is astonishing. URMs are encouraged to apply, indeed begged to apply, to medical school and post-graduate medical training programs. Everyone at this level is trying incredibly hard to be fair, generous, forgiving, thoughtful, kind, and encouraging to these applicants. But if the pool of candidates is actually declining, no amount of effort, exhortation, or threat will achieve diversity. It's one thing to do poorly on the MCAT; it's another not even to bother taking it. The latter is now the bigger problem because the academy has already relaxed its standards and come up with all kinds of ways to explain away the need to do well on these tests.[7]

When it comes to underrepresented minorities, math deficits show up at the earliest ages. It is only there where the achievement gap can be overcome, through more rigorous, structured classrooms and through a change in family culture to put a high premium on academic achievement. The institutional response to the achievement gap, however, is racial preferences. As we saw in chapter 3, those inaptly named preference "beneficiaries" drop out of their STEM studies at high rates. This experience of academic failure only exacerbates the anti-acting-white syndrome acknowledged in the UCLA study. You can read through report after report on achieving diversity in STEM, however, without coming across any acknowledgement of the academic skills gap. As for females, they, too, are the target of constant efforts to boost their representation in STEM environments. Yet we are to believe that highly educated heads of research teams are so benighted that they refuse to hire or promote scientists whose superior qualifications would increase the lab's chance of a scientific breakthrough, just because those scientists are female. The diversity crusade rests on the belief that absent discrimination, every scientific field would show gender parity. That belief is ungrounded. Males outperform females at the highest reaches of mathematical reasoning (and are overrepresented at the lowest level of mathematical incompetence). Differences in math precocity between boys and girls show up as early as kindergarten. For decades, males in every ethnic group have scored higher than females in their same ethnic group on the math SAT. In 2016, the percentage of males scoring above 700 (on an 800-point scale) was nearly twice as large as the percentage of females in that range. There are 2.5 males in the United States in the top .01 percent of math ability for every female, according to a paper published in February 2018 in the journal *Intelligence*. But female high-scorers are more likely than male high-scorers to possess strong verbal skills as well, according to authors Jonathan Wai, Jaret Hodges, and Matthew Makel, giving them a greater range of career options. Traditionally, individuals who score well in both the math and verbal domains are less likely to pursue a STEM career. Moreover, females on average are more interested in people-centered rather than abstract work, which helps explain why females account for 75 percent of health-care-related workers, but only 14 percent of engineering workers and 25 percent of computer workers. Nearly 82 percent of obstetrics and gynecology medical residents in 2016 were female. Is gynecology biased against males or are females selecting where they want to work?

■ ■ ■

The extraordinary accomplishments of Western science were achieved without regard to the complexions of its creators. Now we are to believe that scientific progress will stall unless we pay close attention to identity and try to engineer proportional representation in schools and laboratories. The truth is exactly the opposite: Lowering standards and diverting scientists' energy into combating phantom sexism and racism is reckless in a highly competitive, ruthless, and unforgiving global marketplace. Driven by unapologetic meritocracy, China is catching up fast to the United States in science and technology. Identity politics in American science is a political self-indulgence that we cannot afford.

12

SCANDAL ERUPTS OVER THE PROMOTION
OF BOURGEOIS BEHAVIOR

Were you planning to instruct your child about the value of hard work and civility? Not so fast! According to a recent uproar at the University of Pennsylvania and at the University of San Diego, advocacy of such bourgeois virtues is "hate speech." The controversy, sparked by an op-ed written by two law professors, illustrates the rapidly shrinking boundaries of acceptable thought on college campuses and the use of racial victimology to police those boundaries. The diversity-obsessed administrators and faculty of both schools were a big part of the problem.

On August 9, 2017, University of Pennsylvania law professor Amy Wax and University of San Diego law professor Larry Alexander published an op-ed in *The Philadelphia Inquirer* calling for a revival of the bourgeois values that characterized mid-century American life, including child-rearing within marriage, hard work, self-discipline on and off the job, and respect for authority. The late 1960s took aim at the bourgeois ethic, they say, encouraging an "antiauthoritarian, adolescent, wish-fulfillment ideal [of] sex, drugs, and rock-and-roll that was unworthy of, and unworkable for, a mature, prosperous adult society."

Today, the consequences of that cultural revolution are all around us: lagging education levels, the lowest male workforce participation rate since the Great Depression, opioid abuse, and high illegitimacy rates. Wax and Alexander catalog the self-defeating behaviors that leave too many Americans idle, addicted, or in prison: "the single-parent, antisocial habits, prevalent among some working-class whites; the anti-'acting white' rap culture of inner-city blacks; the anti-assimilation ideas gaining ground among some Hispanic immigrants."

Throwing caution to the winds, Wax and Alexander challenge the core tenet of multiculturalism: "All cultures are not equal," they write. "Or at least they are not equal in preparing people to be productive in an advanced economy." Unless America's elites again promote personal responsibility and other bourgeois virtues, the country's economic and social problems will only worsen, they conclude.

The University of Pennsylvania's student newspaper, *The Daily Pennsylvanian,* spotted a scandal in the making. The day after the op-ed was published, it came out with a story headlined "'Not All Cultures Are Created Equal' Says Penn Law Professor in Op-Ed." Naturally, the paper placed Wax and Alexander's op-ed in the context of Wax's other affronts to left-wing dogma. It quoted a Middlebury College sociology professor who claimed that Middlebury's "students of color were being attacked and felt attacked" by a lecture that Wax gave at Middlebury College in 2013 on black family breakdown. It noted that Penn's Black Law Students Association had criticized her for a *Wall Street Journal* op-ed in 2005 on black self-help. But the centerpiece of the *Daily Pennsylvanian* story was its interview with Wax.

Initially trained as a neurologist at Harvard Medical School, Wax (whom I consider a friend) possesses fearsome intelligence and debating skills. True to form, she stuck by her thesis. "I don't shrink from the word, 'superior'" with regard to Anglo-Protestant cultural norms, she told the paper. "Everyone wants to come to the countries that exemplify" these values. "Everyone wants to go to countries ruled by white Europeans." (This statement responded to the reporter's question about "white European" countries.) Western governments have undoubtedly committed crimes, she said, but it would be a mistake to reject what is good in those countries because of their historical flaws.

The fuse was lit. The rules of the game were the following: ignore what Wax and Alexander had actually said; avoid providing any counterevidence; and play the race card to the hilt as a substitute for engaging with their arguments. First out of the gate was the Penn graduate students' union, GET-UP. On August 11, a day after the *Daily Pennsylvanian* article, GET-UP issued a "Statement about Wax Op-Ed," condemning the "presence of toxic racist, sexist, homophobic attitudes on campus." The "superiority of one race over others is not an academic debate we have in the 21st century," GET-UP wrote. "It is racism masquerading as science."

But the Wax-Alexander op-ed and the Wax interview said nothing about racial superiority (much less about sex or homosexuality). It argued for a set of behavioral norms that are available to all peoples but that had found their strongest expression over the course of a particular culture. As *The Daily Pennsylvanian* itself acknowledged, Wax had emphasized to them that she was not implying the superiority of whites. "Bourgeois values aren't just for white people," she had said. "The irony is: Bourgeois values can help minorities get ahead." No matter. Time to roll out the racial victimology. "The kind of hate Wax espouses is an everyday part of many students' lives at Penn, and we can and must fight against it," GET-UP thundered in its peroration. "For every incident like this that gains press and publicity, we must recognize that there are countless [others that] go unmarked and unchecked."

Fact-check: Wax had attacked no students. Her argument was against the 1960s countercultural revolution that had undermined the legitimacy of bourgeois values. Unanswered question: Were Wax and Alexander wrong that the virtues of self-restraint, deferred gratification, and future orientation are key for economic and personal progress, and that an anti-achievement, anti-authority culture of drug use and a detachment from the workforce is inimical to advancement? GET-UP had nothing to say about those key matters.

The Daily Pennsylvanian followed up with another article on August 13: "Campus Is Abuzz over Penn Law Professor Amy Wax's Controversial Op-Ed, Which Called for a Return of 'Bourgeois' Cultural Values." The August 13 article quoted liberally from the GET-UP statement and added some sarcastic tweets by an assistant professor of educational linguistics at the education school.

Feisty as ever, Wax emailed the paper: "If this is the best Penn professors and grad students can do, our culture really is in trouble."

Missing so far from the reaction was a call for speech restrictions
and more diversity infrastructure. The IDEAL Council, "representing marginalized graduate students at the University of Pennsylvania
through the Graduate and Professional Student Assembly," corrected
the omission with its August 17 "Open Letter to the University of
Pennsylvania Regarding Hate Speech in Our Community." Wax and
Alexander's *Inquirer* op-ed "pivoted on the denigration of a number
of racial and socioeconomic groups," which "will not be surprising to
many students of color, especially those in the law school who have
had to take a course with Wax," IDEAL claimed. "Her racist and homophobic statements are well-documented both on and off campus."

IDEAL and GET-UP both ignored the fact that Wax and Alexander
criticize white underclass behavior, a silence necessary to clear the deck
for full-throated racial victimology. Far from mistreating "students
of color," Wax has received a law school teaching award from Penn's law
students and a second university-wide teaching award, conferred by
faculty committee. If she oppressed "students of color," the faculty
presumably would have heard about it.

A glad cry must have gone out among IDEAL manifesto writers
when they discovered that Wax had taught at the University of Virginia
law school until 2001. Voilà! Irrefutable proof of bigotry! "Prior to
teaching at Penn, Wax was a professor at the University of Virginia
Law School," the manifesto gloats. "On August 12th, White suprem-
acists marched through the University of Virginia carrying torches,
chanting 'You will not replace us,' and yelling racial and anti-Semitic
slurs."

The causality speaks for itself, but in case the reader needs help,
IDEAL explains that white supremacy "can find its intellectual home
in the kind of falsely 'objective' rhetoric in Amy Wax's statement,
which positions (white) bourgeois culture as not only objectively superior, but also under incursion from lesser cultures and races."
"[F]alsely 'objective'" presumably means: "based on facts that one is unable to rebut." Nothing in the Wax-Alexander op-ed claimed that

white culture was under incursion from lesser races. The 1960s attack on bourgeois culture came most forcefully from American "academics, writers, artists, actors, and journalists," they write, "who relished liberation from conventional constraints."

Having established Wax's connection to the "metastasizing KKK chapters of Pennsylvania," IDEAL got down to brass tacks: demands for a "formal policy for censuring hate speech and a schedule of community-based consequences for discriminatory acts against marginalized groups."

Finally, of course, came the demand for booty and bureaucracy: a "formal, centralized Diversity & Inclusion office with staff that are charged directly with . . . providing resources for students experiencing marginalized [sic] or discrimination at Penn." Never mind that Penn has been cranking out "Action Plans for Faculty Diversity and Excellence," "Faculty Inclusion Reports," "Gender Equity Reports," and "Minority Equity Progress Reports" for two decades.

The unanswered question remains: Were Wax and Alexander wrong that the virtues of self-restraint, deferred gratification, and future orientation are key for economic and personal success? Like GET-UP, IDEAL had not one word to say about the Wax-Alexander thesis, confining itself instead to accusations of racism. Well, perhaps Wax's colleagues at the University of Pennsylvania law school would do better?

No such luck. A spokesman for the law school tried to distance the school from the controversy: "The views expressed in the article are those of the individual authors. They are not a statement of Penn Law's values or institutional policies."[1] That was either an anodyne truism or an underhanded dig at the op-ed as contrary to the school's "values." The administration should have made it crystal clear that reasoned argumentation is not "hate speech" or a "discriminatory act." Wax would not be silenced by the fierce deployment of the racism card. But most academics are not so brave.

The dean of the Penn law school, Ted Ruger, published an op-ed in the student newspaper, affirming that free speech was a "bedrock value" at Penn but noting the "contemporaneous occurrence" of the op-ed and the Charlottesville rally and implying that Wax's views were "divisive, even noxious."[2] Nearly half the professors at the University of Pennsylvania law school published an open letter condemning Wax and inviting students to report their experience of bias and stereotypes at Penn Law (read: Wax's class)—a transparent effort to build a case for removing her from teaching first-year classes. The signatories "categorically rejected" her claims,[3] but provided no reasons for doing so. New York University's Jonathan Haidt explained the corrosive effect of such collective, unreasoned denunciations. "Every open letter you sign to condemn a colleague for his or her words brings us closer to a world in which academic disagreements are resolved by social force and political power, not by argumentation and persuasion," he wrote on his website Heterodox Academy. The rest of the faculty remained conspicuously silent, as has University of Pennsylvania president Amy Gutmann.

Dean Ruger then took a page from UCLA education school dean Suárez-Orozco's playbook. He suggested to Wax in December 2017 that she take a year's sabbatical and stop teaching her first-year civil-procedure class, she reports. The poor dean was under pressure to banish Wax, you see, and hoped that the controversy would die down in her absence. Wax declined the invitation to disappear. In March 2018, Ruger's suggestion that she desist from teaching 1-Ls became a non-negotiable order, however, after remarks she made about mismatch at the law school increased the campus fury against her.

Wax's coauthor, Larry Alexander, teaches at the University of San Diego, a Catholic institution. USD at first seemed to take the piece in stride. But then the dean of USD's law school, Stephen Ferruolo, issued a schoolwide memo repudiating Alexander's article and pledging new measures to compensate "vulnerable, marginalized" students for the "racial discrimination and cultural subordination" that they experience.[4]

Ferruolo's letter refused to engage with any of Wax and Alexander's arguments. The dean simply announced that Alexander's "views" were not "representative of the views of our law school community" and suggested that they were insensitive to "many students" who feel "vulnerable, marginalized or fearful that they are not welcomed." He did not raise any specific objections to Alexander's arguments, or even reveal what the arguments were.

Instead, he promised more classes, speakers, and workshops on racism; more training on racial sensitivity; and a new committee to devise further diversity measures. Stronger racial preferences will most certainly follow. The implication of this bureaucratic outpouring is the absurd notion that the law school faculty is full of bigots.

USD's response was more significant than Penn's because it was more surprising. While USD has embraced a "social justice" mission in recent decades, the law school itself has been less politicized. It has one of the highest proportions of nonleftist professors in the country— about a quarter of the faculty. Ferruolo, a corporate lawyer with strong ties to the biotech industry, presented himself until recently as mildly conservative. If USD was willing to match Penn's hysterical response to the Wax-Alexander op-ed, was there any educational institution remaining that would defend its faculty members against false accusations of racism, should they dissent from orthodoxy?

The Wax-Alexander op-ed's primary sin was to talk about behavior. The founding idea of contemporary progressivism is that structural and individual racism lies behind socioeconomic inequalities. Discussing bad behavioral choices and maladaptive culture is out of bounds and will be punished mercilessly by slinging at the offender the usual fusillade of "-isms" (to be supplemented, post-Charlottesville, with frequent mentions of "white supremacy").

The fact that underclass behaviors are increasingly common among lower-class whites, and not at all limited to poor blacks and Hispanics, might have made it possible to address personal responsibility. That does not appear to be the case. What if the progressive analysis of inequality is wrong, however, and a cultural analysis is closest to the truth? If confronting the need to change behavior is punishable "hate speech," it is hard to see how the country can resolve its social problems.

PART IV
THE PURPOSE OF THE UNIVERSITY

13

THE HUMANITIES AND US

In 2011, the University of California at Los Angeles decimated its English major. Such a development may seem insignificant. It is not. What happened at UCLA is part of a momentous shift in our culture that bears on our relationship to the past—and to civilization itself.

Until 2011, students majoring in English at UCLA had to take one course in Chaucer, two in Shakespeare, and one in Milton—the cornerstones of English literature. Following a revolt of the junior faculty, however, during which it was announced that Shakespeare was part of the "Empire," UCLA junked these individual author requirements and replaced them with a mandate that all English majors take a total of three courses in the following four areas: Gender, Race, Ethnicity, Disability, and Sexuality Studies; Imperial, Transnational, and Postcolonial Studies; genre studies, interdisciplinary studies, and critical theory; or creative writing. In other words, the UCLA faculty was now officially indifferent as to whether an English major had ever read a word of Chaucer, Milton, or Shakespeare, but was determined to expose students, according to the course catalog, to "alternative rubrics of gender, sexuality, race, and class."

Such defenestrations have happened elsewhere, of course, and long before 2011. But the UCLA coup was particularly significant because the school's English department was one of the last champions of the historically informed study of great literature, uncorrupted by an ideological overlay. Precisely for that reason, it was the most popular English major in the country, enrolling a whopping 1,400 under-graduates.

Let's compare what the UCLA student has lost and what he has gained. Here's Oberon addressing Puck in *A Midsummer Night's Dream*:

> . . . *once I sat upon a promontory*
> *And heard a mermaid on a dolphin's back*
> *Uttering such dulcet and harmonious breath*
> *That the rude sea grew civil at her song*
> *And certain stars shot madly from their spheres*
> *To hear the seamaid's music.*

To which UCLA's junior English faculty respond: Ho-hum. Here's the description of a University of California postcolonial studies research grant: The "theoretical, temporal, and spatial intersections of postcoloniality and postsocialism will arrive at a novel approach to race, gender, and sexuality in present-day geopolitics." To which UCLA's junior English faculty respond: That's more like it!

Other readers and listeners have not been so obtuse in their literary judgments. Consider the response of a nineteenth-century Frenchman exposed to Shakespeare for the first time. In early 1827, a troupe of British actors arrived in Paris to perform six Shakespeare plays. The young composer Hector Berlioz was in the audience at the Théâtre de l'Odéon and, like most spectators, read along with the English language performances in a French prose translation. Berlioz later recalled the moment in his *Mémoires*:

> Shakespeare, coming upon me unawares, struck me like a thunder-bolt. The lightning flash of that sublime discovery opened before me at a stroke the whole heaven of art, illuminating it to its remotest depths. . . .
> But the shock was too strong, and it was long before I recovered from it. . . . As I came out of *Hamlet*, shaken to the depths by the experience, I vowed not to expose myself a second time to the flame of Shakespeare's genius.

This resolution proved fleeting:

> Next day the playbills announced *Romeo and Juliet*.
>   After Denmark's somber clouds and icy winds, to be exposed to the
> fiery sun and balmy nights of Italy, to witness the drama of that pas-
> sion swift as thought, burning as lava, radiantly pure as an angel's
> glance, . . . was more than I could bear. By the third act, scarcely able
> to breathe—it was as though an iron hand had gripped me by the
> heart—I knew that I was lost.[1]

Berlioz's reaction was typical. Alexandre Dumas, also in the audience,
wrote that Shakespeare arrived in France with the "freshness of Adam's
first sight of Eden." Fellow attendees Eugène Delacroix, Victor Hugo,
and Théophile Gautier, along with Berlioz and Dumas, would create
works inspired by those seminal evenings. The Bard's electrifying
combination of profound human insight and linguistic glory would
continue catapulting across national borders to influence poets, paint-
ers, and composers the world over, as no other writer has done.

Yet the UCLA English department—like so many others—was
more concerned that its students encounter race, gender, and disability studies than that they plunge headlong into the overflowing riches
of actual English literature—whether Milton, Wordsworth, Thack-
eray, George Eliot, or dozens of other great artists closer to our own
day. How is this possible? The UCLA coup represents the character-
istic academic traits of our time: narcissism, an obsession with victimhood, and a relentless determination to reduce the stunning
complexity of the past to the shallow categories of identity and class
politics. Sitting atop an entire civilization of aesthetic wonders, the
contemporary academic wants only to study oppression, preferably his
own, defined reductively according to gonads and melanin. Course
catalogs today babble monotonously of group identity. UCLA's undergraduates can take courses in Women of Color in the U.S., Women
and Gender in the Caribbean, Chicana Feminism, Studies in Queer
Literatures and Cultures, and Feminist and Queer Theory.

Today's professoriate claims to be interested in "difference," or, to
use an even more up-to-date term, "alterity." But this is a fraud. The

contemporary academic seeks only to confirm his own worldview and the political imperatives of the moment in whatever he studies. The 2014 Modern Language Association conference, the annual gathering of America's *literature* (not social work) faculty, for example, addressed "embodiment, poverty, climate, activism, reparation, and the condition of being unequally governed . . . to expose key sites of vulnerability and assess possibilities for change."

It was not always so. The humanist tradition was founded not on narcissism but on the all-consuming desire to engage with the genius and radical difference of the past. The fourteenth-century Florentine poet Francesco Petrarch triggered the explosion of knowledge known today as Renaissance humanism with his discovery of Livy's monumental history of Rome and the letters of Cicero, the Roman statesman whose orations, with their crystalline Latin style, would inspire such philosophers of republicanism as John Adams and Thomas Jefferson.

But Petrarch didn't want to just read the ancients; he wanted to converse with them as well. So he penned heartfelt letters in Latin to Virgil, Seneca, Horace, and Homer, among others, informing them of the fate of their writings and of Rome itself. After rebuking Cicero for the vindictiveness revealed in his letters, Petrarch repented and wrote him again: "I fear that my last letter has offended you. . . . But I feel I know you as intimately as if I had always lived with you."

Petrarch was hardly the only Renaissance scholar to feel so immediate a bond with the classical authors. In 1416, the Florentine clerk Poggio Bracciolini discovered the most important Roman treatise on rhetoric moldering in a monastery library outside Constance, a find of such value that a companion exclaimed: "Oh wondrous treasure, oh unexpected joy!" Bracciolini thought of himself as rescuing a still-living being. The treatise's author, Quintilian, would have "perished shortly if we hadn't brought him aid in the nick of time," Bracciolini wrote to a friend in Verona. "There is not the slightest doubt that that man, so brilliant, genteel, tasteful, refined, and pleasant, could not longer have endured the squalor of that place and the cruelty of those jailers."

This burning drive to recover a lost culture propelled the Renaissance humanists into remote castles and monasteries across Europe to search for long-forgotten manuscripts. Despite their rapport with their Greek and Roman ancestors, they were no historical naïfs. The humanists were well aware, unlike their medieval predecessors, of the chasm between their present and the classical past, as exemplified most painfully in the fallen state of medieval Latin. It was precisely to overcome the effects of time on historical sources that they developed the seminal methods of modern scholarship.

The knowledge that many ancient texts were forever lost filled these scholars with despair. Nevertheless, they exulted in their growing repossession of classical learning, for which they felt, in Emerson's words, a canine appetite. In François Rabelais's exuberant *Gargantua* stories from the 1530s, the giant Gargantua sends off his son to study in Paris, joyfully conjuring up the languages—Greek, Latin, Hebrew, Chaldean, and Arabic—that he expects him to master, as well as the vast range of history, law, natural history, and philosophy. "In short," he concludes, "let me find you a perfect abyss of knowledge."

This constant, sophisticated dialogue between past and present would become a defining feature of Western civilization, prompting the evolution of such radical ideas as constitutional government and giving birth to arts and architecture of polyphonic complexity. And it became the primary mission of the universities to transmit knowledge of the past, as well as—eventually—to serve as seedbeds for new knowledge.

Compare the humanists' hunger for learning with the resentment of a Columbia University undergraduate who had been required by the school's freshman core curriculum to study Mozart. She happens to be black, but her views are widely shared, to borrow a phrase, "across gender, sexuality, race, and class."

"Why did I have to listen in music humanities to this Mozart?" she groused in a discussion of the curriculum reported by David Denby in his book on Columbia's core. "My problem with the core is that it upholds the premises of white supremacy and racism. It's a racist core. Who is this Mozart, this Haydn, these superior white men? There are no women, no people of color." These are not the idiosyncratic thoughts of one disgruntled student; they represent the dominant ideology in the humanities today. Columbia not only failed to disabuse the student of such parochialism; it is also all but certain that some of its faculty strengthened her in her close-mindedness, despite the school's admirable commitment to its beleaguered core.

Of course, the absurd game of reducing all expression to gender or race politics is particularly ludicrous when it comes to music—but the charge of Eurocentrism is even more preposterously leveled against Mozart, who makes a Muslim pasha the only truly noble character in his opera *The Abduction from the Seraglio*, and whose Sarastro in *The Magic Flute* appeals to a universal humanity.

Ralph Ellison anticipated the contemporary multiculturalist's shallow self-definition and sphere of interest. Ellison read Marx, Freud, T. S. Eliot, Pound, Gertrude Stein, and Hemingway as a young man in Macon County, Alabama—books, he said, which "seldom, if ever, mentioned Negroes," but that were to release him "from whatever 'segregated' idea I might have had of my human possibilities." He was liberated not by black political writers like Richard Wright, he wrote, "but by composers, novelists, and poets who spoke to me of more interesting and freer ways of life." It requires "real poverty of the imagination" to think that self-understanding "can come to a Negro *only* through the example of *other Negroes*," Ellison concluded.[2]

That constricting narcissism has now leaped out of the campus and into the arts world at large. Directors in Europe and the United States are dragooning poor defenseless operas to serve as mouthpieces for their own hobbyhorses. These egotistical stage directors wrench centuries-old works into the present and force them to ape the political and sexual obsessions of today's cultural elite. Audiences can expect to see lots of nudity and kinky sex on stage, as well as cell phones, Big Macs, and snide put-downs of American capitalism. Mozart's aristocratic seducer, Don Giovanni, is infallibly a charmless, drug-addicted lout wallowing in the detritus of consumer culture and surrounded by sluts, psychopaths, and slobs.

The official excuse for such mutilation is that a work can only be "relevant" to a modern audience if it is tricked out in modern garb and forced to speak, however incoherently, of modern concerns. As the director of the Frankfurt opera declared, no one should care what Handel wanted in his operas; what matters is "what interests us . . . what we want."

Actually, the *only* thing that matters is what Handel, Mozart, and Tchaikovsky wanted. It is their artistic genius that allows us to enter worlds radically different from our own and expand our understanding of what it is to be human. (The revisionist director, like the contemporary academic, detests any values, such as nobility, grandeur, or sexual decorum that differ from his own), and will shamelessly rewrite an opera's plot to eliminate them. But in an era of twerking and drunken hookups, there is much to be gained by experiencing, if only for a few hours, a courtly ethic where desire can be expressed by the slightest inclination of a hand or an almost imperceptible darkening of the voice.

As for the visual arts, artists learned their craft for centuries by lovingly studying and copying the masters. No more. Today's would-be artist need only stage his own predictable politics to claim artist status, a view that has given us such performance pieces as the publicly performed loss of anal virginity at a London art school or a video-recorded use of a cement sex toy at the San Francisco Art Institute.

There is, in other words, much bad news today about the humanist impulse. What we rarely hear is the good news: Thanks to enlightened philanthropy, the enduring lure of beauty, and, yes, market forces, the humanist impulse is thriving in many places beyond the university.

The most important classical music development of our time is a direct rebirth of the Renaissance spirit: a loose group of performers known as the "early-music" movement is determined to re-create how music from the baroque and classical eras was originally performed. Like the Renaissance scholars who realized that the classical texts that had come down to them had been corrupted by errors, these musicians believe that twentieth-century performance styles veered drastically from how baroque music was intended to be played. The results have been a revelation, releasing submerged dance rhythms and res-urrecting long-forgotten composers—such as Hasse, Porpora, and Steffani—who urgently deserve to be heard again.

But even those musicians not seeking the holy grail of authentic period performance are driven by the same humanist reverence for past genius. At the 2013 Texas State International Piano Festival (that de-spised Red State hosts many such festivals), an eleven-year-old Asian-American pianist (and violinist) proudly recounted that her first piano instructor boasted a teaching lineage stretching back to Haydn. "I was so excited to learn that. I respect Haydn *so* much," she told the NPR program *From the Top*, apparently untroubled by Haydn's lamentable white-male status and thinking of him, like Petrarch of Cicero, as an almost-contemporary.

Regarding the visual arts, New Yorkers are particularly fortunate: Many of New York's museums still present the best of human cre-ation, relatively untainted by identity politics. At the Metropolitan Museum of Art, former director Philippe de Montebello consciously fought off pressures for trendy relevance. His successor, Thomas Camp-bell, squandered resources on misguided contemporary art initiatives (and was ousted in 2017), but still mounted some superlative shows, such as the 2016 exhibit on Hellenistic art. The Frick's and the Mor-gan's commitment to standards and taste is almost terrifyingly superb.

None of this accomplishment can be taken for granted; leadership is crucial, and it can turn in an instant. New York's music press has been baying for the Metropolitan Opera to give over the house com-pletely to revisionist opera directing. Yet New York audiences, unlike those in Europe, can still see productions that take the composer's in-tention as their lodestar, however much such fidelity enrages the commentariat.

The demand side for the humanities is also robust, as we will see in the next chapter. Publishing has capitalized on this thirst for knowl-edge. The success of one book after another on the American Found-ing proves that the public's appetite for urbane explorations of American history is boundless.

Yet though the humanist spirit is chugging along nicely outside the university, the university remains its natural home, from which it should not be in exile. We have bestowed on the faculty the best job in the world: Freed from the pressures of economic competition, professors are actually *paid* to spend their days wandering among the most sublime creations of mankind. All we ask of them in return is that they sell their wares to ignorant undergraduates. Every fall, insistent voices should rise from the faculty lounges and academic departments saying: Here is greatness, and this is your best opportunity to absorb it. Here is Aeschylus, whose hypnotic choruses bear witness to dark forces more unsettling than you can yet fathom. Here is Mark Twain, Habsburg Vienna, and the *Saint Matthew Passion*. Here is the drama of Western civilization, out of whose constantly battling ideas there emerged unprecedented individual freedom and unimagined scientific progress.

Instead, the professoriate is tongue-tied when it comes to promoting the wonders of its patrimony. These privileged cowards can't even summon the guts to prescribe the coursework that every student must complete in order to be considered educated. Need it be said? Students don't know anything. That's why they're in college. They certainly don't know enough to select courses that will give them the rudiments of culture. The transcripts that result from the professoriate's abdication of its intellectual responsibility are not a pretty sight, featuring as many movie and video courses as a student can stuff into each semester.

When the academy *is* forced to explain the value of the humanities, the language that it uses is pathetically insipid. You may have heard the defense du jour, tossed out en route to the next gender studies conference. The humanities, we are told, teach "critical thinking." Is this a joke? These are the professorial critical thinkers who write sentences like this:

> It is because the proper names are already no longer proper names because their production is their obliteration, because the erasure and the imposition of the letter are originary, because they do not supervene upon a proper inscription; it is because the proper name has never been anything but the original myth of a transparent legibility present

under the obliteration; it is because the proper name was never possible except through its functioning within a classification and
therefore within a system of differences, within a writing retaining the
traces of difference, that the interdict was possible, could come into
play, and, when the time came, as we shall see, could be transgressed;
transgressed, that is to say restored to the obliteration and the non-
self-awareness at the origin.[3]

And we're supposed to believe that they can think? Moreover, the
sciences provide critical thinking skills as well—far more rigorous
ones, in fact, than the hackneyed deconstructions of advertising that
the left-wing academy usually means by critical thinking.

It is no wonder, then, that we have been hearing that the humanities are in crisis. A 2013 Harvard report, cochaired by the school's
premier postcolonial studies theorist, Homi Bhabha, lamented that
57 percent of incoming Harvard students who initially declare interest in a humanities major eventually change concentrations. Why may
that be? Imagine an intending lit major who is assigned something *by*
Professor Bhabha: "If the problematic 'closure' of textuality questions
the totalization of national culture. . . ."[4] How soon before that student concludes that a psychology major is more up his alley?

No, the only true justification for the humanities is that they provide the thing that Faust sold his soul for: knowledge. It is knowledge
of a particular kind, concerning what men have done and created over
the ages. The American Founders drew on an astonishingly wide range
of historical sources and an appropriately jaundiced view of human nature to craft the world's most stable and free republic. They invoked
lessons learned from the Greek city-states, the Carolingian Dynasty,
and the Ottoman Empire in the Constitution's defense. And they assumed that the new nation's citizens would themselves be versed in
history and political philosophy. Indeed, a closer knowledge among
the electorate of Hobbes and the fragility of social order might have
prevented the more brazen social experiments that we've undergone
in recent years. Ignorance of the intellectual trajectory that led to the
rule of law and the West's astounding prosperity puts those achievements at risk.

But humanistic learning is also an end in itself. It is simply better to have escaped one's narrow, petty self and entered minds far more subtle and vast than one's own than never to have done so. The Renaissance philosopher Marsilio Ficino said that a man lives as many millennia as are embraced by his knowledge of history. One could add: A man lives as many different lives as are embraced by his encounters with literature, music, and all the humanities and arts. These forms of expression allow us to see and feel things that we would otherwise never experience—society on a nineteenth-century Russian feudal estate, for example, or the perfect crystalline brooks and mossy shades of pastoral poetry, or the exquisite languor of a Chopin nocturne.

Ultimately, humanistic study is the loving duty we owe those artists and thinkers whose works so transform us. It keeps them alive, as well as us, as Petrarch and Poggio Bracciolini understood. The academic narcissist, insensate to beauty and nobility, trapped in the diversity delusion, knows none of this.

And as politics in Washington and elsewhere grows increasingly unmoored from reality, humanist wisdom provides us with one final consolation: There is no greater lesson from the past than the intractability of human folly.

14
GREAT COURSES, GREAT PROFITS

The canon of great literature, philosophy, and art is thriving—in the marketplace, if not on college campuses. For the last quarter-century, a company called the Great Courses has been selling recorded lectures in the humanities and sciences to an adult audience eager to brush up its Shakespeare and its quantum mechanics. The company produces only what its market research shows that customers want. And that, it turns out, is a curriculum in the monuments of human thought, taught without the politically correct superiority and self-indulgent theory common in today's colleges.

To open a Great Courses catalog is to experience an intellectual seduction. "When was the last time you read the classics of American literature?" teases one course description. "Possibly not as recently as you'd like. These carefully crafted lectures are your royal road to recapturing the American experience—and our intellectual and cultural heritage." A course on Plato's *Dialogues*—"for millennia the objects of devoted study by the noblest minds"—invites you to "become engrossed in the 'romance of the intellect.'" The company uses words to describe learning—such as "joy," "beauty," "pleasure," "classic," and its favorite, "greatness"—that have long disappeared from the academy's discourse. "As you read or reread these masterpieces, you will likely experience such joy from great reading that you may wonder why you have spent so much time on contemporary books," asserts one course description, committing several transgressions against the reigning post-poststructuralist orthodoxy.

And the company offers a treasure trove of traditional academic content, which undergraduates paying $60,000 a year may find nowhere on their Club Med–like campuses. In the 2017 to 2018 academic year, for example, a Bard College student interested in American history could have taken "Inclusion at Bard," "When Race Morphed: Understanding the Peoples of the United States, from 1900 to the Civil Rights Era," or "Crusading for Justice: On Gender, Sexuality, Racial Violence, Media, Rights," but the only traditional American political history course was "The Civil War and Reconstruction."[1] A Great Courses customer, by contrast, can choose from a cornucopia of American history not yet divvied up into the fiefdoms of race, gender, and sexual orientation, with multiple offerings in the American Revolution, the constitutional period, the Bill of Rights, and the intellectual influences on the country's founding. There are lessons here for the academy, if it will only pay them heed.

The Great Courses, originally called The Teaching Company, wasn't begun with the goal of creating an antidote to today's politicized academy. Tom Rollins, chief counsel and chief of staff to Senator Ted Kennedy's Labor and Human Services Committee, quit his post in 1989 with the idea of finding the most charismatic college professors and having them tape college-level courses for the adult-education market.

Rollins, then thirty-three, soon discovered that his assumptions about the university—that it existed, in his words, "to transmit to the young everything the civilization has figured out so far and to discover new things"—were not shared by everyone in the academy. "My first baptism came quickly," he said. One of his earliest hires was Rick Roderick, a philosophy professor at Duke University, whom Rollins describes as to the left of Karl Marx. Nothing disqualifying there, so long as a professor injects his political views into a course only if relevant. Roderick had already recorded two popular courses for the company and was in the middle of his third when he let fly the observation that we shouldn't bother to listen to anyone—Ronald Reagan came immediately to mind, he said—who scored too low on the "DQ index." (That would be the "Dan Quayle index," after the purportedly stupid vice president.) Roderick went on to speculate on tape that the only reason Nancy Reagan had ever had power was that she "gave the best head in Hollywood." At this point, Rollins, who had considerable capital resting on the success of Roderick's course, intervened: "Rick, I'm deleting this material." Roderick coolly replied: "Tom, truth is a defense to libel." Ultimately, the index stayed in; Nancy Reagan's alleged source of power was out.[2]

An American literature course by two theory-drenched Ivy League professors provided another early learning experience. The professors made little effort to conceal their contempt for the presumed racism and sexism of their audience and of the authors they were discussing. Within a month of the course's release, customers were calling the company to complain about the lecturers' condescending tone. In an institution that would live or die according to its customers' satisfaction, Rollins couldn't afford to alienate his audience. He destroyed all the master tapes of the course, so that no further copies could ship out, even accidentally. "Teaching shouldn't be an opportunity for a professor to get off his chest burning issues that no one would listen to except students," Rollins said, sadder but wiser about the academy. "People want to know what the field has discovered; they aren't interested in your personal views."

Some of the early surprises involved the camera's power to terrify even seasoned lecturers. By 1992, Rollins was living in an attic, after burning through his retirement savings to invest in his company. Maxed out on his credit cards and having sold twelve of his thirteen Washington power suits, he had bet everything he had left on a history of Western philosophy course, for which his customer polling indicated a huge demand. A $10,000-a-day film crew had set up in the basement of the Georgetown University School of Medicine, ready to tape the course's Machiavelli lecture—but the Columbia University professor who was supposed to deliver it was nowhere to be found. Rollins assumed that he was having a last smoke in the stairwell; instead, he found him there curled into a fetal position. "If I have to leave this stairwell, I will either throw up or faint," vowed the professor, a large, strapping fellow. "I need Machiavelli in thirty seconds!" Rollins called out. Michael Sugrue, one of the two other lecturers in the course and a historian of colonial America, volunteered. He gave a superb talk, and the series became one of the company's biggest sellers. Another professor in a different course actually did throw up before the taping—but then gave an excellent presentation on Greek civilization.

Despite several brushes with mortality in its start-up years, after a decade, the firm was earning $20 million in sales. From the start, some customers developed an intensely personal relationship with the product, accusing Rollins of failing if he wasn't constantly putting out new material. "They'd call me to say, 'C'mon, Tom, I'm done with your latest; when's the next one out?' It was like intellectual crack." The audience—mostly older professionals with successful careers—sees the liberal arts as a life-changing experience, observes Louis Markos, an English professor at Houston Baptist University who has recorded courses on C. S. Lewis and on literary criticism for the company. "They are hungry for this material."

The company markets deftly to that hunger. The catalogs are learning opportunities in their own right, tantalizingly laying out the material that each course will cover, such as the contributions and foibles of the Renaissance popes. This peekaboo strategy presumes a burning desire for knowledge on the reader's part. "Starting with the Renaissance, the culture of the West exploded," begins the description of a Western civilization series. Then it irresistibly reels the reader in: "Over the next 600 years, rapid innovations in philosophy, technology, economics, military affairs, and politics allowed what once had been a cultural backwater left by the collapse of the Roman Empire to dominate the world. But how—and why—did this happen? How did the decentralized agrarian principalities of medieval Europe remake themselves into great industrial nation-states? How and why did absolutism rise and then yield to democratic liberalism?"

In promoting its wares, the Great Courses breaks one academic taboo after another. The advertising copy for "Books That Have Made

History: Books That Can Change Your Life" asserts: "Beginning with the definition of a great book as one that possesses a great theme of enduring importance, noble language that elevates the soul and ennobles the mind, and a universality that enables it to speak across the ages, Professor [J. Rufus] Fears examines a body of work that offers an extraordinary gift of wisdom to those willing to receive it"—a statement so reckless that it would get its proponent thrown out of the Modern Language Association's annual convention. Indeed, one could take the company's definition of literature in another course description as a rebuke to the prevailing academic mores, not least in its very use of the word "literature" rather than the usual "text": "While we sometimes think of literature as anything written, it is in fact writing that lays claim to consideration on the grounds of beauty, form, and emotional effect." The Great Courses' uninhibited enthusiasm is so alien to contemporary academic discourse that several professors who have recorded for the firm became defensive when I asked them about their course descriptions, emphatically denying any part in writing the copy—as if celebrating beauty were something to be ashamed of.

The most striking thing about the Great Courses' humanities curriculum, however, is how often the same thinkers appear across a large range of courses. The canon has been "problematized" in the academy, but it is alive and well in these recordings. Plato, Aristotle, Cicero, Paul, Erasmus, Galileo, Bacon, Descartes, Hobbes, Spinoza, Dante, Chaucer, Spenser, Shakespeare, Cervantes, Milton, Molière, Pope, Swift, Goethe, and others are foregrounded again and again as touchstones of our civilization. This repetition occurs not because the company is on a mission to resuscitate the canon but because customers want it. The insatiability of the demand for such courses surprises even the producers themselves. "We were reexamining the same material," said Rollins, "and I kept wondering: 'How can customers keep buying "Great Ideas of Philosophy" *and* "Great Minds of the Western Intellectual Tradition"?' But people bought both. They wanted different takes on Kant, Socrates, and the Enlightenment."

So totalitarian is the contemporary university that some professors wrote to Rollins complaining that his courses were too canonical in content and do not include enough of the requisite "silenced" voices. It is not enough, apparently, that identity politics dominate college humanities departments; they must also rule outside the academy. Of course, outside the academy, theory encounters a little something called the marketplace, where it turns out that courses like "Queering the Alamo," say, can't compete with "Great Authors of the Western Literary Tradition."

The Great Courses is by no means a theory-free zone; it even offers a course in canon formation. The title of another course, "Representing Justice: Stories of Law and Literature," uses the mannered gerundial construction so beloved of theory-besotted academics—not surprising in a course built on the briefly trendy idea that law is a form of literature. But the incursions of identity studies and other post-1960s academic developments remain minimal—and are inevitably denounced by some customers on the company's website. Overwhelmingly, the professors act as handmaidens to their subjects, laying out their material clearly and objectively, rather than avenging four thousand years of injustice by unmasking the power relations supposedly hidden in a hapless text. Whitman College classics professor Elizabeth Vandiver notes in a course on Homer's *Iliad* that ancient Greek culture was patriarchal, *unlike* the modern era. Seth Lerer, a literature professor at the University of California at San Diego, does not chastise Milton for sexism in the famous description of Adam and Eve in *Paradise Lost*:

> For contemplation he and valour form'd,
> For softness she and sweet attractive grace,
> He for God only, she for God in him.

If the Great Courses were a college, its students would graduate with a panoramic view of human accomplishment and the natural world. Their knowledge of the past would be bolstered with courses in ancient Mesopotamia, Greece, Rome, and Egypt; the early, high, and late Middle Ages; the Renaissance and the Reformation; Chinese, Russian, and African history; and modern European history, including the Enlightenment, Victorian England, and World Wars I and II. In science and mathematics, they could study cosmology, algebra, calculus, differential equations, quantum mechanics, chemistry, chaos theory, basic biology, probability, the history of mathematics, the great ideas of classical physics, and the science of consciousness. To understand how mankind has thought about human life, they could plunge into Aristotle's *Ethics*, Plato's *Republic*, medieval philosophy, Eastern philosophy, Nietzsche, Tocqueville, Voltaire, the philosophical underpinnings of capitalism, and modern philosophy since Descartes. In literature, they could read the Greek tragedies, Homer, the *Aeneid*, the *Divine Comedy*, Shakespeare, the English Romantic poets, Mark Twain, the English novel, and masterpieces of Russian literature. Their appreciation of beauty could be enhanced by studying the Dutch masters, cathedral architecture, Michelangelo, Mozart's operas and chamber works, northern and Italian Renaissance art, the lives and times of Stravinsky and Shostakovich, and Beethoven's piano sonatas, symphonies, and string quartets.

True, the Great Courses emphasizes breadth over depth and offers largely introductory material. In literature and intellectual history, the survey format predominates, with relatively few courses on individual writers or philosophical schools. The company planned a series dedicated to single authors but changed its mind after its Chaucer and Milton series didn't sell as well as expected. "People don't want to spend six hours on a single author," Rollins said. (What about Dickens or Trollope? I asked. "You should have seen their polling numbers," Rollins responded.) The company offers little genre or period specialization, and there is insufficient close reading of literary and philosophical language. But there is also none of the specious specialization of such courses as Wesleyan's "Circulating Bodies: Commodities, Prostitutes, and Slaves in Eighteenth-Century England," which "explores the period's circulating bodies as they were passed from hand to hand, valued and revalued, used, abused, and discarded,"[3] or Bowdoin's "Renaissance Sexualities," which "reimagines the canon of Renaissance literature from the perspective of desires that have not yet been named, [and] explores homoeroticism, sodomy, and heteronormativity . . .

with special attention to the politics and poetics of same-sex desire and the erotics of theatrical performance by boy actors."[4]

In the past, the company used polling to determine not only which courses to offer, but even the individual lecture topics within each course. Seth Lerer was told to omit Old English from what would become his extremely popular lectures on the history of the English language because only 10 percent of likely buyers wanted it. Lerer insisted on including it anyway. "The company was good at understanding its audience but at the time not good at understanding what college professors were like," he said. "Professors generate content and teach it because they think something should be taught, not because it meets a market." (This lofty conception of academic freedom and intellectual responsibility sounds admirable in theory; in current practice, the results are less impressive.) Ultimately, however, the company agreed with Lerer and a substantial fraction of its audience that there were commonsense limits to the consumer model of education. "We don't know what should be in each course," the polled customers told the company, according to Rollins, "and neither do our fellow customers!"

Beyond the promise of knowledge, the Great Courses markets itself by invoking the Eros of the great teacher. It claims to have identified the very best of the country's more than half-million college professors. Company recruiters sit in on classes of professors who have won awards or been recognized for their teaching; the most promising are invited to the Great Courses headquarters to record an audition lecture. That recording then goes to the company's most valued customers. If enough of them like it, the company asks the professor to create a lecture course.

In the company's "heroic" early period, as insiders call it, professors, once chosen, received carte blanche in crafting their courses. Now, however, the company closely involves itself in the creation of each course to make sure that it isn't being sold "five pounds of manure in a ten-pound bag," as Rollins put it. Professors must submit a detailed outline of each lecture according to strict deadlines before taping begins. Company employees work with each professor to make sure that courses are logically coherent in parts as well as the whole. Each lecture must be thirty minutes long: no ignoring the clock or deferring material to the next week, as on a college campus. Such a quality-control regime contrasts sharply with the academy and has led some professors who recorded in the freewheeling "heroic" era to part ways amicably with the company. The amount of work required to create a course is fully equivalent to writing a book, said Columbia University professor John McWhorter, whose linguistics lectures are among the company's most popular.

In its emphasis on teaching, the company differs radically from the academic world, where "teaching is routinely stigmatized as a lower-order pursuit, and the 'real' academic work is research," noted Allen Guelzo, an American history professor at Gettysburg College.[5] Though colleges ritually berate themselves for not putting a high enough premium on teaching, they inevitably ignore that skill in awarding tenure or extra pay. As for reaching an audience beyond the hallowed walls of academe, perhaps a regular NPR gig would gain notice in the faculty lounge, but not a Great Courses series. Jeremy McInerney, a University of Pennsylvania history professor, told *The Chronicle of Higher Education* in 1998 that he wouldn't have taped "Ancient Greek Civilization" for the company if his tenure vote had been in doubt: "This doesn't win you any further respect. If anything, there's a danger of people looking down on it, since many people are suspicious of anything that reeks of popularism." So much for the academy's supposed stance against elitism.

Do the Great Courses' professors live up to their billing? Not always. A few ramble in their presentations or oversimplify (even sugarcoat) their material—making Nietzsche, for example, sound almost like a self-help guru. But most of the professors are solid to very good, with the best exhibiting an infectious enthusiasm for their subject matter, whether expressed through the debonair showmanship of an Allen Guelzo or the ingenuous directness of his colleague on the company's superb American history survey, Emory professor Patrick Allitt.

The Great Courses' highest-selling lecturer—music professor Robert

Greenberg—unquestionably deserves his devoted following. Greenberg's patent love for the music of the past is utterly endearing. During one course, he implores: "My friends, if it wasn't an unseemly thing to do, I would go down on my knees and beg all of you to go out and get a recording of [Robert Schumann's] magnificent piano quintet. You will never regret it." Recounting how Johannes Brahms destroyed his first twenty string quartets, Greenberg says mournfully: "We rightly ask: 'J.B., J.B., did you *have* to?'"[6] Greenberg's blue-collar New Jersey persona ("I grew up in Levittown," he explains; "if you spoke hoity-toity, you got the shit kicked out of you") might put off some super-serious listeners—to their loss, since his composer biographies are superb, vividly drawn portraits of quixotic geniuses and their cultural environment. "When Brahms started his first concert tour in 1853," Greenberg narrates, "the not-quite-20-year-old was an insignificant bit of blond lint from a bad neighborhood who played some piano and wrote some music. Seven months later, he would be hailed as the heir to Beethoven."[7] The only flaw in Greenberg's courses is the frequent mediocrity of the anonymous performances that he uses to illustrate them, the result of strict copyright rules on recordings, which have also limited the composers he can cover.

Predictably, the Great Courses has come under pressure for not having enough "diversity" in its teaching ranks. Rollins received angry letters from women complaining about the paucity of female lecturers; his nonstop efforts to recruit them have yielded few results, in part because women lecture less than men. As for the truly big-name female professors, they command speaking fees so high that the Great Courses' pay scale looks insignificant. The same applies to the black superstars, one of whom told Rollins: "Tom, honestly, I make several thousand dollars a night from Martin Luther King Day through Black History Month; you're not even on my radar screen." A Great Courses lecturer earns a royalty that varies according to how highly viewers rate his performance; the base royalty is 4 percent of the course's gross revenue, but that rate can rise to 6 percent if a course receives high enough evaluations. The average royalty is about $25,000 a year for a course.

The very fact that the Great Courses has found professors who teach without self-indulgence may suggest that academia is in better shape than is sometimes supposed. But the firm's two-hundred-plus faculty make up a minute percentage of the country's college teaching corps. And some Great Courses lecturers feel so marginalized on their own campuses, claimed Guelzo, that "if the company granted tenure, they would scramble to abandon their current ships and sleep on couches to work for the firm." Further, it isn't clear that the Great Courses professors teach the same way back on their home campuses. A professor who teaches the Civil War as the "greatest slave uprising in history" to his undergraduates because that is what is expected of him, said University of Pennsylvania history professor Alan Kors, will know perfectly well how to teach a more intellectually honest course for paying adults.[8]

Unfortunately, even some Great Courses faculty demonstrate the narrowing of the academic mind. I contacted another Penn history professor to interview him about his experiences with the company. After a positive initial response to my request, he suddenly announced that he wouldn't speak with me. "I ought to have looked up the Manhattan Institute before I replied to your first e-mail," he wrote. "I cannot in good conscience contribute in any way to any project associated with an institution which rejects everything I believe. It says something about the undeclared civil war in U.S. life that I have to say that to you."

While the Great Courses, then, is only an ambiguous marker of the academic scene, the meaning of the audience's response is far clearer: There is a fervent demand in the real world for knowledge about history and the high points of human creation. Public libraries have formed discussion groups around the most popular courses. Customers accost Great Courses professors in airports as though they were celebrities. Alan Kors has received fan letters from forest rangers and from prison convicts. By contrast, "students never thank you; college is simply what they do next," says Patrick Allitt.[9]

The company releases no information about its buyers, but professors say that they have been told to think of their audience as just as

educated as they are, but in a different field. The customers must be
well-off enough to pay what can be a hefty sum for the courses; a
typical twenty-four-lecture course costs around $200 on DVD, and
Greenberg's thirty-two-lecture course on Verdi runs $520, though
patient customers wait for sales to snap up courses for around $60. A
few professors suggested that the company has pegged the audience
as leaning conservative. Seth Lerer claimed that the firm told him in
the 1990s that some of its clientele would be uncomfortable with his
including Black English in his "History of the English Language"
course. "They were very conscious of their political demographic," he
said. Lerer got an angry email from a customer asking how he could
include that "leftist son of a bitch" Noam Chomsky in the course. John
McWhorter was told to omit from his linguistics lectures his usual
argument that the idea of grammatical "correctness" is an "arbitrary
imposition." Such caveats on the company's part, however, could simply reflect the desire to avoid alienating any customers.

Some popular professors make more money from their Great
Courses royalties and the resulting speaking engagements than from
their academic salaries. Greenberg's "Understanding the Fundamen-
tals of Music" sells twenty thousand units a year, according to *Forbes*;
Lerer said that his "History of the English Language," which the company told him was a high midrange seller, sold tens of thousands of
units over a dozen years. All in all, the firm has sold more than 9 million courses since 1990.

Brentwood Associates, a private-equity firm, acquired a majority
stake of the Great Courses in 2006, spotting a thriving company with
huge growth potential. "The foundation that Rollins created was unlike anything we'd seen," said Brentwood's Eric Reiter. "He was a brilliant entrepreneur, building the company brick by brick through
rigorous testing."[10] Profits soon doubled, thanks to major investments
in advertising—visible to anyone who reads *The New York Times Book
Review*, *The Atlantic*, or *Science News* or who is on the receiving end of
some of the 70 million catalogs that the company sent out last year.
"Few businesses have such a passionate customer base," said Reiter.

"Nine out of ten people on the street have never heard of it, but nine out of ten, upon learning about the product, want it."

Annual sales reached $150 million by 2016, according to *The New York Times*. The firm opened a high-tech headquarters in Virginia for its two hundred employees and has beefed up the visual learning aids on its DVDs—a sorely needed correction. But the Great Courses confronts a major challenge as it tries to expand its course offerings: "finding great lecturers, a talent that seems to be increasingly rare these days," said Lucinda Robb, the company's former director of professor development. In fact, the company has been recycling its most popular professors on topics increasingly remote from their official competencies. It is also diversifying into nonacademic realms, such as wine appreciation and personal health. The growing reach of free online university courses might seem to pose a competitive challenge, but for now, the Great Courses adds enough value to its lecturers to justify the product's sticker price.

The biggest question raised by the Great Courses' success is: Does the curriculum on campuses look so different because undergraduates, unlike adults, actually demand postcolonial studies rather than the Lincoln-Douglas debates? "If you say to kids, 'We're doing the regendering of medieval Europe,' they'll say, 'No, let's do medieval kings and queens,'" asserted Allitt. "Most kids want classes on the French Revolution, the Russian Revolution, World War I, and the American Civil War." Creative writing is such a popular concentration within the English major, Lerer argues, because it is the one place where students encounter attention to character and plot and can nonironically celebrate literature's power.

But even if Allitt and Lerer are right, the educational market works very differently inside the academy and outside it, and the consumers of university education are largely to blame. Almost no one comparison-shops for colleges based on curricula. Parents and children select the school that will deliver the most prestigious credentials and social connections. Presumably, some of those parents are Great Courses customers themselves—discerning buyers regarding their own continuing education, but passive check writers when it comes to their children's. Employers, too, ignore universities' curricula when they decide where to send recruiters, focusing only on the degree of IQ-sorting that each college exercises sub rosa.

Universities are certainly doing very well for themselves, despite ignoring their students' latent demand for traditional learning. But they would better fulfill their mission if they took note of the Great Courses' wild success in teaching the classics. "I wasn't trying to fix something that was broken in starting the company," Rollins said. "I was just trying to create something beautiful." Colleges should replicate that impulse.

15

THE TRUE PURPOSE OF THE UNIVERSITY

In 2016, Yale University's president provided a window into the modern university's self-conception—an understanding embraced by both liberals and conservatives but flawed in essential ways. A primary purpose of a Yale education, President Peter Salovey told Yale's freshman class, is to teach students to recognize "false narratives." Such narratives, Salovey claimed, are ubiquitous in American culture: "My sense is that we are bombarded daily by false narratives of various kinds, and that they are doing a great deal of damage." Advocates may "exaggerate or distort or neglect crucial facts," Salovey said, "in ways that serve primarily to fuel your anger, fear, or disgust."[1] (Salovey repeated this trilogy of "anger, fear, and disgust" several times; it was impossible not to hear a reference to Donald Trump, though Salovey tried to stay nonpartisan.) According to Salovey, the Yale faculty is a model for how to respond to false narratives: They are united by a "stubborn skepticism about narratives that oversimplify issues, inflame the emotions, or misdirect the mind," he said.

Two things can be said about Salovey's theme: First, it is hilariously wrong about the actual state of "stubborn skepticism" at Yale. Second, and more important, Salovey mistakes the true mission of a college education. To assess whether Yale is, in fact, a bastion of myth-busting, it is necessary to return to one of the darkest moments in Yale's history: the university's response to the mass outbreak of student narcissism in October 2015. As discussed in chapter 1, the wife of a college master had sent an email to students, suggesting that they were capable of deciding for themselves which Halloween costume to wear and didn't need advice from Yale's diversity commissars. (Halloween costumes have been the target of the PC police nationally for allegedly "appropriating" minority cultures.)

The email sparked a furor among minority students across Yale and beyond, who claimed that it threatened their very being. In one of many charged gatherings that followed, students surrounded the college master, cursing and screaming at him, calling him a racist, and demanding that he resign from Yale.

Of all the Black Lives Matter–inspired protests that were sweeping campuses at that moment, the episode was the most grotesque. In reaction, Yale groveled. President Salovey sent around a campus-wide letter proclaiming the need to work "toward a better, more diverse, and more inclusive Yale"—implying that Yale was not "inclusive"—and thanking students for offering him "the opportunity to listen to and learn from you." That many of the students had refused to listen to their college master—or to give him an opportunity to speak—was never mentioned. Salovey went on to pledge a reinforced "commitment to a campus where hatred and discrimination have no place," implying that hatred and discrimination currently did have a place at Yale. Salovey announced that the entire administration, including faculty chairs and deans, would receive training on how to combat racism at Yale and reiterated a promise to dump another $50 million into Yale's already all-consuming diversity efforts.

If ever there were a narrative worthy of being subjected to "stubborn skepticism," in Salovey's words, the claim that Yale was the home of "hatred and discrimination" is it. During the hours-long scourging of Nicholas Christakis, a student loudly whines: "We're dying!" To say it again: Not only are Yale's minority students most decidedly *not* dying, there is not a single faculty member or administrator at Yale (or any other American college) who does not want minority students to succeed. Yale has been trying to admit and hire as many "underrepresented minorities" as it possibly can without eviscerating academic standards. There has never been a more tolerant social environment in human history than Yale (and every other American college)—at least if you don't challenge the reigning political orthodoxies. Any Yale student who thinks himself victimized by the institution is in the throes of a terrible delusion, unable to understand his supreme good fortune in ending up at one of the most august and richly endowed universities in the world.

But the ubiquitous claim that American campuses are riven with racism is not, apparently, one of the "false narratives" that Salovey had in mind. Not only did the president endorse that claim, but the husband-and-wife team who had triggered the Halloween costume furor penned a sycophantic apology to minority students in their residential college: "We understand that [the original email] was hurtful to you, and we are truly sorry," wrote Professors Nicholas and Erika Christakis. "We understand that many students feel voiceless in diverse ways and we want you to know that we hear you and we will support you."[2] Yale's minority students may "feel voiceless," but that feeling is just as delusional as the feeling that Yale is not "inclusive."

So Salovey's claim that Yale resolutely seeks out and unmasks "false narratives" is itself a false narrative. But is the routing of "false narratives" even an apt description of what a college education should ideally be? It is not, even though that goal, in different iterations, is widely embraced across the political spectrum. The most urgent task of any college is the transmission of knowledge, pure and simple. American students arrive at college knowing almost nothing about history, literature, art, or philosophy. If they aspire to a career in STEM fields, they may have already picked up some basic math and physics, and possibly some programming skills. But their orientation in the vast expanse of Western civilization is shallow; they have likely been traveling on a surface of selfies and pop culture with, at best, only fleeting plunges into the past.

A postmodern theorist, the prime product of today's university culture, would immediately object that there is no such thing as neutral knowledge. But this hypersophisticated critique is irrelevant to the problem of widespread student ignorance. There exists a bedrock of core facts and ideas that precede any later revisionist interpretation. They would include, at a bare minimum: the events that led to the creation of the nation-state in Europe; the achievements of Greco-Roman civilization; familiarity with key works of Shakespeare, the Greek tragedians, Twain, Dickens, Wordsworth, and Swift, among others; an understanding of genetics and the functioning of neurons; and the philosophical basis for constitutional democracy, among hundreds of other essential strata of the human geology.

The concept of "false narratives" is simply irrelevant to the vast bulk of what students do not know. Before you can challenge a received narrative about the past, you should be expert in its established contours. President Salovey gives examples of the Yale faculty's overturning of "distorted narratives." One example was undoubtedly selected to resonate with more conservatively inclined listeners and readers: a professor of medieval history who allegedly demonstrated the religious roots of the secular legal tradition.[3] Such scholarship is an essential part of any university; but when it comes to undergraduates, it would be triumph enough if Yale gave them even a foggy notion of the difference between medieval canon law and British common law.

Moreover, it is inaccurate to define a received understanding of the common-law tradition as a "false narrative," a term that connotes an ideological agenda and that is itself highly ideological. That Salovey would insert the work of a medievalist into the "false narratives" conceit reflects several streams in contemporary academic thought. In the 1970s, a fantastical idea took hold throughout the humanities—that the goal of criticism was to unmask the alleged deceptions afflicting, and perpetrated by, "texts." The assumption was that all language carried hidden meanings that either subverted alleged power structures or reinforced them. The French philosopher Paul Ricoeur labeled this outlook the "hermeneutics of suspicion." Ricoeur traced its roots to Marx, Freud, and Nietzsche, who advanced the view that humans live in a tissue of lies and illusions about the world, whether with regard to economic relations, the rational self, or philosophical truth.

A less precious antecedent to Salovey's "false narratives" paradigm is the progressive-education mantra from the late 1990s that "critical thinking" should be the goal of education. The internet has made the allegedly mindless transmission of facts obsolete, the educrats proclaimed, since students can always look up such boring things as facts on the web. Instead, schools should cultivate in their students the capacity to "think critically." A typical exercise was to have students "deconstruct" an advertisement to expose all the ways that big bad corporations were trying to dupe consumers. The "critical thinking" idea conveniently let teachers off the hook for failing to teach their students anything, by declaring that there was nothing substantive that needed teaching anyway.

But the "false narratives" idea really came into its own with the rise of academic identity politics. To the modern academic, the quintessential "false narrative" facilitates the oppression of victim groups by white heterosexual males. Salovey hits all the requisite notes in his final example of a Yale professor debunking a "false narrative." "Professor Hazel Carby [a black feminist theorist] wrote a telling remark in her foreword to a book called *Silencing the Past*," Salovey says, "highlighting the power of challenging false or incomplete narratives about the marginalized: 'We learn how scanty evidence can be repositioned to generate new narratives, how silences can be made to speak for themselves,' Carby wrote." Predictably, the book that Carby was introducing blames the West for distortions regarding a Caribbean slave revolt, the Holocaust, the Alamo, and Christopher Columbus.

In the realm of daily politics, it is fair to say that we are awash in false narratives. But the past is filled with accomplishments that are not "narratives" or not "false" in the sense intended by the phrase "false narratives." These accomplishments should be approached with humility and reverence. The task of both scholar and student should be to understand them on their own terms.

Conservatives have, of late, stressed a process-oriented notion of education that shares certain similarities with the "false narratives" approach. This emphasis reflects their understandable revulsion at the silencing on campus of politically incorrect views. Education should be about reasoned debate and the airing of all opinions in the pursuit of the truth, critics of campus political correctness say. Students should take courses from professors who challenge their views and should attend lectures by visiting scholars whose ideas they find uncongenial, Princeton professor Robert George wrote in *The Wall Street Journal*. Students should not be so "deeply in love with [their] opinions" as to not listen to "others who see things differently," George asserted.[4]

This ideal of the Socratic academy is so reasonable that it may seem foolish to quibble with it. Of course, students should engage with ideas that they disagree with rather than silencing anything that challenges their worldview. But there is a universe of knowledge that does not belong in the realm of "opinion." It would be as absurd for an ignorant eighteen-year-old to say: "I have an opinion about early Mediterranean civilizations, but I am willing to listen to others who see things differently," as it would be to say: "I have an opinion about the laws of thermodynamics, but I am willing to listen to the other side."

The free-speech model of education tends toward a focus on the present. The issues about which students are going to have the strongest opinions concern current political and policy matters: Is Donald Trump a fascist? Is immigration enforcement racist? Does the criminal-justice system discriminate against blacks? Which bathrooms should "trans" individuals use? The fact that only one answer to these questions is acceptable on college campuses is indisputably a problem. But they are not the questions that undergraduate education should focus on; there will be time enough after students graduate to debate current affairs. While defenders of the open university rightly fight for free speech, they should not lose sight of the knowledge that is the university's core mission to transmit. If students had been more deeply immersed in acquiring that knowledge and less taken with challenging "false narratives" about the marginalized, we might not have seen the narcissistic campus meltdowns after the 2016 presidential election.

16
FROM CULTURE TO CUPCAKES

Even before its students rioted in the streets, distressed that right-wing provocateur Milo Yiannopoulos would dare to open his mouth in their presence, the University of California at Berkeley presented a visual illustration of the academy's decline from a place of learning to a victimology hothouse. Within walking distance on the Berkeley campus were emblems of both a vanished academic world and the diversity-industrial complex that has ousted it.

A first-time visitor to the Berkeley law school would be startled by the two long quotations, in Bauhaus-era typography, that adorn its otherwise brutalist facade, so anachronistic has their rhetoric become. On the left is a passage by Supreme Court Justice Benjamin Cardozo, from a 1925 speech at the Albany Law School:

> You will study the wisdom of the past, for in a wilderness of conflicting counsels, a trail has there been blazed. You will study the life of mankind, for this is the life you must order, and, to order with wisdom, must know. You will study the precepts of justice, for these are the truths that through you shall come to their hour of triumph. Here is the high emprise, the fine endeavor, the splendid possibility of achievement, to which I summon you and bid you welcome.

As if that were not antique enough, on the right side of the entrance are words from Oliver Wendell Holmes, whose seat on the Supreme

Court Cardozo filled in 1932. The passage comes from an 1885 address to the Suffolk Bar Association:

> When I think thus of the law, I see a princess mightier than she who once wrought at Bayeux, eternally weaving into her web dim figures of the ever-lengthening past—figures too dim to be noticed by the idle, too symbolic to be interpreted except by her pupils, but to the discerning eye disclosing every painful step and every world-shaking contest by which mankind has worked and fought its way from savage isolation to organic social life.

No law school today, if erecting itself from scratch, would think of parading such sentiments on its exterior. They are as alien to the reigning academic ideology as the names of the great thinkers, virtually all male, carved into the friezes of late-nineteenth-century American campus buildings. Cardozo's and Holmes's invocation of "mankind" is alone cause for removal, of course, but equally transgressive is their belief that there is wisdom in the past and not just discrimination. They present learning as a heroic enterprise focused not on the self and its imagined victimization but on the vast world beyond the self, both past and present. Education is the search for objective knowledge that takes the learner into a grander universe of thought and achievement. Stylistically, Cardozo's elevated tone is as old-fashioned as his complicated syntactical cadences; his exhortation to intellectual mastery is too "masculinist" and triumphal for today's identity-obsessed university.

To Cardozo's ornate grammatical style, Holmes adds poetical imagery combining classical mythology with historical legend; this allusive rhetorical tradition has disappeared from public discourse. Holmes's Whig view of history as an upward progression violates the current academic obsession with the alleged ongoing oppression of the "other" in Western society. Both thinkers' celebration of the law overlooks the teachings of critical race theory, which purports to expose the racial subtext of seemingly benign legal concepts. And they fatally omit any mention of "inclusion" and "diversity."

There's not a trace of the heroic on the Berkeley law school's website today; the closest it comes to any ennobling inspiration is the statement: "We believe that a Berkeley Law degree is a tool for change, both locally and globally." What the study of the past can offer is left unspecified.

But this bland expression of progressive ideology is positively Miltonic compared with the bromides that were, until recently, on display just meters away from the law school. UC Berkeley's Division of Equity and Inclusion had hung vertical banners across the main campus reminding students of the contemporary university's paramount mission: assigning guilt and innocence within the ruthlessly competitive hierarchy of victimhood. Each banner showed a photo of a student or a member of the student-services bureaucracy, beside a purported quotation from that student or bureaucrat. No rolling cadences here, no mythical imagery, no exhortations to intellectual conquest. Instead, just whining or penitential snippets from the academic lexicon of identity politics. "I will acknowledge how power and privilege intersect in our daily lives," vowed an Asian female member of the class of 2017. Just how crippling is that "intersection" of "power and privilege"? The answer came in a banner showing a black female student in a backward baseball cap and a male Hispanic student, who together urge the Berkeley community to "Create an environment where people other than yourself can exist." (In 2018, placards celebrating Berkeley's 150th anniversary supplanted most of the diversity banners—for now, at least.)

A naïve observer of the Berkeley campus would think that lots of people "other than himself" exist there, and would even think that Berkeley welcomes those "other" people with overflowing intellectual and material riches. Such a misperception, however, is precisely why Berkeley funds the Division of Equity and Inclusion with a cool $20 million annually and staffs it with 150 full-time functionaries: It takes that much money and personnel to drum into students' heads how horribly Berkeley treats its "othered" students.

A member of the student-services bureaucracy reinforced the message of continual oppression on her banner. "I will be a brave and sympathetic ally," announced Bene Gatzert of University Health Services. Cardozo and Holmes saw grandeur in the mastery of the common law; today's campus functionary sees herself in a heroic struggle against the ubiquitous forces of white-male heterosexual oppression. The *au courant* concept of "allyship" divides the campus into the oppressed, their allies, and the oppressors. If you are not in either of the first two categories, you're by definition in the third. "Allies" are needed if oppressed students at UC Berkeley—the country's most elite public university, endowed with libraries and laboratories that are the envy of the world—are simply to survive their ordeal.

One of Berkeley's likely oppressors offered a suitably self-abasing banner: "I will think before I speak and act," promised a white male student from the class of 2016. Ordinarily, such a vow of self-control might seem like the sort of bourgeois virtue celebrated by Amy Wax and Larry Alexander (chapter 12). In the current academic context, however, it means: "I will mentally scan the University of California's official list of microaggressions before I open my mouth to avoid expressing an offensive belief in color blindness, meritocracy, or the value of hard work."

A former head of the bureaucracy that created the banner campaign weighed in with her own banner. "Respect the full humanity of others," urged Na'ilah Suad Nasir, who pulled in $215,000 a year as vice chancellor for equity and inclusion. This admonition would be appropriate when trying to mediate, say, between warring tribes given to slaughtering one another's members. But the diversocrat assumption that Berkeley's pacific students, raised from nursery school on the pablum of tolerance and diversity, are at risk of seriously violating one another's humanity, beyond the ordinary slights of everyday social interaction, is absurd. What this seemingly gratuitous admonition really means is: "Do not violate any politically correct taboo around race, gender identity, or any other favored category in the armamentarium of narcissistic grievance."

Equally officious was the charge to "Keep an open mind and listen with integrity," from Joseph Greenwell, the associate vice chancellor and dean of students. The nauseatingly pop-psychological coinage of "listening with integrity" is a tip-off that student-services bureaucrats think of themselves as leading an encounter session, not an institution of higher learning. Students arrive at Berkeley shockingly ignorant of the most basic rudiments of history and Western culture. Berkeley's adults should feel haunted by the need to cram as much knowledge as possible into their students' heads before they depart. But the only reference in the banner campaign to the academic resources lying open to those knowledge-deficient students is: "Take advantage of the American Cultures curriculum," from a Hispanic student in the class of 2015. As we have seen, American Cultures is Berkeley's diversity requirement: "a more inclusive curriculum that reflect[s] the diverse racial groups of the U.S.," in the words of the official website, and that allows "collaborative social justice projects alongside community organizations." A more appropriate admonition for an incoming student would have been: "Take some American history before you leave."

Holmes and Cardozo invited students to the life of the mind. The diversocrats who have commandeered the American university invite students to a cultural reeducation camp where they can confess their political sins or perfect their sense of victimhood. The post-Trump nervous breakdown was a direct consequence of the diversocrats' reign; reaction to his election will only solidify their power, and deepen the delusion that students and recent graduates bring into the larger world. Rather than emerging with minds broadened and informed by the best that our heritage offers, students increasingly are narrowed into groups defined by grievance. Who—other than a vast administrative bureaucracy—benefits from such diminishment? And what will replace what has been lost?

NOTES

Introduction

1. W. E. B. Du Bois, *The Souls of Black Folk*, with an introduction by John Edgar Wideman (New York: The Library of America, 2009, pbk.), 438.

2. *The Frederick Douglass Papers, Series Two: Autobiographical Writings, vol. 2: My Bondage and My Freedom*, eds. John W. Blassingame, John R. McKivigan, and Peter P. Hinks (New Haven and London: Yale University Press, 2003), 90–91.

3. Victor Wang, "Student Petition Urges English Department to Diversify Curriculum," *Yale Daily News*, May 16, 2016, accessed May 7, 2018, http://yaledailynews.com/blog/2016/05/26/student-petition-urges-english -department-to-diversify-curriculum/.

4. Allison Stanger, "Understanding the Angry Mob at Middlebury That Gave Me a Concussion," op-ed, *New York Times*, Mar. 13, 2017, accessed May 7, 2018, https://www.nytimes.com/2017/03/13/opinion/understanding -the-angry-mob-that-gave-me-a-concussion.html.

5. Middlebury Faculty for an Inclusive Community, "An Initial Statement of Our Principles," *Middlebury Campus*, May 10, 2017, accessed May 7, 2018, http://middleburycampus.com/35724/opinions/an-initial-statement -on-the-principles-of-inclusivity-civil-freedoms-and-community/.

Chapter One: *The Hysterical Campus*

1. Steven Glick, "Claremont Students Plan to Protest 'Anti-Black Fascist' Heather Mac Donald," *Claremont Independent*, Apr. 6, 2017, accessed May 7, 2018, https://claremontindependent.com/students-plan-to-protest -anti-black-fascist-heather-mac-donald/.

2. Hiram Chodosh, "Last Night's Ath Talk," email message to Claremont McKenna faculty, staff, and students, Apr. 7, 2017.

3. Editorial Board, "Ath Talks Aren't Neutral," *Student Life*, Apr. 7, 2017, accessed May 7, 2018, http://tsl.news/opinions/6698/.

4. Dray Denson, Avery Jonas, and Shanaya Stephenson, "Open letter to David Oxtoby: In Response to Academic Freedom and Free Speech," Apr. 17, 2017, accessed Apr. 24, 2018, http://archive.is/Dm2DN#selection -147.10-147.127.

5. Haruka Senju,"Violence as Self-defense," *Daily Californian*, Feb. 7, 2017, accessed May 7, 2018, http://www.dailycal.org/2017/02/07/violence-self -defense/.

6. Neil Lawrence, "Black Bloc Did What Campus Should Have," *Daily Californian*, Feb. 7, 2017, accessed Apr. 24, 2018, http://www.dailycal.org /2017/02/07/black-bloc-campus/.

7. Elizabeth Abel, Wendy Brown, Judith Butler, Ian Duncan, Donna Jones, David Landreth, Saba Mahmood, et al., Letter to Chancellor Nicholas Dirks, Jan. 3, 2017, accessed Apr. 22, 2018, https://docs.google .com/document/d/13mTOQ7wVst6voLMg6Pvr-3uJ2Fbn7zcXg _Bkx8mGDOk/edit.

8. "Yale University Student Protest Halloween Costume Email," YouTube video, posted Nov. 6, 2015, accessed Apr. 22, 2018, https://www.youtube .com/watch?v=9IEFD_JVYd0&feature=youtu.be.

9. "Part III: Yale Students and Nicholas Kristachis [sic]," YouTube video, Nov. 5, 2015, posted Nov. 14, 2015, accessed Apr. 22, 2018, https://www .youtube.com/watch?v=u-q3Y8pRoj8&feature=youtu.be&t=2m; "Part IV: Yale Students and Nicholas Kristachis [sic]," YouTube video, Nov. 5, 2015, posted Nov. 14, 2015, https://www.youtube.com/watch?v =es1W9cREZAs&feature=youtu.be&t=2m.

10. "President and Yale College Dean Underscore Commitment to a 'Better Yale'" statement, Yale University website, Nov. 6, 2015, accessed Apr. 22, 2018, https://news.yale.edu/2015/11/06/president-and-yale-college-dean -underscore-commitment-better-yale.

11. Sam Budnyk, "Emory Students Express Discontent with Administrative Response to Trump Chalkings," *Emory Wheel*, Mar. 22, 2016, accessed Apr. 22, 2018, http://emorywheel.com/emory -students-express-discontent-with-administrative-response-to-trump -chalkings/.

12. Jim Galloway, "Chalk One Up for Donald Trump at Emory University," *Political Insider* (blog), *Atlantic Journal–Constitution*, Mar. 22, 2016, accessed Apr. 22, 2018, https://politics.myajc.com/blog/politics/chalk -one-for-donald-trump-emory-university/6pgzUuEj8T4bhrGT2RFMjL/.

13. BWOG Staff, "Columbia Class of 2018 Facebook Page Debates POC Core Professors," *BWOG Columbia Student News*, Nov. 15, 2015, accessed Apr. 21, 2018, http://bwog.com/2015/11/15/columbia-class-of-2018 -facebook-page-debates-poc-core-professors/.

14. "Note to Employees from CEO Sundar Pichai," Google blog, Aug. 8, 2017, accessed Apr. 22, 2018, https://www.blog.google/topics/diversity/note -employees-ceo-sundar-pichai/.

15. Yonatan Zunger, "So, About This Googler's Manifesto," Medium, Aug. 5, 2017, accessed Apr. 22, 2018, https://medium.com/@ yonatanzunger/so-about-this-googlers-manifesto-1e3773ed1788.

16. Sarah Emerson, Louise Matsakis, and Jason Koebler, "Internal Reaction to Google Employee's Manifesto Show Anti-Diversity Views Have Support," Motherboard, Aug. 5, 2017, accessed Apr. 22, 2018, https://motherboard.vice.com/en_us/article/ywpamw/internal-reaction-to -google-employees-manifesto-show-anti-diversity-views-have-support.

Chapter Two: *Elites to Affirmative Action Voters: Drop Dead*

1. John Searle, interview, Dec. 1, 2006.

2. Interview with University of California-San Diego professor, Dec. 4, 2006.

3. Richard Sander, interview, Nov. 4, 2006.

4. Nina Robinson, interview, Nov. 30, 2006.

5. Brent Bridgeman and Cathy Wendler, Characteristics of Minority Students Who Excel on the SAT and in the Classroom, Policy Information Report (Princeton, NJ: Educational Testing Service, 2005), accessed Apr. 22, 2018, https://www.ets.org/Media/Research/pdf/PICMINSAT.pdf.

6. Mark Rashid, interview, Nov. 21, 2006.

7. Richard H. Sander, "A Systematic Analysis of Affirmative Action in American Law Schools," *Stanford Law Review* 57 (Nov. 2004), 367–483, accessed Apr. 22, 2018, http://www.adversity.net/Sander/Systemic _Analysis_FINAL.pdf.

8. Katherine S. Mangan, "Combatants Over Affirmative Action in Admissions Await Law Review Issue That's Their Next Battleground,"

Chronicle of Higher Education, Apr. 15, 2005, accessed Apr. 22, 2018, https://www.chronicle.com/article/Combatants-Over-Affirmative/120448.

9. Goodwin Liu, "A Misguided Challenge to Affirmative Action," Commentary, *Los Angeles Times,* Dec. 20, 2004, accessed Apr. 22, 2018, http://articles.latimes.com/2004/dec/20/opinion/oe-liu20.

10. Katherine S. Mangan, "Does Affirmative Action Hurt Black Students?" *Chronicle of Higher Education,* Nov. 12, 2004, accessed Apr. 22, 2018, https://www.chronicle.com/article/Does-Affirmative-Action-Hurt /19206.

11. "Robert Birgeneau: 'We Serve California Extremely Well,'" Berkelyan, *UC Berkeley News,* October 18, 2006, accessed Apr. 22, 2018, https://www .berkeley.edu/news/berkeleyan/2006/10/18_Birgeneau.shtml.

Chapter Three: *Affirmative Disaster*

1. Peter Arcidiacono, Esteban M. Aucejo, and Ken Spenner, "What Happens after Enrollment? An Analysis of the Time Path of Racial Differences in GPA and Major Choice," *IZA Journal of Labor Economics* 1, no. 5 (Oct. 2012), accessed Apr. 22, 2018, https://izajole.springeropen.com /articles/10.1186/2193-8997-1-5.

2. Ibid.

3. "Black Students at Duke Upset Over Study," UrbanMecca, *Herald-Sun* (Durham, NC), Jan. 13, 2012, accessed Apr. 22, 2018, http://urbanmecca .net/news/2012/01/13/black-students-at-duke-upset-over-study/.

4. karla fc holloway (@ProfHolloway), "#Duke authors' unpublished study of #race + #AffirmativeAction lacks academic rigor," Jan. 16, 2012, https:// twitter.com/ProfHolloway/status/159011440831901697.

5. Timothy B. Tyson, "The Econometrics of Rwandan Pear Blossoms at Duke University," *Mike Klonsky's Blog,* Jan. 27, 2012, accessed Apr. 22, 2018, http://michaelklonsky.blogspot.com/2012/01/econometrics-of -rwandan-pear-blossoms.html.

6. "Politics of Grievance at Duke," ZetaBoards, Jan. 22, 2012, accessed May 7, 2018, http://s1.zetaboards.com/Liestoppers_meeting/topic/4662188/1/.

Chapter Four: *The Microaggression Farce*

1. Cathryn Dhanatya, interview, July 7, 2014.

2. Rosalind Raby, interview, July 17, 2014.

3. Rosalind Raby, "Val Rust: A Lifetime of Achievement," SSCE Newsletter (Spring 2013), 5, accessed Apr. 22, 2018, https://www.yumpu.com/en/document/view/19168727/spring-2013-ssce-newsletter-ampersand-ucla.

4. Interview with recent graduate, July 20, 2014.

5. Daniel Solorzano, Sayil Camacho, William Dandridge, Johanna Drucker, Alma Flores, Annamarie Francois, Patricia Garcia, Sandra Graham, Timothy Ho, Tyrone Howard, et al., "Final Report of the GSE&IS Committee on Race and Ethnic Relations," UCLA Ed & IS, GSE&IS Resources (June 2014), accessed Apr. 22, 2018, https://portal.gseis.ucla.edu/incident-resolution/gse-is-committee-on-race-and-ethnic-relations-final-report.

6. Elie Mystal, "Racists' T-Shirts on Campus? Only If You Bother to Think About It," *Above the Law*, Nov. 22, 2013, accessed Apr. 22, 2018, https://abovethelaw.com/2013/11/racists-t-shirts-on-campus-only-if-you-bother-to-think-about-it/.

7. "Substantively Respond to BLSA's Suggestions for a Less Hostile Campus Climate," petition from BLSA at UCLA School of Law to Dean Rachel Moran, UCLA School of Law, Change.org, accessed Apr. 22, 2018, https://www.change.org/p/dean-rachel-moran-ucla-school-of-law-substantively-respond-to-blsa-s-suggestions-for-a-less-hostile-campus-climate-2.

8. Rachel Moran, "Initial Steps to Enhance Diversity and Inclusion in Our Community," email message to Classes of 2014, 2015, and 2016, Feb. 28, 2014.

9. Institute of Education Sciences, "The Nation's Report Card: Reading, 2013, State Snapshot Report, California Grade 8 Public Schools," accessed May 7, 2018, http://nces.ed.gov/nationsreportcard/subject/publications/stt2013/pdf/2014464CA8.pdf.

10. "Quick Facts About UCLA," UCLA Undergraduate Admission website, accessed Apr. 22, 2018, http://www.admissions.ucla.edu/campusprofile.htm.

11. UCLA Office of Media Relations, "Statement on Video by African American Student Group," UCLA Newsroom, Nov. 7, 2013, accessed Apr. 22, 2018, http://newsroom.ucla.edu/stories/statement-on-video-by-african-249314.

12. Gene D. Block, "The Impact of Proposition 209 and Our Duty to Our Students," UCLA Office of the Chancellor website, Feb. 24, 2014, accessed Apr. 22, 2018, https://chancellor.ucla.edu/messages/the-impact-of -proposition-209-and-our-duty-to-our-students/.

13. Sy Stokes guest appearance, NewsNation with Tamron Hall, Nov. 11, 2013, YouTube video, posted Nov. 11, 2013, accessed Apr. 22, 2018, http://www.youtube.com/watch?v=FpaZv-YM4kE.

Chapter Five: *Are We All Unconscious Racists?*

1. "Our Teams: Vice Chancellor's Team, Vice Chancellor for Equity, Diversity and Inclusion, Jerry Kang," UCLA website, accessed Apr. 23, 2018, https://equity.ucla.edu/about-us/our-teams/vice-chancellor/.

2. Frederich R. Lynch, "Why Trump Supporters Distrust Immigration and Diversity," op-ed, *New York Times,* Aug. 4, 2017, accessed Apr. 23, 2018, https://www.nytimes.com/2017/08/04/opinion/trump-supporters -immigration-diversity.html.

3. Joelle Emerson, interview, Aug. 14, 2017.

4. "Why Family Income Differences Don't Explain the Racial Gap in SAT Scores," *Journal of Blacks in Higher Education,* no. 20 (Summer 1998), 6, DOI: 10.2307/2999198. Accessed May 7, 2018, http://www.jstor.org/stable /2999198.

5. California Department of Education News Release, "Schools Chief Torlakson Reports Across-the-Board Progress Toward Career and College Readiness in CAASPP Results," Release: 16–57, Aug. 24, 2016, accessed Apr. 23, 2018, https://www.cde.ca.gov/nr/ne/yr16/yr16rel57.asp.

6. Roland G. Fryer, Jr. "An Empirical Analysis of Racial Differences in Police Use of Force," National Bureau of Economic Research Working Paper 22399, issued July 2016, revised Jan. 2018, accessed Apr. 23, 2018, http://www.nber.org/papers/w22399; Ted R. Miller, Bruce A. Lawrence, Nancy N. Carlson, Delia Hendrie, Sean Randall, Ian R. H. Rockett, and Rebecca S. Spicer, "Perils of Police Action: A Cautionary Tale from US Data Sets," Injury Prevention 23, no. 1 (June 16, 2016), accessed Apr. 23, 2018, http://injuryprevention.bmj.com/content/early/2016/06/16/injuryprev -2016-042023; Phillip Atiba Goff, Tracey Lloyd, Amanda Geller, Steven Raphael, and Jack Glaser, The Science of Justice: Race, Arrests, and Police Use of Force, Center for Policing Equity, UCLA (July 2016), accessed Apr. 23, 2018, http://policingequity.org/wp-content/uploads/2016/07/CPE

_SoJ_Race-Arrests-UoF_2016-07-08-1130.pdf; Lois James, Stephen M. James, and Bryan J. Vila, "The Reverse Racism Effect: Are Cops More Hesitant to Shoot Black Than White Suspects?" *Criminology & Public Policy* 15, no 2 (May 2016), 457–79, accessed Apr. 23, 2018, http://onlinelibrary.wiley.com/doi/10.1111/1745-9133.12187/abstract.

7. James P. O'Neill: Crime and Enforcement Activity in New York City, Jan. 1–December 31, 2016, NYPD Commissioner's report, accessed Apr. 23, 2018, http://www1.nyc.gov/assets/nypd/downloads/pdf/analysis _and_planning/year-end-2016-enforcement-report.pdf.

8. Federal Bureau of Investigation, "2015 Law Enforcement Officers Killed & Assaulted," Table 41: 2015 Law Enforcement Officers Feloniously Killed: Race and Sex of Known Offender, 2006–2015, accessed Apr. 23, 2018, https://ucr.fbi.gov/leoka/2015/tables/table_41_leos_fk_race_and_sex_of _known_offender_2006-2015.xls.

Chapter Six: *The Campus Rape Myth*

1. Kristi Tanner, "Database: 2016 FBI Crime Statistics by U.S. City," Detroit Free Press, Sept. 25, 2017, accessed Apr. 23, 2018, https://www .freep.com/story/news/2017/09/25/database-2016-fbi-crime-statistics-u-s -city/701445001/.

2. Claire Kaplan, interview, Oct. 30, 2007.

3. Bonnie S. Fisher, Francis T. Cullen, and Michael G. Turner, "The Sexual Victimization of College Women" (Washington, D.C.: U.S. Department of Justice, National Institute of Justice, Dec. 2000), accessed Apr. 23, 2018, https://www.ncjrs.gov/pdffiles1/nij/182369.pdf.

4. David Cantor, Bonnie Fisher, Susan Chibnall, Carol Bruce, Reanne Townsend, Gail Thomas, and Hyunshik Lee, "Report on the AAU Campus Climate Survey on Sexual Assault and Sexual Misconduct," report prepared for Harvard University (Rockville, MD: Westat, Sept. 21, 2015), accessed Apr. 28, 2018, http://sexualassaulttaskforce.harvard.edu/files/taskforce/files /final_report_harvard_9.21.15.pdf?m=1442784546.

5. Stanford University, "Safety, Security, and Fire Report," 2017 (Stanford, CA: Stanford University Department of Public Safety, 2017), accessed Apr. 25, 2018, https://police.stanford.edu/pdf/ssfr-2017.pdf.

6. Julie Shaw, "Suspect in Rape Case Cops a Plea," *Inquirer and Daily News,* June 29, 2007, accessed Apr. 23, 2018, http://www.philly.com/philly /hp/news_update/20070629_Suspect_in_rape_case_cops_a_plea.html.

7. Rebecca D. Robbins, "Students Call for Beefed Security After Reported Rapes," *Harvard Crimson*, Aug. 25, 2012, accessed Apr. 23, 2018, http://www.thecrimson.com/article/2012/8/25/students-security-after-rapes/.

8. T. Rees Shapiro and Nick Anderson, "U-Va. Seeks to Cope with Trauma after Sophomore Hannah Graham Vanished," *Washington Post*, Oct. 4, 2014, accessed Apr. 23, 2018, http://www.washingtonpost.com/local/education/u-va-seeks-to-cope-with-trauma-after-sophomore-hannah-graham-vanished/2014/10/04/4f5adcb4-4a80-11e4-891d-713f052086a0_story.html.

9. Carole T. Goldberg, "Confronting Sexual Assault," *Yale Health Care* 10, no. 2, (March/Apr. 2007), 4, accessed Apr. 25, 2018, https://yalehealth.yale.edu/resources/yale-health-care-newsletter.

10. Brett A. Sokolow, "Who's Helping Whom: Are Our Sexual Assault Response Protocols Working?" *Campus Safety & Student Development* 4, no. 5 (May/June 2003), 657–70, accessed May 7, 2018, http://www.civicresearchinstitute.com/online/article_abstract.php?pid=11&iid=395&aid=2621.

11. Elizabeth Bartholet, Nancy Gertner, Janet Halley, and Jeannie Suk Gersen, "Fairness for All Students Under Title IX," Harvard Law School, Digital Access to Scholarship at Harvard, Aug. 21, 2017, accessed Apr. 23, 2018, http://nrs.harvard.edu/urn-3:HUL.InstRepos:33789434.

12. Janet Halley, "Trading the Megaphone for the Gavel in Title IX Enforcement," *Harvard Law Review* 128 (Feb. 18, 2015), accessed May 7, 2018, https://harvardlawreview.org/2015/02/trading-the-megaphone-for-the-gavel-in-title-ix-enforcement-2/.

13. Interview with Columbia University security official, Oct. 26, 2007.

14. Memorandum Opinion by Judge Norman K. Moon, John Doe v. Washington and Lee University, 6:14-cv-00052, U.S. District Court for the Western District of Virginia, Lynchburg Division (2015), accessed on May 7, 2018, https://law.justia.com/cases/federal/district-courts/virginia/vawdce/6:2014cv00052/96678/54/.

15. Brett A. Sokolow, Esq. and NCHERM Group Partners, An Open Letter to Higher Education about Sexual Violence, May 27, 2014.

16. Jeremy Bauer-Wolf, "Student Accused of Sexual Assault Wins Big in Court," *Inside Higher Ed*, Feb. 13, 2018, accessed Apr. 23, 2018, https://www.insidehighered.com/quicktakes/2018/02/13/student-accused-sexual-assault-wins-big-court.

17. Alan Charles Kors, interview, Oct. 26, 2007.

18. Alan D. Berkowitz, "Guidelines for Consent in Intimate Relationships," *Campus Safety & Student Development* 4, no. 3, (March/Apr. 2002), 49–50, accessed Apr. 23, 2018, http://www.alanberkowitz.com/articles/consent.pdf.

19. B well Health Promotion, Sex 101, "Sex Toys," Brown University, accessed Apr. 23, 2018, https://www.brown.edu/campus-life/health/services/promotion/sexual-health-sex-101/sex-toys.

20. Tumblr page for Oberlin Sexual Information Center, accessed Apr. 23, 2018, http://oberlinsic.tumblr.com/post/76579281747/is-the-sex-toy-sale-happening-this-semester.

21. Harvard Sex Week, "Sex Week 2017," Harvard University, accessed Apr. 23, 2018, https://www.harvardsexweek.org/sex-week-2017/.

22. Go Ask Alice!, Columbia University website, accessed Apr. 23, 2018, http://goaskalice.columbia.edu/answered-questions/im-sure-i-was-drunk-im-not-sure-if-i-had-sex.

23. Interview with Rutgers University freshman, Nov. 7, 2007.

Chapter Seven: *Neo-Victorianism on Campus*

1. Tovia Smith, "A Campus Dilemma: Sure, 'No' Means 'No,' but Exactly What Means 'Yes'?" *All Things Considered*, NPR, June 13, 2014, accessed Apr. 23, 2018, https://www.npr.org/2014/06/13/321677110/a-campus-dilemma-sure-no-means-no-but-exactly-what-means-yes.

2. "Move the 'Sleepwalker' Inside the Davis Museum," petition from Wellesley student to Wellesley president, Change.org, accessed Apr. 23, 2018, https://www.change.org/p/president-h-kim-bottomly-move-the-sleepwalker-inside-the-davis-museum.

3. OSU Marching Band Culture Task Force, "OSU Marching Band Cultural Assessment and Administrative Oversight Review," Nov. 18, 2014, accessed Apr. 23, 2018, https://www.osu.edu/assets/pdf/Task%20Force%20Report%20Final.pdf.

4. Michael Kimmel and Gloria Steinem, "'Yes' Is Better Than 'No,'" op-ed, *New York Times*, Sept. 4, 2014, accessed Apr. 23, 2018, https://www.nytimes.com/2014/09/05/opinion/michael-kimmel-and-gloria-steinem-on-consensual-sex-on-campus.html.

5. Exhibit 4, screen shots of text messages submitted as evidence in John Doe v. Occidental College, accessed Apr. 23, 2018, https://d28htnjz2elwuj

.cloudfront.net/wp-content/uploads/2014/06/John-Doe-Full-Lawsuit
-against-Occidental-Part-2.pdf.

6. John Doe v. Occidental College, Los Angeles County Superior Court,
Feb. 13, 2014, accessed Apr. 23, 2018, https://d28htnjz2elwuj.cloudfront
.net/wp-content/uploads/2014/02/John-Doe-Full-Lawsuit-against
-Occidental-Part-1_Redacted.pdf.

7. Jeffrey Rosen, "Ruth Bader Ginsburg Opens Up About #MeToo, Voting
Rights, and Millennials," *Atlantic,* Feb. 15, 2018, accessed Apr. 23, 2018,
https://www.theatlantic.com/politics/archive/2018/02/ruth-bader-ginsburg
-opens-up-about-metoo-voting-rights-and-millenials/553409/.

Chapter Eight: *The Fainting Couch at Columbia*

1. *Columbia University Sexual Respect* website, accessed Apr. 23, 2018,
https://sexualrespect.columbia.edu/2017-18-sexual-respect-and-community
-citizenship-initiative.

2. Email message to author, July 7, 2015.

3. Paul Nungesser complaint filed against Columbia University trustees
Lee C. Bollinger and Jon Kessler, 15 CV 03216, United States District
Court, Southern District of New York, Apr. 29, 2015), accessed Apr. 23,
2018, https://www.scribd.com/doc/262956362/Nungesser-Filed-Complaint.

Chapter Nine: *Policing Sexual Desire: The #MeToo Movement's Impossible Premise*

1. Alexa Valiente and Angela Williams, "Matt Damon Opens Up about
Harvey Weinstein, Sexual Harassment and Confidentiality Agreements,"
ABC News, Dec. 14, 2017, accessed Apr. 23, 2018, https://abcnews.go.com
/Entertainment/matt-damon-opens-harvey-weinstein-sexual-harassment
-confidentiality/story?id=51792548.

2. Jessica Bennett, "When Saying 'Yes' Is Easier Than Saying 'No,'" *New
York Times* Sunday Review, Dec. 16, 2017, accessed Apr. 23, 2018,
https://www.nytimes.com/2017/12/16/sunday-review/when-saying-yes-is
-easier-than-saying-no.html?rref=collection%2Fsectioncollection%2Fsund
ay&action=click&contentCollection=sunday&region=stream&module
=stream_unit&version=latest&contentPlacement=7&pgtype
=sectionfront.

3. Jacob Bernstein, Matthew Schneiner, and Vanessa Friedman, "Male
Models Say Mario Testino and Bruce Weber Sexually Exploited Them,"

New York Times, Jan. 13, 2018, accessed Apr. 23, 2018, https://www
.nytimes.com/2018/01/13/style/mario-testino-bruce-weber-harassment
.html.

4. Bonnie Wertheim, "The #MeToo Moment: Covering 'The New Red
Carpet,'" *New York Times,* Jan. 6, 2018, accessed on April 23, 2018, https://
www.nytimes.com/2018/01/06/us/the-metoo-moment-covering-the-new
-red-carpet.html.

5. Jim Fusilli, "The Grammys' Boys' Club," *Wall Street Journal,* Jan. 23,
2018, accessed Apr. 23, 2018, https://www.wsj.com/articles/the-grammys
-boys-club-1516745617.

6. Julia Reiss, "Six Female Music Executives Respond to Neil Portnow
with Letter to Recording Academy," *Complex,* Feb. 5, 2018, accessed
Apr. 23, 2018, http://www.complex.com/music/2018/02/six-female
-music-executives-respond-neil-portnow-with-letter-to-recording
-academy.

7. Joelle Emerson, email message to author, Jan. 21, 2018.

8. Carolina A. Miranda, "What the Sexual Harassment Allegations at
Artforum Reveal about Who Holds the Power in Art (Hint: Not
Women)," *Los Angeles Times,* Nov. 1, 2017, accessed Apr. 23, 2018, http://
www.latimes.com/entertainment/arts/miranda/la-et-cam-knight
-landesman-artforum-20171101-htmlstory.html.

9. Robin Pogrebin and Jennifer Schuessler, "Chuck Close Is Accused of
Harassment. Should His Artwork Carry an Asterisk?" *New York Times,*
Jan. 28, 2018, accessed Apr. 23, 2018, https://www.nytimes.com/2018/01
/28/arts/design/chuck-close-exhibit-harassment-accusations.html.

10. Interview with orchestra conductor's agent, Nov. 28, 2017.

11. Deirdre McCloskey, email to author, January 24, 2018.

12. James Damore and David Gudeman v. Google LLC, 18CV321529,
Class Action Complaint, filed Jan. 8, 2018, Superior Court of
California, County of Santa Clara, accessed Apr. 23, 2018, https://www
.scribd.com/document/368694136/James-Damore-vs-Google-class
-action-lawsuit.

13. Editorial Board, "The Quest for Transgender Equality," *New York
Times* Opinion Section, May 4, 2015, accessed Apr. 23, 2018, https://www
.nytimes.com/2015/05/04/opinion/the-quest-for-transgender-equality
.html.

Chapter Ten: *Multiculti U.*

1. "President Clark Kerr, a National Leader in Higher Education, Dies at 92," press release, *UCBerkeleyNews,* Dec. 2, 2003, accessed Apr. 23, 2018, https://www.berkeley.edu/news/media/releases/2003/12/02_kerr.shtml.

2. Kassy Cho, "Assistant Dean for Campus Climate Selected," *Daily Bruin,* May 10, 2011, accessed Apr. 23, 2018, http://dailybruin.com/2011/05/10 /assistant_dean_for_campus_climate_selected/.

3. Lisa Cisneros, "UCSF Appoints First-Ever Vice Chancellor for Diversity, Outreach," *UCSF News Center,* Dec. 2, 2010, accessed Apr. 23, 2018, https://www.ucsf.edu/news/2010/12/5854/ucsf-appoints-first-ever -vice-chancellor-diversity-outreach.

4. "UCLA's Core Mission can Be Expressed in Just Three Words: Education, Research, Service," *UCLA Mission and Values,* accessed Apr. 23, 2018, http://www.ucla.edu/about/mission-and-values.

5. Interview with electrical and computer engineering professor, July 27, 2012.

6. Maria Herrera Sobek, interview, July 18, 2012.

7. "Astrophysics Jobs Rumor Mill—Faculty & Staff," *AstroBetter,* accessed Apr. 23, 2018, http://www.astrobetter.com/wiki/Rumor+Mill+2012 -2013+Faculty-Staff.

8. "UC Advisory Council on Campus Climate, Culture and Inclusion named," press release, University of California Office of the President, June 16, 2010, accessed Apr. 23, 2018, http://www.fresno.ucsf.edu /newsroom/newsreleases/2010-6-16Flores.pdf.

9. University of California, Diversity Annual Accountability Sub-Report, September 2010, accessed May 7, 2018, https://www.ucop.edu/graduate -studies/_files/diversity_subreport_2010.pdf.

10. Berkeley Academic Guide, American Cultures Requirement, accessed Apr. 23, 2018, http://guide.berkeley.edu/undergraduate/colleges-schools /engineering/american-cultures-requirement/.

11. UC Berkeley Spring 2016 course: Gender and Women's Studies 130AC—Gender, Race, Nation, and Health, accessed Apr. 23, 2018, https://ninjacourses.com/explore/1/course/GWS/130AC/.

12. "College Faculty Vote Down Community and Conflict General Education Requirement," *UCLA Today,* June 1, 2012, accessed Apr. 28, 2018, http:// newsroom.ucla.edu/stories/college-faculty-vote-down-community-234674.

13. Phil Hampton, "Faculty Approve Undergraduate Diversity Requirement for UCLA College," *UCLA Newsroom*, Apr. 10, 2015, accessed Apr. 23, 2018, http://newsroom.ucla.edu/releases/faculty-approve -undergraduate-diversity-requirement-for-ucla-college.

14. University Committee on Planning and Budget, The Choices Report (Oakland: Systemwide Academic Senate of the University of California, March 2010), accessed Apr. 23, 2018, http://gsa.ucsd.edu/sites/gsa.ucsd.edu /files/SW%20UCPB%20Choices%20Rpt%20Apr%202010.pdf.

15. UC Newsroom, "How UC Serves Low Income Students," Jan. 29, 2014, accessed Apr. 23, 2018, https://www.universityofcalifornia.edu/news /how-uc-serves-low-income-students.

16. Berkeley Financial Aid & Scholarships website, Blue and Gold Opportunity Plan, accessed Apr. 23, 2018, https://financialaid.berkeley.edu /blue-and-gold-opportunity-plan.

Chapter Eleven: *How Identity Politics is Harming the Sciences*

1. UCLA scientist, email message to author, Jan. 16, 2018.

2. "Advance Partnership: Faculty Intervention Guide and Decision Tool for Improving the Academic Workplace," award abstract 1726351, accessed Apr. 24, 2018, https://www.nsf.gov/awardsearch/showAward?AWD_ID =1726351&HistoricalAwards=false; National Science Foundation, "IUSE/ PFE: RED: REvolutionizing Diversity Of Engineering (REDO-E)," award abstract 1730693, accessed Apr. 24, 2018, https://www.nsf.gov/awardsearch /showAward?AWD_ID=1730693&HistoricalAwards=false.

3. Stuart H. Hurlbert, "Politicized External Review Panels as Unguided 'Diversity' Missiles: California University Administrators Remain Ultra-slow Learners," Center for Equal Opportunity, Sept. 13, 2017, accessed Apr. 23, 2018, http://www.ceousa.org/about-ceo/docs/1140-politicized-external -review-panels-as-unguided-diversity-missiles.

4. Sharon Zhen, "Engineering School Introduces Associate Dean of Diversity and Inclusion," *Daily Bruin*, Sept. 17, 2017, accessed Apr. 24, 2018, http://dailybruin.com/2017/09/17/engineering-school-introduces -associate-dean-of-diversity-and-inclusion/.

5. Association of American Colleges & Universities, "Teaching to Increase Diversity and Equity in STEM (TIDES)," accessed Apr. 24, 2018, https://www.aacu.org/sites/default/files/files/LEAP/LEAPChallenge TIDES.pdf.

6. James Damore and David Gudeman v. Google LLC, 18CV321529, Superior Court of California, County of Santa Clara, accessed Apr. 24, 2018, https://www.scribd.com/document/368694136/James-Damore-vs -Google-class-action-lawsuit.

7. Physician-scientist, email message to author, February 4, 2018.

Chapter Twelve: *Scandal Erupts Over the Promotion of Bourgeois Behavior*

1. Dan Spinelli, "'Not All Cultures Are Created Equal,' Says Penn Law Professor in Op-Ed," *Daily Pennsylvanian*, Aug. 10, 2017, accessed Apr. 24, 2018, http://www.thedp.com/article/2017/08/amy-wax-penn-law-cultural -values.

2. Ted Ruger, "On Charlottesville, Free Speech, and Diversity," *Daily Pennsylvanian*, Aug. 14, 2017, accessed Apr. 24, 2018, http://www.thedp .com/article/2017/08/guest-column-dean-ted-ruger-penn-law -charlottesville-amy-wax.

3. 33 Penn Law Faculty Members, "Open Letter to the University of Pennsylvania Community," *Daily Pennsylvanian*, Aug. 30, 2017, accessed Apr. 24, 2018, http://www.thedp.com/article/2017/08/open-letter-penn-law -faculty.

4. Stephen Ferruolo, email, "To the USD School of Law Community," Sept. 12, 2017.

Chapter Thirteen: *The Humanities and Us*

1. *The Memoirs of Hector Berlioz*, trans. and ed. David Cairns, (New York: Alfred A. Knopf/Everyman's Library, 2002), 70, 72.

2. *The Collected Essays of Ralph Ellison*, rev. and updated, ed. and with an introduction by John F. Callahan (New York: Modern Library, 2003), 164.

3. Jacques Derrida, *Of Grammatology*, trans. Gayatri Chakravorty Spivak (Baltimore and London: Johns Hopkins University Press, 1976), 109.

4. Homi K. Bhabha, ed., *Nation and Narration* (New York: Routledge, 1990), 3.

Chapter Fourteen: *Great Courses, Great Profits*

1. Bard College Catalogue 2017–2018, pages 165, 169, 170, accessed Apr. 24, 2018, http://www.bard.edu/catalogue/index.php?aid =1204742&sid=670341pp.

2. Tom Rollins, interview, May 18, 2011.

3. Wesleyan University Catalog 2017–2018, https://iasext.wesleyan.edu /regprod/!wesmaps_page.html?stuid=&facid=NONE&crse=013261 &term=1179.

4. Bowdoin College's class schedule for "Renaissance Sexualities," https:// www.bowdoin.edu/register/course-information/course-info/Spring/ sched-s17.pdf.

5. Allen Guelzo, email message, Apr. 21, 2011.

6. Robert Greenberg, "Great Masters: Robert and Clara Schumann—Their Lives and Music," Great Courses, accessed Apr. 23, 2018, https://www .thegreatcourses.com/courses/great-masters-robert-and-clara-schumann -their-lives-and-music.html. Robert Greenberg, "Great Masters: Brahms— His Life and Music," Great Courses, accessed Apr. 24, 2018, https://www .thegreatcourses.com/courses/great-masters-brahms-his-life-and-music .html.

7. Robert Greenberg, "Great Masters: Brahms."

8. Alan Kors, interview, Apr. 29, 2011.

9. Patrick Allitt, interview, Apr. 28, 2011.

10. Eric Reiter, interview, May 17, 2011.

Chapter Fifteen: *The True Purpose of the University*

1. Peter Salovey, "Countering False Narratives," *Yale Alumni Magazine,* Aug. 27, 2016, accessed Apr. 24, 2018, https://yalealumnimagazine.com /articles/4394-countering-false-narratives.

2. David Shimer, "Admins Speak Out on Racial Tensions," *Yale Daily News,* Nov. 6, 2015, accessed Apr. 24, 2018, https://yaledailynews.com /blog/2015/11/06/holloways-email-addresses-campus-controversies/.

3. Salovey, "Countering False Narratives."

4. Robert P. George, "Why I Wanted to Debate Peter Singer," op-ed, *Wall Street Journal,* Dec. 18, 2016, accessed Apr. 24, 2018, https://www.wsj.com /articles/why-i-wanted-to-debate-peter-singer-1482098245.

INDEX

The Abduction from the Seraglio (Mozart), 216
Above the Law (blog), 72–74
achievement gaps
  for African Americans, 80–81
  in California, 78
  in diversity, 98–99
  in higher education, 198–99
  politics of, 49, 61
  psychology of, 101–2
  for students, 40–47
administration
  at Claremont McKenna College, 14, 16–17
  faculty and, 33, 39
  free speech for, 205–6
  goals for, 26–27, 43–44
  microaggressions for, 68–70, 76–78
  at Middlebury College, 17
  politics for, 16–17, 23–24, 82, 139–40
  at Princeton University, 2
  psychology of, 121
  for safe spaces, 150
  students and, 23–25, 238, 246–47
  at UC, 35
  at UC Davis, 47
  for UC system, 171–72
  at UCLA, 14
  victimology for, 11, 73–75, 241–42
  at Yale University, 237–42

admissions
  affirmative action in, 53–61
  diversity in, 39–40
  GRE in, 194
  identity politics in, 194
  for law school, 41, 58–59
  lotteries for, 46–47
  for minorities, 37–41
  racism in, 40, 44–46
  SAT scores in, 37–38, 40–43
  for UC system, 51–52
affirmative action. *See* Proposition 209
African Americans. *See also* Black Lives Matter; minorities
  achievement gaps for, 80–81
  Asians compared to, 107–8
  Black Law Students Association for, 74–76
  campus for, 61
  Caucasians compared to, 54, 110–12
  in higher education, 180–81
  Hispanics compared to, 39–48, 75–77
  law school for, 101
  in UC system, 78
Agness, Karin, 125
Alexander, Larry, 201–7, 246
Allen, Woody, 5
Allitt, Patrick, 233, 235
alumni, 24, 55–56
anarchy, 21–22

Arcidiacono, Peter, 54, 58
Asians. *See also* minorities
  African Americans compared to, 107–8
  Caucasians compared to, 77–78, 95, 177
  racism and, 44–45, 64–65
  stereotypes for, 51
athletics, 22–24
Atkinson, Richard, 43–44
Aucejo, Esteban, 54, 58

Banaji, Mahzarin, 88–94, 107
Bannon, Steve, 16–17
Barlowe, Alexandra Zina, 25
Bartholet, Elizabeth, 124
Bawer, Bruce, 4
behavioral realism, 90–94, 98–99, 107–8
Bennett, Jessica, 156, 158–59
Berdahl, Robert, 39
Berkowitz, Alan D., 132
Berlioz, Hector, 212–13
Bhabha, Homi, 220
Birgeneau, Robert, 35, 50
Black Law Students Association, 74–76
Black Lives Matter, 9–13, 104, 106,
  109–10, 238
Blacks. *See* African Americans; minorities
Blasio, Bill de, 161
Blink (Gladwell), 89–90
Block, Gene, 79–80, 181–82
Blocker, Déborah, 22
Bok, Derek, 57
Bolus, Roger, 59
Book of the Courtier (Castiglione), 152
bourgeois class, 201–7
Bowen, William, 57
Boyle, Susan, 104
Bracciolini, Poggio, 214, 221
Brahms, Johannes, 232
Brentwood Associates, 234–35
Britain's Got Talent (TV show), 104
Brown, Jerry, 179, 183
Brown, John, 19
Brown, Michael (Ferguson, MO), 82
Brown, Michael (UC System), 51–52
Brown, Sandra, 104–7
Brown, Willie, 35–36

Brown University, 2–3, 133–34
Brownmiller, Susan, 124
Busch, Andrew, 14

California. *See also* Proposition 209; UC
  System; *specific schools*
  achievement gaps in, 78
  discrimination in, 108–13
  economics of, 179
  goals in, 99–100
  higher education in, 40–48
  law school in, 185
  minorities in, 51
  Oakland in, 108–13
  policy in, 142–43, 166, 183
  politics in, 35–38, 140–41
Campbell, Kashawn, 59–61
campus. *See also* higher education
  for African Americans, 61
  free speech on, 16–17, 29
  ideology of, 243–47
  neo-victorianism on, 139–47
  politics on, 149–54
  protests on, 1–4, 204–5
  racism on, 239
  risk management for, 131–37
  victimology on, 131
  violence on, 12, 14, 81–82, 121–22
campus rape. *See* rape
Carby, Hazel, 241
Cardozo, Benjamin, 243–44, 247
Castiglione, Baldassare, 152
Caucasians, 54, 77–78, 95, 110–12, 177
Cech, Erin, 193
CEO Action for Diversity and Inclusion,
  97–98, 102
Chodosh, Hiram, 14, 16
Chomsky, Noam, 234
Christakis, Erika, 24–26, 239
Christakis, Nicholas, 238–39
The Chronicle of Higher Education, 231
Cisco, 97–98
Citrin, Jack, 43–44, 46–47
Civil Rights Commission, 94–95
C.K., Louis, 158
Claremont colleges. *See specific colleges*

Claremont McKenna College, 9–12, 14, 16–17, 140–41
Clery Act, 122–23, 128–30
Clinton, Hillary, 89
Clydesdale, Timothy, 49–50
"The Coddling of the American Mind" (Lukianoff/Haidt), 28–29
Collins-Eaglin, Jan, 11
Columbia University
    faculty at, 225–26, 231
    ideology at, 134–35
    mattress girl at, 153–54
    policy at, 149–54
    students at, 29, 215–16
Comey, James, 89
The Communist Manifesto (Engels/Marx), 26
companies, 31–32
comprehensive review, 43, 45
Connerly, Ward, 35, 37, 185
consent policy, 140–42, 147
Correll, Joshua, 102–3, 106
critical race theory, 66–67, 89–90
critical thinking, 219–20, 241
cultural bias, 99–100
curriculum, 1–2, 180–87

Damon, Matt, 155–56
Damore, James, 30–32, 164, 197–98
Dauber, Michele Landis, 49
Day of Action Statements, 65–67
Delacroix, Eugène, 213
Denby, David, 215–16
Department of Education, 142
Derrida, Jacques, 5, 168
Desmond-Hellmann, Susan, 175
DeVos, Betsy, 124
Dhanatya, Cathryn, 64
Dialogues (Plato), 223
DiSciullo, Megan, 97–98
discrimination
    behavioral realism in, 91–92
    in California, 108–13
    implicit bias in, 96–104
    in labor markets, 98–99
    for media, 89–90
    policy for, 37, 40, 168, 238–39

    politics of, 94
    poverty and, 41
    psychology of, 32–33, 93
    racism and, 36–37, 242
    science and, 30–31, 88–89
    at UC, 44
    at UCLA, 44–45
diversity
    achievement gaps in, 98–99
    in admissions, 39–40
    CEO Action for Diversity and Inclusion, 97–98, 102
    Civil Rights Commission for, 94–95
    for companies, 31–32
    at Duke University, 53–59
    economics of, 94–95, 102–3, 190–91, 238, 245
    faculty for, 15, 18
    free speech and, 15–16
    goals for, 96
    for Google, 95, 100
    "Google's Ideological Echo Chamber" (Damore), 30–31
    in higher education, 6, 80, 189–90
    identity politics and, 2–3
    ideology of, 27, 38–39
    for Labor Department (US), 30–31
    in labor markets, 37, 94–95, 102
    for LGBTQ community, 193
    merit compared to, 46
    for minorities, 23, 59
    NAACP for, 44
    for NLRB, 32
    as policy, 35–36, 56–58, 163, 174, 176, 186, 232
    politics of, 178, 245–46
    PricewaterhouseCoopers for, 97–98
    Proposition 209 for, 35–40
    at Stanford University, 164
    STEM fields and, 195–99
    at UC, 245
    at UCLA, 181–82
    at UCSB, 179
    UN for, 37
    webinars for, 196
    at Yale University, 195

Don Giovanni (Mozart), 152
Douglass, Frederick, 1, 19
Dow Jones, 164
Du Bois, W. E. B., 1
Duberman, Martin, 167
Duke University, 53–59, 125
Dumas, Alexandre, 213
Dutoit, Charles, 162

Eberhardt, Jennifer, 104–5, 108–13
Eccles, Tom, 162
economics
    behavioral realism in, 98–99
    California, 179
    of diversity, 94–95, 102–3, 190–91,
        238, 245
    for faculty, 218–19
    of feminism, 162
    of Great Courses, 225–26, 234–36
    of higher education, 185–86, 236
    of #MeToo movement, 163–64
    of rape, 131
    of social justice, 184
    stereotypes and, 93
    for students, 224
    of systematic oppression, 37
    UC, 171–72
    UC system, 174
education. *See* higher education
Eliot, George, 213
Ellison, Ralph, 216
Emerson, Joelle, 98, 161
Emory University, 26–28
Engles, Richard, 26
Erdely, Sabrina Rubin, 138
Evergreen State College, 3–4

Facebook, 75
faculty
    administration and, 33, 39
    at Columbia University, 225–26, 231
    for diversity, 15, 18
    economics for, 218–19
    free speech for, 80–81
    for Great Courses, 231–34
    in higher education, 43, 68–69

humanities for, 230–31
ideology and, 213–14, 219–20
morality for, 225
politics for, 16, 18–19, 57
social justice for, 83–85
at UC, 22
at University of Chicago, 16–17
victimology for, 9
The Faerie Queen (Spenser), 152
false narratives, 240–42
Farrar, Geraldine, 159
fascism, 15–16
feminism. *See also* #MeToo movement
    economics of, 162
    gender in, 156–57
    goals for, 159–60
    at Harvard University, 118
    in higher education, 5, 140, 163,
        228–29
    in media, 119, 158–59
    #MeToo movement for, 155–58
    microaggressions for, 142–43
    policy for, 139
    politics of, 117, 123, 130–31, 135, 141,
        145, 152–53
    psychology of, 122
    in science, 164–66
    *SLUT: A Play and Guidebook for
        Combating Sexism* (book) for, 149
    social justice for, 158–59
    Title IX for, 126–28
Ferruolo, Stephen, 206
Ficino, Marsilio, 221
Fox, Charles James, 1
free speech
    for administration, 205–6
    on campus, 16–17, 29
    diversity and, 15–16
    for faculty, 80–81
    at Google, 197–98
    hate speech and, 201–7
    Heterodox Academy for, 16
    in higher education, 87, 219–21, 223,
        226–27
    for LGBTQ community, 150
    politics of, 77–78, 202–3, 243–47

as protests, 19
Silencing the Past (book), 241
for students, 27
for Trump, 20–21
at UC, 173–74, 243–47
Fridell, Lori, 104
Fryer, Roland, 103
Fucaloro, Anthony, 11
Fusilli, Jim, 160

Gardner, Alexis Morgan, 74–75
Gargantua (Rabelais), 215
Gatzert, Bene, 245–46
Gautier, Théophile, 213
gender. *See also* LGBTQ community;
    neo-Victorianism
  in feminism, 156–57
  goals for, 199
  in higher education, 166–68, 211, 213
  in identity politics, 174
  identity politics in, 152–53
  ideology of, 165–66
  in media, 158–60
  politics of, 84–85, 142–44, 162–63,
      197–98, 216
  in SAT scores, 163–64, 199
  in science, 193
  in US, 180–81
George, Robert, 241–42
Georgetown University, 225–26
Gersen, Jeannie Suk, 124
Gertner, Nancy, 124
Gettysburg College, 231
Gilbert, Neil, 119–20
Ginsburg, Ruth Bader, 145, 167
Gladwell, Malcolm, 89–90
Glazer, Nathan, 173
Glegg, Roger, 94–95
Glick, Steven, 11
Go Ask Alice!, 134–35
goals
  administration, 26–27, 43–44
  in California, 99–100
  for diversity, 96
  feminist empowerment, 159–60
  gender parity, 199

higher education, 27–28, 33, 50–52, 54
  for identity politics, 195–96
  for minorities, 182–83
  multiculturalism, 180–86
  psychology of, 61
  for SAT scores, 100–101
  for students, 47–48
  UC system, 172–73
Google, 30–32, 95, 100, 164, 197–98
"Google's Ideological Echo Chamber"
    (Damore), 30–31
Graduate Record Exam (GRE), 194
Great Courses
  economics of, 225–26, 234–36
  faculty for, 231–34
  in higher education, 225–29
  ideology of, 223–25, 228–29
  politics of, 229–31
Greenburg, Robert, 231–32, 234
Greenwald, Anthony, 88–94, 98, 101–2,
    107
Greenwell, Joseph, 246–47
Guelzo, Allen, 231, 233

Haidt, Jonathan, 28–29, 206
Haight, Henry, 172
Halley, Janet, 124–25
Hamer, Fannie Lou, 2
Harvard University
  feminism at, 118
  law enforcement at, 128–29
  law school, 123–24
  policy at, 142
  politics at, 120
  protests at, 81
  *Saturday Night: Untold Stories of Sexual
      Assault at Harvard* (magazine),
      126–27
  students at, 220
hate speech, 201–7
Hayashi, Patrick, 41–42, 51
Heldman, Caroline, 146
Henderson, Thelton, 36
Heterodox Academy, 16n
Hewlett Packard, 97–98
Higdon, Jennifer, 163

higher education
  achievement gaps in, 198–99
  affirmative action in, 95
  African Americans in, 180–81
  alumni and, 24
  in California, 40–48
  The Chronicle of Higher Education, 231
  Clery Act in, 122–23, 128–30
  diversity in, 6, 80, 189–90
  economics of, 185–86, 236
  faculty in, 43, 68–69
  feminism in, 5, 140, 163, 228–29
  free speech in, 87, 219–21, 223,
    226–27
  gender in, 166–68, 211, 213
  goals of, 27–28, 33, 50–52, 54
  GRE for, 194
  Great Courses in, 225–29
  Hispanics in, 64–65, 195–96, 245–47
  humanities in, 213–14, 218–21, 240
  ideology and, 2, 17–18, 151, 172–73,
    215–16, 234–36, 237–42
  leadership in, 50–51, 59
  #MeToo movement in, 166–68
  multiculturalism in, 5, 171–80, 187
  policy in, 42
  politics in, 217, 231–32
  poverty in, 48, 99–100
  Proposition 209 in, 40–48, 51–52
  punishments in, 17
  racism in, 95–96, 100–102, 211,
    215–16
  rape in, 120–24, 130–31
  safe spaces in, 28–29
  science in, 5–6, 60–61
  social justice in, 207
  social media and, 11
  Society of Comparative and
    International Education for, 63–64
  STEM fields in, 164–66, 190–93
  systematic oppression in, 78–79
  victimology in, 63–64, 201–7
Hispanics, 39–48, 64–65, 75–77, 195–96,
  245–47. *See also* minorities
Hodges, Jaret, 199
Holloway, Karla, 55

Hollywood, 95, 155–56, 158–61
Holmes, Oliver Wendell, 243–44, 247
Holt, Lester, 89
Houston Baptist University, 226
Hugo, Victor, 213
humanities
  for faculty, 230–31
  in higher education, 213–14, 218–21,
    240
  ideology of, 211–15
  for LGBTQ community, 229–30
  politics of, 215–17
  science compared to, 55–56
  in US, 217–19
Hume, David, 76

IAT. *See* Implicit Association Test
identity politics, 57–58
  in admissions, 194
  diversity and, 2–3
  in gender, 152–53
  gender in, 174
  goals for, 195–96
  ideology of, 79–81, 189–90
  in science, 190–93, 195–99
  as social justice, 164–66
  in US, 199–200
  victimology and, 4–5
ideology
  of affirmative action, 39–48
  of behavioral realism, 90, 107–8
  of Black Lives Matter, 9–13
  of campus, 243–47
  at Columbia University, 134–35
  of comprehensive review, 45
  of cultural bias, 99–100
  of diversity, 27, 38–39
  faculty and, 213–14, 219–20
  of fascism, 15–16
  of gender, 165–66
  "Google's Ideological Echo Chamber"
    (Damore), 30–31
  of Great Courses, 223–25, 228–29
  higher education and, 2, 17–18, 151,
    172–73, 215–16, 234–36, 237–42
  of humanities, 211–15

of IAT, 103–4, 107
of identity politics, 79–81, 189–90
of merit, 42–43
of #MeToo movement, 155–58, 160–63
of microaggressions, 63–65, 78–81
of multiculturalism, 202
politics of, 18, 239–40
of Proposition 209, 36
of protests, 15
of racism, 87–91
of safe spaces, 18–19
of social justice, 70–71
of stereotypes, 57
of systematic oppression, 22–23, 69–70,
    245–46
of victimology, 29–30, 33
immigrants, 13
Implicit Association Test (IAT), 88–94,
    103–4, 107
implicit bias
    in discrimination, 96–104
    in law enforcement, 108–13
    psychology of, 87–94, 104–8

Jaccard, James, 92
Jackson, Jesse, 2
James, Lois, 103
Johnson, Chip, 111
Johnson, K.C., 124

Kahneman, Daniel, 98
Kang, Jerry, 89–91, 96, 107, 182
Kay, Herma Hill, 39–40
Kennedy, Ted, 224
Kerr, Clark, 173–74
Khosla, Pradeep, 183–84
Kimball, Roger, 4
Klein, Dianne, 178–79
Kors, Alan, 233
Koss, Mary, 119–20

Labor and Human Services Committee, 224
Labor Department (US), 30–31
labor markets
    CEO Action for Diversity and
        Inclusion in, 97–98, 102

discrimination in, 98–99
diversity in, 37, 94–95, 102
#MeToo movement in, 163–66
minorities in, 30–32, 98
LaFosse, Alyssa, 133
Lai, Calvin, 94
Laird, Robert, 37–38
Lange, Peter, 56–57
Lau, Kimberly C., 155
Lauer, Matt, 157
law enforcement
    affirmative action in, 96
    at Harvard University, 128–29
    implicit bias in, 108–13
    #MeToo movement for, 158–59
    protests against, 9–16
    racism in, 82, 89, 96, 102–13
    stereotypes in, 105–6
    violence and, 102–4, 113, 120–21
law school
    admissions, 41, 58–59
    affirmative action in, 48–52
    for African Americans, 101
    Bar exam, 48–49
    in California, 185
    at Harvard University, 123–24
    policy in, 243–47
    Proposition 209 for, 48–51
    at UC, 39, 46
    at UCLA, 39, 41, 71–80, 90–91
    at University of Pennsylvania, 201–7
leadership, 50–51, 59, 70–71
lectures, 14–16
Lee, Tyshawn, 12
Lehmann, Lotte, 159
Lerer, Seth, 234–35
Levine, James, 162
Lewis, C. S., 226
LGBTQ community, 150, 160–67, 193,
    195, 229–30
Lisak, David, 125, 136
Liu, Goodwin, 49
Lockyer, Bill, 37
The Los Angeles Times, 59–61
Lukianoff, Greg, 28–29
Lynch, Frederick, 95

MacKinnonite, Catharine, 136
The Magic Flute (Mozart), 216
Makel, Matthew, 199
Man, Paul de, 5
Markos, Louis, 226
Marx, Karl, 26, 224
mattress girl, 153–54
Mazumder, Bhashkar, 101–2
McAuliffe, Terry, 142–43
McCloskey, Deirdre, 163–64
McDavid, Bob, 23
McInerney, Jeremy, 231
McWhorter, John, 231, 234
media. *See also* social media
    Black Lives Matter in, 104, 109–10
    consent policy in, 141–42
    discrimination for, 89–90
    feminism in, 119, 158–59
    gender in, 158–60
    #MeToo movement in, 160–61
    minorities in, 90–91
    politics of, 5–6
    protests for, 23
    racism for, 59–61
    rape and, 137–38, 146
    social justice in, 81, 117
    for students, 121–22
    Sulkowicz in, 153–54
Medical schools. *See* science; STEM fields
Mémoires (Berlioz), 212–13
merit, 42–43, 45, 46, 48–49
#MeToo movement
    economics of, 163–64
    in higher education, 166–68
    ideology of, 155–58, 160–63
    for labor markets, 163–66
    for law enforcement, 158–59
    in media, 160–61
    politics of, 159–60
microaggressions
    for administration, 68–70, 76–78
    in critical race theory, 66–67
    for feminism, 142–43
    ideology of, 63–65, 78–81
    policy for, 73–74
    politics of, 70–72

psychology of, 74–76
as victimology, 65–68, 72–73, 81–85
Middlebury College, 3, 16–17
A Midsummer Night's Dream
        (Shakespeare), 212
Miller, Ted, 103
minorities
    admissions for, 37–41
    in California, 51
    diversity for, 23, 59
    goals for, 182–83
    in labor markets, 30–32, 98
    in media, 90–91
    policy for, 42–52, 65, 83–84
    politics for, 14, 55–57
    at Pomona College, 18–20
    protests by, 238
    safe spaces for, 74–75
    SAT scores for, 47, 53, 92, 95–96
    science for, 53–54
    Trump impact on, 26–27
    URMs, 51–52, 191–92, 194–98
    victimology for, 105–6, 110–11
    violence for, 20
    writing for, 60
Mitchell, Gregory, 92
Mollerstrom, Johanna, 164
Montero, Janina, 79
Moores, John, Sr., 45
morality, 156–57, 158, 167–68, 225
Moran, Rachel, 73, 75–77
Morrison, Toni, 172
Mozart, Wolfgang Amadeus, 152, 215–16
Ms. (magazine), 117–18
multiculturalism
    goals of, 180–86
    in higher education, 5, 171–80, 187
    ideology of, 202
    politics of, 63–64
    at Yale University, 24–26
Murray, Charles, 3, 16–17
Muti, Riccardo, 163

NAACP. *See* National Association for the
        Advancement of Colored People
Napolitano, Janet, 82–85, 184

Nasir, Na'ilah Suad, 246
National Association for the
    Advancement of Colored People
    (NAACP), 44
National Institutes of Health (NIH),
    191–92
National Labor Relations Board (NLRB),
    32
National Science Foundation (NSF),
    189–90
Naughton, Eileen, 31
Nelsons, Andris, 161
neo-Victorianism, 139–47
New York Life, 97–98
New York University, 124–25, 133–34
NIH. *See* National Institutes of Health
Nixon, Jay, 23
NLRB. *See* National Labor Relations
    Board
Nosek, Brian, 94
NSF. *See* National Science Foundation

Oakland (California), 108–13
Obama, Barack, 89, 144, 166
Occidental College, 140–41, 143–46
Ohio State University, 142
Open Society Foundation, 90
oppression. *See* systematic oppression
Oswald, Fred, 92
Oxford University, 194
Oxtoby, David, 18

Pacific Legal Foundation, 36–37
Palmer, Erin, 196
Peraza, Jonathan, 26
Perkins, Djuna, 141–42
Petrarch, Francesco, 214, 221
Pichai, Sundar, 30
Pinker, Steven, 157
Pitt, William, 1
Plato, 223
police. *See* law enforcement
policy
    in California, 142–43, 166, 183
    at Claremont McKenna College,
        140–41

at Columbia University, 149–54
comprehensive review as, 43
consent policy, 140–42, 147
for discrimination, 37, 40, 168, 238–39
diversity as, 35–36, 56–58, 163, 174,
    176, 186, 232
for feminism, 139
at Harvard University, 142
in higher education, 42
in law school, 243–47
for microaggressions, 73–74
for minorities, 42–52, 65, 83–84
morality and, 158
for NIH, 191–92
at Occidental College, 140–41, 145–46
for rape, 126–27, 131–35
of UC system, 61
at UCLA, 67–70, 211–13
political correctness. *See* free speech
politics. *See also* identity politics
    of achievement gaps, 49, 61
    for administration, 16–17, 23–24, 82,
        139–40
    of Black Lives Matter, 106
    at Brown University, 133–34
    in California, 35–38, 140–41
    on campus, 149–54
    of discrimination, 94
    of diversity, 178, 245–46
    for faculty, 16, 18–19, 57
    of feminism, 117, 123, 130–31, 135,
        141, 145, 152–53
    of free speech, 77–78, 202–3, 243–47
    of gender, 84–85, 142–44, 162–63,
        197–98, 216
    at Google, 30–32, 164
    of Great Courses, 229–31
    at Harvard University, 120
    in higher education, 217, 231–32
    of Hollywood, 95, 155–56, 158–61
    of humanities, 215–17
    of ideology, 18, 239–40
    of lectures, 15–16
    of LGBTQ community, 160–67, 195
    of media, 5–6
    of merit, 42–43

politics (*continued*)
  of #MeToo movement, 159–60
  of microaggressions, 70–72
  for minorities, 14, 55–57
  of morality, 156–57, 167–68
  of multiculturalism, 63–64
  in New York, 218
  at Occidental College, 143–44
  psychology in, 102–3
  of race theory, 5
  of racism, 70, 82
  of rape, 125–29, 146–47
  Silencing the Past (book), 241
  of social justice, 67–68, 191, 226–28,
    234, 247
  of STEM fields, 189–91, 239
  of stereotypes, 51–52
  of students, 1–2, 235, 237–38
  at UC, 37, 39–41, 172–74
  of UC system, 43–51, 179–80
  at UCLA, 174–75
  at UCSB, 176
  at UCSD, 174–76
  in US, 221
  at Yale University, 124
Pomona College, 18–20
Portman, Natalie, 160
poverty, 41, 48, 99–100
PricewaterhouseCoopers, 97–98
Princeton University, 2
Proctor & Gamble, 97–98, 102
Proposition 209, 35–39
  in higher education, 40–48, 51–52
  for law school, 48–51
protests
  anarchy in, 21–22
  on campus, 1–4, 204–5
  Day of Action Statements as, 65–67
  on Facebook, 75
  free speech as, 19
  at Harvard University, 81
  ideology of, 15
  against law enforcement, 9–16
  media covering, 23
  by minorities, 238
  on social media, 9–10, 29–30, 55, 72–74

Take Back the Night (rally) as, 118–19
  totalitarianism in, 28
  at UCLA, 12–14, 63–67
  victimology in, 11–12
  at Yale University, 24
  on YouTube, 74, 77
psychology
  of achievement gaps, 101–2
  of administration, 121
  of behavioral realism, 90
  at Claremont McKenna College,
    10–11
  "The Coddling of the American Mind"
    (Lukianoff/Haidt), 28–29
  of critical thinking, 219–20
  of discrimination, 32–33, 93
  of false narratives, 240–42
  of feminism, 122
  of goals, 61
  IAT for, 88–94
  of implicit bias, 87–94, 104–8
  of merit, 45
  of microaggressions, 74–76
  of morality, 157
  in politics, 102–3
  of racism, 91–94
  of safe spaces, 27–28
  science of, 91–92
  of social justice, 196–97, 216–17
  of students, 22
  of US, 139–40
  of victimology, 3, 14–15, 17, 120,
    151–52
  of violence, 21–22, 104–5, 135

Qualcomm, 97–98
Quayle, Dan, 225

Rabelais, François, 215
Raby, Rosalind, 64
race theory, 5
racism
  in admissions, 40, 44–46
  Asians and, 44–45, 64–65
  on campus, 239
  discrimination and, 36–37, 242

in higher education, 95–96, 100–102, 211, 215–16

ideology of, 87–91

in law enforcement, 82, 89, 96, 102–13

for media, 59–61

politics of, 70, 82

poverty and, 99–100

psychology of, 91–94

in US, 22, 94–95, 97–99, 107–8

as victimology, 203

rape

consent policy and, 140–42

at Duke University, 125

economics of, 131

in higher education, 120–24, 130–31

media covering, 137–38, 146

policy for, 126–27, 131–35

politics of, 125–29, 146–47

rape culture, 118, 149, 167

Saturday Night: Untold Stories of Sexual Assault at Harvard (magazine), 126–27

among students, 135–37

Take Back the Night (rally) for, 118–19

in US, 131–32

victimology and, 117–20, 124–25, 129–30

Rashid, Mark, 47, 50–51

Reagan, Nancy, 225

Reagan, Ronald, 224–25

Reiter, Eric, 234–35

Renaissance. *See* Great Courses; humanities

risk management, 131–37

Robb, Lucinda, 235

Robinson, Jacoby, 121

Robinson, Labrente, 121

Robinson, Nina, 40

Roderick, Rick, 224–25

Rolling Stone (magazine), 137–38

Rollins, Tom. *See* Great Courses

Rose, Charlie, 157

Rose Institute for State and Local Government, 9–12

Rosemund, Sabriya, 196

Ross, Alex, 162–63

Ross, Howard, 90, 96

Rubio, Marco, 166

Ruckh, Veronica, 156–57

Ruger, Ted, 205–6

Rust, Val, 18–19, 63–71

Rutgers University, 136

Ryan, Garrett, 11

safe spaces

administration for, 150

in companies, 32

in higher education, 28–29

ideology of, 18–19

for minorities, 74–75

psychology of, 27–28

for students, 2, 239–40

Sakaki, Judy, 182

Salovey, Peter, 25, 28, 237–41

San Diego State University, 187, 192

Sander, Richard, 39, 46–50, 58–59, 71–75

SAT scores, 37–38, 40–43

gender in, 163–64, 199

goals for, 100–101

for minorities, 47, 53, 92, 95–96

in science, 54–55

Saturday Night: Untold Stories of Sexual Assault at Harvard (magazine), 126–27

Saussure, Ferdinand de, 56

Schmidt, Eric, 32

Schoenfeld, Michael, 57–58

Schrag, Peter, 171–72

Schumann, Robert, 232

science

discrimination and, 30–31, 88–89

feminism in, 164–66

gender in, 193

in higher education, 5–6, 60–61

humanities compared to, 55–56

identity politics in, 190–93, 195–99

INCLUDES for, 190–91

for minorities, 53–54

NSF for, 189–90

of psychology, 91–92

SAT scores in, 54–55

stereotypes in, 32

Sessions, Laura, 126
Shakespeare, William, 212–13
The Shape of the River (Bowen/Bok), 57
Sheridan, Richard, 1
Silencing the Past (book), 241
Singal, Jesse, 92–93, 107
SLUT: A Play and Guidebook for Combating Sexism (book), 149
Sobek, Maria Herrera, 176–77, 179
social justice. *See also* politics
  economics of, 184
  for faculty, 83–85
  for feminism, 158–59
  in higher education, 207
  identity politics as, 164–66
  ideology of, 70–71
  in media, 81, 117
  politics of, 67–68, 191, 226–28, 234, 247
  psychology of, 196–97, 216–17
  in TED Talks, 151–53
social media
  Facebook, 75
  higher education and, 11
  Above the Law (blog), 72–74
  lectures on, 14
  protests on, 9–10, 29–30, 55, 72–74
  webinars for, 151
  YouTube, 74, 77
Society of Comparative and International Education, 63–64
Sokolow, Brett, 122, 129–30
Solórzano, Daniel, 66–68
Solovey, Peter, 237–38
Sonoma State University, 182
Sophir, Jayme, 32–33
Soros, George, 90
The Souls of Black Folk (Du Bois), 1
Spenner, Ken, 54, 58
Spenser, Edmund, 152
sports, 22–24
Stanford University, 164
Steele, Claude, 47
Steinem, Gloria, 142–43
STEM fields, 164–66, 189–93, 195–99, 239. *See also* science

stereotypes, 29–32, 51–52, 57, 93, 105–6
Stokes, Sy, 77–79, 81
students
  achievement gaps for, 40–47
  administration and, 23–25, 238, 246–47
  alumni and, 55–56
  at Brown University, 2–3
  at Columbia University, 29, 215–16
  critical thinking for, 241
  economics for, 224
  at Evergreen State College, 3–4
  free speech for, 27
  Go Ask Alice! for, 134–35
  goals for, 47–48
  at Harvard University, 220
  leadership for, 70–71
  media for, 121–22
  at Middlebury College, 3, 16
  politics of, 1–2, 235, 237–38
  psychology of, 22
  rape among, 135–37
  safe spaces for, 2, 239–40
  stereotypes of, 29–30
  at UCSD, 5
  victimology for, 18, 28, 81–85, 245–47
Suárez-Orozco, Marcelo, 66–67, 69, 71, 206
Sugrue, Michael, 226
Sulkowicz, Emma ("mattress girl"), 153–55
systematic oppression, 22–24, 37, 69–70, 78–79, 245–46

Take Back the Night (rally), 118–19
Taylor, Stuart, 124
The Teaching Company. *See* Great Courses
TED Talks, 151–53
Tenured Radicals (Kimball), 4
Testino, Mario, 157
Tetlock, Philip, 90, 92
Texas State International Piano Festival, 218
Title IX, 126–28

Torre, Adela de la, 187
Toscanini, Arturo, 159
totalitarianism, 28
triggering. *See* microaggressions
Trump, Donald, 20–21, 26–27, 167,
    237
Twain, Mark, 219
Tyson, Tim, 55–56

UC. *See* University of California, Berkeley
UC Davis. *See* University of California,
    Davis
UC system, 181–87. *See also specific schools*
    administration for, 171–72
    admissions for, 51–52
    African Americans in, 78
    economics of, 174
    goals of, 172–73
    policy of, 61
    politics of, 43–51, 179–80
UCLA. *See* University of California,
    Los Angeles
UCSB. *See* University of California,
    Santa Barbara
UCSD. *See* University of California,
    San Diego
UN. *See* United Nations
underrepresented minorities (URMs),
    51–52, 191–92, 194–98
Unhooked (Sessions), 126
United Nations (UN), 37
United States (US)
    bourgeois class in, 201–7
    Civil Rights Commission for, 94–95
    Clery Act in, 122–23, 128–30
    "The Coddling of the American Mind"
        (Lukianoff/Haidt), 28–29
    Department of Education in, 142
    gender in, 180–81
    humanities in, 217–19
    identity politics in, 199–200
    immigrants in, 13
    Labor and Human Services Committee
        in, 224
    Labor Department of, 30–31
    NLRB in, 32

politics in, 221
psychology of, 139–40
racism in, 22, 94–95, 97–99, 107–8
rape in, 131–32
violence in, 118–19
universities. *See* higher education
University of California, Berkeley (UC)
    administration, 35
    affirmative action at, 59–61
    discrimination at, 44
    diversity at, 245
    economics for, 171–72
    faculty at, 22
    free speech at, 173–74, 243–47
    law school, 39, 46
    politics at, 37, 39–41, 172–74
    victimology at, 21–22
University of California, Davis (UC
    Davis), 47
University of California, Los Angeles
    (UCLA)
    administration, 14
    Black Law Students Association,
        74–76
    critical race theory at, 89–90
    discrimination at, 44–45
    diversity at, 181–82
    law school, 39, 41, 71–80, 90–91
    policy at, 67–70, 211–13
    politics at, 174–75
    protests at, 12–14, 63–67
    STEM fields at, 193
University of California, San Diego
    (UCSD), 5, 174–76
University of California, Santa Barbara
    (UCSB), 176, 179
University of Chicago, 16–17
University of Missouri, 22–24
University of Pennsylvania, 201–7
University of San Diego, 201–7
University of Virginia, 137–38
Until Proven Innocent (Taylor/Johnson,
    K. C.), 124–25
URMs. *See* underrepresented minorities
US. *See* United States
Uvin, Peter, 14

Vandiver, Elizabeth, 228
Velasco, David, 162
victimology, 4–5, 9, 74–75, 241–42
    on campus, 131
    at Emory University, 26–28
    in higher education, 63–64, 201–7
    ideology of, 29–30, 33
    microaggressions as, 65–68, 72–73,
        81–85
    for minorities, 105–6, 110–11
    in protests, 11–12
    psychology of, 3, 14–15, 17, 120,
        151–52
    racism as, 203
    rape and, 117–20, 124–25, 129–30
    for students, 18, 28, 81–85, 245–47
    systematic oppression as, 23–24
    at UC, 21–22
The Victims' Revolution (Bawer), 4
violence. *See also* rape
    in Berkeley (California), 16, 20–22
    on campus, 12, 14, 81–82, 121–22
    Clery Act and, 128–30
    law enforcement and, 102–4, 113,
        120–21
    for minorities, 20
    psychology of, 21–22, 104–5, 135
    *Saturday Night: Untold Stories of Sexual
        Assault at Harvard* (magazine),
        126–27
    in US, 118–19

Wagner, James, 26–28
Wai, Jonathan, 199
Walmart, 95
The War on Cops (Mac Donald), *9*
Warren, Elizabeth, 15–16

Washington and Lee University, 127–28
Watson, Kenjus, 65, 67–68, 70–71
Wax, Amy, 201–7, 246
Weber, Bruce, 157
webinars, 151, 196
Wehrheim, Katrin, 22
Weiner, Steve, 185
Weinstein, Bret, 3–4
Weinstein, Harvey, 155, 157
Welle, Brian, 100
Wellesley College, 142
Wertheim, Bonnie, 158–59
White, Miles, 94–95
Whitman College, 228
Wilkins, David, 49
Williams, Gabrielle, 60
Winfrey, Oprah, 161
Wing-Richards, Hillary, 130–31
Wolfe, Timothy, 22–23
Wong, Scott, 106
Wright, Richard, 216

Yagan, Danny, 74
Yale University
    administration, 237–42
    consent policy at, 147
    curriculum at, 1–2
    diversity at, 195
    multiculturalism at, 24–26
    politics at, 124
    protests at, 24
Yang, Henry, 179
Yiannopoulos, Milo, 16, 20–22, 243
YouTube, 74, 77
Yudof, Mark, 177, 179, 184–85

Zachariah, Abdul-Razak Mohammed, 25